THE AUTOBIOGRAPHY

HEWITT'S LAW

Jack Hewitt

with Dave Argabright

HEWITT'S LAW
the autobiography

By Jack Hewitt
with Dave Argabright

© 2003 Dave Argabright

ISBN 0-9719639-1-6

Published by:
Books by Dave Argabright
P.O. Box 84
Fishers, IN 46038
(317) 598-9773
www.daveargabright.com

Front cover photo/Jim Haines
Back cover photo/Skip Peterson

Printed with pride in the USA by Print Communications, Inc.
Indianapolis, Indiana

ACKNOWLEDGEMENTS

It took the help of many people to make this book possible. The authors would like to thank the following: Corinne Economaki for her superb editing; Jody Hewitt for her invaluable record-keeping; Linda Burchett of Print Communications for her cover design; and Randy Steenbergen and the staff at Print Communications for helping us through the printing process.

In the midst of an intense media tour following his Winston Cup championship, Tony Stewart found time to write the foreword for this book. That's truly above and beyond the call of duty and his effort, along with Bones Bourcier, is greatly appreciated.

Steven Cole Smith, an excellent writer and a good friend, provided some helpful insights regarding the "voices" found in this book, and we are grateful for his contribution.

For their research help, we thank: Dick Jordan of the United States Auto Club; Scott Hall of the All Stars Circuit of Champions; and Richard Day of the World of Outlaws. Australian "spell-checking" was provided by Brian "Scruff" Donaldson and Jon Evans. Bill Holder and Buzz Rose also provided research material.

Background information and research data was gained from several sources, including *National Speed Sport News*; *Sprint Car and Midget Magazine*; past issues of *Open Wheel Magazine*; and the Witness Productions book, *Dirt Road to a Silver Crown*, by Bob Gates, Patrick Sullivan, Ed Watson, and John Mahoney.

A number of additional people deserve thanks for their contribution: Sherry Argabright, for her sharp proofreading and endless encouragement; Doug Auld of *Sprint Car and Midget Magazine*; Tom Johnson of Acordia Insurance; Mike Kerchner and others at *National Speed Sport News*; Tom Schmeh of the National Sprint Car Hall of Fame; Jeff Walker; and many others who helped in their own special way.

CONTENTS

FOREWORD

Tony Stewart on Jack Hewitt

It's kind of funny, because he's one of my all-time heroes, but I have absolutely no idea when I might have first watched Jack Hewitt race. For me, it's like he's always been there, always been a big part of the racing scene around the Midwest. I'm sure it was long before I had gotten serious about my own racing, in the days before I'd even started racing TQ midgets around Indiana. I do remember watching Hewitt run Stan Shoff's sprinter, and all the cars he drove for Bob Hampshire and J.W Hunt. But, like I said, I don't recall exactly when I first saw him race.

But I do have a really good memory of the first time we ever raced together. It was in the first USAC national midget race I ever ran, in April of 1991 at Winchester, Indiana. It has nothing to do with where I finished-tenth, I guess-or how the race went, or even how big and fast that track seemed to a kid like me. My main recollection from that day is of sitting in my car on the front straightaway, getting ready for the B-main. I was starting third and Hewitt was started fourth, so our two cars were staged side by side, waiting for the push trucks to roll up and get us fired off. And I was sitting there, thinking, Man, I'm starting right next to Jack Hewitt. *Jack Hewitt!* He raced winged sprint cars, he raced non-wing sprint cars, he raced Silver Crown cars, he raced midgets, he raced dirt late models. He raced everything, and he was strong wherever he went. He was a guy I had always paid lots of attention to, and here I was, starting alongside him. Just thinking about that moment still brings a smile to my face.

I didn't know Jack at all back then, and even once we started competing on a regular basis it took a little bit of time for me to get close to him. That's probably because Hewitt was a lot like Dale Earnhardt; there was a little bit of intimidation there. See, Jack always had this reputation: If you did him wrong on the race track, you were probably going to be in for some trouble in the pits later on. The old joke was, "If you're going to wreck Hewitt, you'd better wreck him hard enough to hurt him. Otherwise, *he's* going to hurt *you*." I saw him win enough really good fights to know that he'd earned that reputation legitimately, and, I'll admit, that did enter my mind a couple of times when I was getting ready to race him.

Thankfully, even though we've run a ton of races together, I never did get on Jack's bad side. Of course, neither one of us has officially retired from racing yet, and we're both awfully competitive guys, so I'm not going to say that it *won't* happen. I just hope that by now, our relationship has gotten to the point where if I did mess him up, he'd realize that it had to be strictly an accident, just hard racing.

Today, I realize that Hewitt was a lot like Earnhardt in other ways, too. Once you got past what a great racer he was, you came to see that Jack was just a regular guy who loved his family, loved his fishing, and genuinely loved his friends. If you're his friend, he'll do whatever he can to take care of you. He'll treat you just like you're one of his own kids.

One of the favorite souvenirs I have from my racing career involves Jack. It comes from 1995, my Triple Crown season with USAC. That September we all went to Eldora, Jack's home track in Ohio, for the 4-Crown Nationals. I was fortunate enough to win both the midget and sprint car features that night, and I finished second to Hewitt in the Silver Crown feature. At the 4-Crown, they pose all the winners together at the end of the night, and they take one collective Victory Lane shot. Well, I've still got that photo of Jack and I standing together on the Eldora stage. To have shared that moment with Jack, at a track where he has always been the king, is something I'll always cherish.

One more Hewitt memory, also from Eldora, at another 4-Crown weekend. This was in 1998, when I was at a point in my life and my career when things were just starting to get really stressful. I was juggling a full Indy Racing League schedule and a partial NASCAR Busch Series schedule, and I was having to deal with more pressure than I'd ever been through. Well, the 4-Crown fell on a rare open weekend for me, so I went over there strictly as a fan, and parked my motorhome right beside Hewitt's. On the afternoon of the race, while Jack was in the pits getting ready to practice, I got wrapped up in a huge water-gun fight with Jack's wife, Jody, and their son, Cody. It was probably the hardest I laughed that whole season, and, like I said, this had been in the middle of a really tense time for me.

If you remember, that was the year that Jack won all four of the 4-Crown features, and I sat in the grandstands and watched every lap he ran that night. That was probably the first time in my life when I actually had an opportunity to race and decided not to, because, like I said, I went to Eldora just to have fun. And I'm glad it worked out that way, because it was an awesome thing to watch Hewitt do what he did. Of course, I've always kidded him that if I had been out there, he wouldn't have won all four features. But that's the kind of relationship Jack and I have: I bust him, and he busts me. It's a very real kind of friendship.

I'll tell you, if you ever need to get grounded in a hurry, all you have to do is go and find the Hewitt's. They're the kind of people who will never, ever let you get a big head, or get too big for your britches. They've always been great at reminding me exactly where I came from. It's not like I feel that I really *need* reminding, because I'm very proud of the way I came up. But they've got a way of letting you know that no matter what you might have done elsewhere, you're still just the same guy they've always known. That attitude of theirs is something I really respect.

I guess the best way to sum up Jack is to say that he is a racer's racer. If you're a race driver and you want to try to be like somebody, as far as I'm concerned there are only two guys to pattern yourself after: A.J. Foyt and Jack Hewitt.

Jack is always saying that it means a lot to him that I've mentioned in several interviews that he's one of my heroes. He says he's honored that I would still think that way. Well, the way I look at it, I'm the one who should feel honored. I not only got to race against my hero, I also got to know him, and to call him my friend. I think I got the better end of that deal.

TONY STEWART
2002 NASCAR Winston Cup Champion

INTRODUCTION

by Dave Argabright

U.S. 36 was smooth and carefree, winding across the Indiana countryside and stretching effortlessly into Ohio. That was the route to Jack's: I-69 to Pendleton, U.S. 36 east across the state line, and a simple country road through Darke and Miami counties to the home where I would find the man of deep convictions, strong opinions, and an endless passion for fun and laughter.

It is an interesting role, collaborating with a man who is telling his life story. I approach the project with both relish and excitement, coupled with a sobering responsibility that I simply must do it right. Through my earlier adventure with Brad Doty to this assignment with Jack Hewitt, I found both men to be open, honest, friendly, and supportive, all the things we needed to tell the story as best we could.

Before I begin to tell you about doing this story with Jack Hewitt, first I must talk about the man himself. My first memory of Jack comes in the early 1980's, when I saw him race at Indiana's Kokomo Speedway. He had long hair and a beard, and he looked rough and rowdy. Not long after, I read about him in *Open Wheel Magazine*, and his startling candor and sense of humor made me feel that I knew him, even though we had never met. Looking back, that was a critical element to the career of Jack Hewitt: his honesty and irreverence allowed people to strongly identify with him, and made them feel that he was not just another star, but a star who was also a regular guy.

Jack was rough around the edges in those early years, but it was clear he had talent. He started his racing career late, making his first sprint car start in 1973 at age 22. When I look back at the sterling numbers he posted in his Hall of Fame career, I can't help but wonder if he could have enjoyed even more success had he begun racing at age 17 or 18. Then again, he was definitely on the wild side at 21, so it was probably in the kid's best interests to keep him away from race cars as long as possible, to save him from himself.

By the mid-1980's the Hewitt legend blossomed. He raced prolifically, winning races and championships. He offered entertaining and provocative interviews, and he was frequently featured in newspapers and magazines. He conquered Eldora Speedway, one of the most intimidating and daunting tracks in America, and his trademark introduction there seemed to symbolize the essence of Jack Hewitt: *"He rides it high, 'cause he ain't afraid to die!"*

In the early 1990's Jack enjoyed even more success. Then came a terrible accident in late 1993 which threatened to cut short his brilliant career. But his tenacity and determination carried the day, and he rose from the ashes to reclaim his skills and return to his winning ways.

By the year 2001, Jack had put up some prodigious numbers in the sport, and he was named as one of the top 25 sprint car racers of the 20th century. He was inducted into the National Sprint Car Hall of Fame, had vast legions of fans, and he had finally got his Indy 500 start. Jack Hewitt, it seems, had become a legitimate superstar.

Yet it was obvious that Jack had never changed from the hardscrabble kid from Troy, Ohio, nor from the hungry and eager young man with the long hair and beard. Stardom be damned, Jack was committed to the principal of Jack being Jack. Nothing more, nothing less.

I got to know him in the mid-1980's, as I was covering races for *National Speed Sport News* and *Open Wheel Magazine*. Like all reporters, I appreciated his candor and his outrageous quotes. Plus, if you've spent any time around Jack, you'll know that something interesting is always about to happen when Dew-It Hewitt is in the house.

We had long discussions both over the phone and in person about fighting at the race track. I am not a fan of fisticuffs; it's just not the right way to settle a disagreement. I tried to impart that philosophy to Jack, just as he tried to convince me that he had the right idea.

"Jack," I would explain, "you can't fix it by punching a guy. If you worked at the factory and didn't like the way a guy was doing his job, you can't just knock his lights out. You'd be in jail."

"Dave," he would answer, "I don't work at the factory. I drive a race car. That guy is gonna kill me if I don't get his attention. If I sweet-talk him, I might not live long enough for him to change his ways. If I give him a black eye, maybe he'll understand better what I'm trying to say."

As the years passed and I spent more and more time with Jack and his family, I began to look at him simply as a friend, and not a star. In that realm, he had a capacity at times to just irritate the hell out of me.

I abhor political correctness, and Jack is truly the antithesis of political correctness. However, his views and opinions were sometimes clearly out of bounds, coming off as harsh and crass. He seemed to know this, because once he knew certain things made me uncomfortable, he would make sure to impart a couple of verbal zingers when I was nearby, grinning and studying me for a response. Hewitt is excellent with the needle.

No matter what, Jack had the uncanny ability to come out on top. Whether it was a debate or argument, or an on-track shunt, he was a hard man to keep down. His 1995 encounter with Tony Elliott was a perfect example of that.

It was Lawrenceburg, Indiana, at a USAC sprint car race. Doug Kalitta was leading, but both Elliott and Hewitt were obviously faster. Elliott slid slightly in front of Jack, and there was contact, sending Elliott into the infield. Hewitt later passed Kalitta and won the race.

It's not that Jack did it on purpose, but I couldn't help but be disappointed at the sequence of events. I hate it anytime the guy who makes contact wins; it seems cheapened, and hollow. Jack was very honest afterwards, saying that Tony had changed his line slightly from the lap before, and he couldn't miss him. Just as he was telling me this, Elliott came strolling into the picture, and there was a confrontation. Hewitt was calm and poised, and he said later that since he had it coming, he would have taken a shot from Elliott had he swung. But USAC official Rollie Beale intervened, and Elliott walked away.

A week later, the series was at Paragon Speedway in Indiana. I was still slightly annoyed at Jack from the Lawrenceburg incident, and when they announced the feature lineup I couldn't help but notice that of all the drivers, Jack Hewitt's name elicited by far the loudest, lustiest roar from the grandstands. Didn't those people remember what happened a week earlier? How can they like him so much?

The race was a classic showdown between Jack and Tony Elliott, who was driving Paul Hazen's car. Elliott drew close behind Hewitt, and as they were making the corner, Elliott put a bumper on Hewitt and spun him. It was a payback, pure and simple.

But Hewitt was unflappable. He throttled the car and with a brilliant flex of his wrists and arms, completed the spin and regained control, immediately chasing after Elliott. *That son-of-a-gun!* How did he do that? I couldn't help but shake my head and laugh out loud, in genuine appreciation of a man who simply never gives up, no matter what. A few laps later he caught Elliott, passed him cleanly, and won the race.

(Hewitt and Elliott were parked side-by-side in the pits, and after the victory celebration, Hewitt had his needle in full swing. "If that's all the harder you can hit me, Tony, you might as well go home!" Elliott laughed, they shook hands, and the incident was history.)

Two years ago, Jack and I began to toss around the idea of doing his autobiography. He was warm to the idea, but concerned: "I've not been a choirboy," he said. "I'm afraid kids would read about me and think that's okay. I don't want to do anything that would be bad for kids."

We both tabled the idea for a while, until December 2001. Jack had decided it was time to move forward with the project, and after some preliminary discussions we pushed ahead.

It began a one-year period that was as interesting as any in my career. There were interviews in his garage, in his pickup truck going down the highway, at the races. It was quickly obvious that as well as I thought I knew Jack Hewitt, there was infinitely more below the surface.

Despite his blue-collar persona, he is sharply intelligent. His outgoing nature and acute comfort around people seemed boundless. Beyond anything else, I was moved by his deep and genuine compassion for the people around him. He says he doesn't care what people think, but nothing could be further from the truth: Jack Hewitt loves people immensely, and he both craves and requires their affection.

He is very much a man who is comfortable with himself. He wears his emotions on his sleeve, holding very little inside. Despite his great success in racing, he is happy to enjoy life as a regular guy, wearing a flannel shirt and eating Wendy's hamburgers.

His deep convictions sometimes make for headstrong stances on issues, and it's very challenging to get him to change his mind. That said, he was an absolute joy to work with on this project. He always made time for the book, even when he was tired or busy. As he recovered from his July accident at North Vernon, we often talked at a time when any movement sent a wince of pain dancing across his face.

Jack approached this book with a firm commitment to being honest in every regard. He was extremely candid with his descriptions of his early life, and he was very willing to discuss his own flaws and mistakes without varnish. There are stories here of others that will surely make them uncomfortable, and we spent long discussions about that. It was never his goal to throw anyone under the bus; but his position was this: how can he protect others when he didn't protect himself and his family, telling stories that are likely to be as difficult to read as they were for him to tell? What is the use of doing a book if you're not willing to be completely honest?

As we spent many hours together on this project, we developed a sturdy, warm friendship. Oh, Jack can still be a pain in the butt; I point that out to him quite often. But we discovered many common interests, including a mutual love for the "hillbilly" music enjoyed by our fathers a generation ago. Sometimes, as the music played in the background, our interview would be interrupted when a new song began and we each tried to be the first to "name that tune."

On another night we rolled out the karaoke machine, and Jack, Jody and I sang (that's a loose definition of the word) tune after tune, laughing and tapping our toes to the music. It was another memorable moment from a memorable project during a memorable year.

As the project began to wind down, it seemed bittersweet. We were both excited about seeing the book in print, but at the same time I knew I would miss those long conversations, the hillbilly music, and the rides home along U.S. 36 as I tumbled the words through my mind and wondered how they would ever make it on paper.

Ultimately, this book tells the story of a proud, straightforward man who rose above humble and difficult beginnings to become one of the greatest short track racers in history. I'm very proud to have helped with the telling of that story, and eternally grateful for the experience.

As you read about this interesting, provocative, sentimental, brave, and driven man, I hope you're a bit better for the experience of knowing him. I know I am.

HEWITT'S
LAW

To Mom and Dad, whom I miss dearly;

to Ted and Larry, who left us much too soon;

and to the fans, who were always there for me.

J.H.

PRELUDE
July 22, 2002
11:25 p.m.
North Vernon, Indiana

I'm laying here in a little hospital, with my body hurting and wondering what all this means. Am I hurt bad? Is it permanent? How long am I going to be laid up?

I started this deal 29 years ago, and it's one bad-ass profession. Race cars are mean by nature, and there ain't any race cars meaner than sprint cars. That's what I've done best, drive sprint cars. Now they've bit me.

One more time. Bit me, chewed me up, spit me out and left me to heal up.

Somehow, I will. I'm a survivor, the type of guy who never quits. Some people might say it's because a guy is tough, or determined, but in my case I just don't know any better. Racing was all I've ever had, and I didn't know anything other than coming back, even after I busted my ass.

I busted my ass tonight, that much I know. I don't know much else; everything else is a blur, like a fog that wraps you up and makes everything disappear. I feel really intense pain in my neck, and they've got me in a collar that won't let my head move. I can't move my right arm or my right leg.

I'm in North Vernon, Indiana. I was racing at Twin Cities Raceway Park, about 10 minutes from here, a little dirt track just like a hundred other tracks I've seen through the years. What happened is simple: another car and I got together, and I started flipping down the backstretch.

Getting me out of the car wasn't fun. I was conscious, but my bell was rung. I could hear the voices; rescue people and my wife, Jody. And Tony Elliott, another driver who came down to help me. I could talk to them just a little bit, and my eyes were squinted closed because I hurt so bad. I told them my neck hurt, so they were careful trying to get me out.

Watching somebody get pried out of a race car is pretty ugly. Most racers don't watch; we keep our distance, and look the other way. If you're sitting in the grandstands, you don't really see what's happening. A guy is usually groaning or crying and everybody is trying to help him. Our seats wrap around us and they have to squeeze our butt out and up through the roll cage, all the while trying not to move our neck.

It ain't pleasant.

I'm worried about my neck. Almost 10 years ago I got hurt big-time, and broke my neck. This pain I'm feeling is very, very familiar, and that isn't a good thing. The last time I wore a big metal halo and it took a long time to get feeling good again.

It's really quiet inside this little emergency room. Quiet, and very chilly. It's about 1 a.m., and I'm all alone, laying here on my back, with my sweaty driver's suit pulled off my shoulders and gathered at my waist. They've covered me with a blanket, but I'm still cold.

A couple of hours ago we were burning up at the race track, it must have been 90 degrees with very high humidity. Just miserable. We'd sweat just thinking about working on the race car. Now, here I am shivering in this chilly room.

Jody has already kicked into survival mode. She's been with me before in this situation. She doesn't get all emotional and bent out of shape, she just braces herself for whatever comes. I guess it's like that, being married to a race driver. We're pretty selfish, and most of us go through this world thinking about what we want and to heck with everybody else. I try not to be that way, but here I am, putting Jody through this again just because it's the kind of work I want to do. She's outside in the hallway, trying to deal with all the decisions and stress and complications. Are you going to transfer him? Can they give him something for the pain? What about all these visitors in the hallway, who can go in and who stays outside?

Meanwhile I lay real still on this bed, wrapped up in a blanket and wearing a cut-up racing uniform, a uniform I might not ever get to wear again. I'm cold and I'm trying to lie real still, because it hurts even when I blink my eyes. Hurts, hurts, hurts. Damn, it hurts.

Already there are people here, friends and racers who are concerned about me. Sitting outside are Dennis and Chris Kaser, who owned the car I was driving tonight. Dennis is feeling really, really bad, because we're very good friends and he knows I'm hurting. If he were hurting like this I'd take his place if I could; I know right now he's feeling the same way.

These car owners, they make you promise you won't get hurt in their car, because that thought just eats 'em up. And I always say, "Oh, I ain't getting hurt. Quit worrying about it." Even though I know you can kill yourself at this business. But you just go right on and act like it ain't gonna happen. If you didn't deny it, it would make you crazy, and you couldn't race. So I deny it like every other racer, and here I am in the hospital. There ain't no denying it now.

I want to go to Indianapolis, to Methodist Hospital. When I got hurt in 1993, that's the hospital that helped me the most. Dr. Terry Trammel is there, and I trust Dr. Trammel and his guys with my life. Literally. Jody has whispered to me that she's going to try and get me to Methodist. Tonight.

They have finally given me a shot for the pain, and everything is beginning to get kind of blurred. I try to sleep, but a lot is going through my mind. I'm thinking about my life, and remembering some of the days and nights from long ago, and how all this got started.

It seems like so long ago...

1

THE BEGINNING

Dad used to tell me that members of the Hewitt family were river pirates down on the Ohio River in the 1800s. Maybe I was born too late, because being a notorious river pirate sounds pretty exciting to me.

My name is Jackie Lee Hewitt, but everybody calls me Jack. My dad, Don Hewitt, was a racer and I always knew I was going to be a racer.

My dad's family was from Piqua, Ohio, and my mom, Lois Irene Wesco, was from Troy. Nobody called Mom by her real name; everybody called her "Jake." My grandfather wanted a son, so goes the story, and my mom was the second daughter. He called her "Jake" just for fun, and the nickname stuck.

Troy and Piqua are not too far from Dayton. Those two towns were always fierce rivals; maybe that's why Mom and Dad raised all kinds of hell with each other.

I loved my parents, and I had a good, close relationship with both almost every day of my life. But I long ago realized that their values and their culture was very different from most other families.

Early on, I recognized that I wasn't raised like most other kids.

I was born July 8, 1951, and when I was a kid we lived on the river in a one-room house, near Pleasant Hill, a town not far from Troy. I can remember how cold it was in the winter, and the river was frozen solid. My dad, he didn't work a 40-hour week, and he was never the kind of guy who was interested in a lot of material things. If he'd win a race, he might go out drinking for three days at a time, and when he came home he had blown all the money.

I hate navy beans. Maybe that's because when I was a kid, we might have 'em every night for a week. We'd eat the soup until the beans were gone, and then it was broth. We would wear holes in our pants, and just keep wearin' them. Each year before school started my younger brother John and I would get a brand new pair of engineer's boots. That's what we wore to school, and they would last us the entire school year.

My dad was not a drunk, and I don't want to give you that idea. He was a partier; he liked to have fun and drink beer and raise hell. Through the week he might not drink at all, just hang around home. He was the type of guy who didn't worry about saving money for a rainy day, he worked to pay the bills he had to and that was it. No bills; no need to work.

Dad used to say, "If the sun doesn't come up tomorrow, don't worry about it. We'll just turn the lights on." If they ever dropped the big bomb, you'd want to be with Don Hewitt, because he was a survivor.

My dad would hit the bars on Friday and Saturday night. My mom might walk into the bar, and maybe my dad was sitting there at the bar talking to a girl. Well, Mom would walk up and just nail him, knocking him clear off the barstool. He would get up off the floor and slap her. My dad would come home sometimes and beat my mom up. It's hard to say a lot of it, but it's just the way it was. You can't hide it.

We were poor kids from a poor family on the poor side of town. Very few people in the Hewitt family seemed interested in amounting to much; we were kind of stuck in the life we'd been born into, without a lot of ideas on how to improve ourselves. I have six or seven uncles and aunts on the Hewitt side of the family, and my two cousins -Sandy and Eva- who are just a little bit older than me, they were the first two Hewitts to ever graduate from high school. I was the first male Hewitt to graduate from high school.

If you looked it up in the dictionary under "dysfunctional," you saw our family's picture.

My dad never went to my ball games, things like that, the things you do together as a normal family. The only thing I can remember us doing together was when I was in the third grade, and he won a 100-lap race at Indianapolis Raceway Park when it was dirt. We took his winnings and went to Florida in a '56 Buick Special, to see Clarence Hewitt, my grandpa on my dad's side. His nickname was "Jew," but I don't know where he got that. He was a really cool guy, and we became very close years later, after I got out of school. He lived in a little room behind my uncle Dallas' house.

One day Grandpa and I were sitting and talking, and he said, "Jack, I really don't lust for women...but you don't suppose I'll go to hell for having nasty dreams about women, do you?" I said, "Well, Grandpa, you can't really control what you dream, so I don't think that will be a problem." That was before I believed in anything.

Growing up without many material things, and with parents who raised a lot of hell, you might think it was sad, and painful. But truthfully it wasn't, and even though things were difficult sometimes, I was a happy, carefree boy, optimistic that things would always get better. That attitude carried over to my adult life, too.

When you go to school with dirty clothes, you get old enough to start realizing that it's a problem. From seventh grade on, my little brother John and I would drive our car along this path next to the railroad track as far as we could, then carry our laundry baskets a good half-mile to the Laundromat. It got to be where John and I, or my cousin Jimmy and I, we'd go do the laundry for the whole family, because that's the only way we were going to get clean clothes. From seventh grade on it was like that. I can iron my shirts as well as my wife Jody can, and it's not because our mom taught us. We *had* to. And that bothered me, I'll admit.

But at the time I didn't know any better. In later years, when I started to understand that the rest of the world isn't like that, I didn't resent my parents. But I had made up my mind that Cody, my son, wasn't going to be raised like that. As far as resenting Mom and Dad...there are a lot of things that people might criticize them for, but my dad still bought me my first car. It cost $150, maybe $200. He did what he could do.

I grew up a mommy's boy. I favored my mom's side of the family, and my brother was more like my dad's side of the family. In seventh grade, that's the last time I remember my dad hitting my mom. I went and grabbed him, and the next thing I knew he had me on the floor, with his hand over my throat and his hand drawn back to drill me. He didn't hit me, and he never hit Mom again after that.

In school I was a dummy. I'm a dummy to this day in many ways. I don't remember a lot of stuff; I don't comprehend all that well. I guess I was maybe, what do they call it, Attention Deficit Disorder? That would have been me. They didn't have names for that kind of thing when I was a kid. Even as an adult, I feel like I'm not real smart. My comprehension just sucks, period. If it's something I really like, if I want to remember it I have to read it three times. But that's all right, it doesn't bother me. I've adjusted to it.

I did just enough to get by. I'll tell you how bad it was: I flunked the third grade. I was going to have to do third grade again if I didn't go to summer school. So my mom sent me to summer school. I was already a week into it, and realized she was sending me to *Bible* school by mistake. So I had to do the third grade over again.

My mom wasn't a really smart lady. I loved her to death, but she just wasn't real smart. And Dad -he went to 10th grade or something like that- he was one of these guys who had so much common sense, instead of book learning, he could figure out almost anything. He worked as a plumber for a time, and he told me, "The only thing you have to remember about being a plumber is that shit runs downhill, and payday is on Thursday."

As far as school, I got along with the rich kids and the poor kids, the white kids and the black kids. I got along with *everybody* in school. My senior year, hippies were kind of a problem, and there were problems between blacks and whites. There were riots and stuff going on.

I eventually graduated from high school in 1970. I was such a lousy student, if it wouldn't have been for Mr. Dale Hershey -a teacher at Troy High School- I would probably *still* be in high school, at age 51. I had made up my mind that I was going to graduate, but I hated school very much. Now I'm like most other adults, I wish I had more schooling. My junior and senior year I signed up for OWE (Occupational Work Experience) which allowed me to go to school the first half of the day, and work at a job the second half. I eventually got a job working nights in an iron foundry, working a 40-hour week. I'd get up in the morning and go to school, and I'll bet I was making more money at that foundry than my teachers made at the school.

During my senior year in high school I left home, and lived in Indianapolis with a couple of friends. I enrolled at George Washington High School, but the school was so overcrowded I had to attend classes at night. After a little while we moved back to Troy, and that's where I graduated.

Out of fear and respect for my parents, I got myself up every morning to go to school. I played hooky a lot, but I went enough to graduate.

In school I was always quiet, in the back of the room. I've had lots of scuffles as a race driver, and that's part of my reputation. I didn't get into fights much as a kid; I can remember a few little skirmishes in the stands at Eldora Speedway near Rossburg, Ohio. You know, "my dad is better than your dad" kind of stuff.

That started to change when I got older, in high school. Troy High School's big, big rival was Piqua. I guess I ran around with the hoodlum kids, the ones who drank and smoked, all the bad stuff. I ran with them until they did something I didn't want to do, and then I would go be with my other friends. When we played football against Piqua, the group I ran around with would go looking for that same kind of group from Piqua, and we'd go out in the country and have us a fight like you wouldn't believe. Like we were worst enemies. Not even fighting for anything, just to prove who was the toughest. That's all it was about.

I was on the varsity fight squad. Wonder why I never got a letter jacket?

The next day after a big fight we'd run into those kids, and you'd think we were long-lost friends.

One night some hoodlum kids from Miami East (that's where my wife Jody went to school) came to Troy and said, "We've got to go down to fight Tipp City, but we don't have enough people to make up our team. Would you mind getting a couple of guys together and coming to Tipp City with us?" So we went with them, there were four carloads of us. We were all squared off, 20 kids on each side, ready to fight at a Frisch's restaurant there. But the cops pulled in. So we all jumped in our cars and hauled ass. Two or three miles down the road, we stopped in front of a housing development. We had stopped to regroup, and go back to Troy, but there was a party going on in one of the houses near where we stopped. These boys came running out from the party, they were from a high school in Dayton.

"What are you guys doin'?"

"Aw, man, we came down here to fight Tipp City, and the cops came and we had to leave."

"Well, if you want to fight, we'll fight ya!"

"Okay, but we're not fighting in your front yard."

We all hopped in our cars and went a little ways down the road, jumped out, and went into the ditches fighting like you wouldn't believe. Probably 12 kids on each side. Somebody yelled, "Cop!" so we all stopped and ran back up onto the road. The car went by, and we said, "Hell, that ain't no cop!" So we all went to the ditch again, with a different partner. Whoever was close.

The next day we went down there to look for our watches, our wallets, our combs, all the stuff we lost, and we're looking in the ditch. This car pulls up behind us, it was their big heavyweight, his name was Willoughby, with two or three other kids. They had lost the same shit we lost. You would have thought we were best friends.

They said, "Aw, man, wasn't that fun!"

"Look at this...I fell on a Coke bottle, and I got seven stitches in my back!"

There wasn't anything to it, it was just plain fighting. We didn't have knives or guns or anything, it was just about trying to see who was the toughest. Nobody was mad afterward; we were just grinning and bragging.

I've got to admit: not very many people were raised like that.

I was very close to my grandparents on my mom's side. I would go to the sale barn with Grandpa Wesco, and we had fun. He chewed tobacco, and always wore a gray felt hat. He was my good friend, and I thought he was very cool. When I was in high school we were living in a house trailer (today it's politically correct to call it a mobile home) on the north side of town. But lighting struck the trailer and started a fire, and it burned completely down. We moved in with Grandpa and Grandma Wesco until we could get another place to live.

Grandpa Wesco had diabetes, though, and eventually they had to amputate his leg. It was a really tough deal; after his leg was taken off, he would just sit there and cry, because he was in so much pain. Grandpa couldn't sleep because of the pain, and he was beginning to drag Grandma's health down, because he would keep her awake, too. So he began to call me on the phone, saying, "Come and get me." I'd go to his house, help him into my car, and we'd go driving around. He's over there crying, and I'm driving around, crying with him. After he rode around an hour or so, he would get tired enough to go home and sleep for a couple of hours. But it wasn't enough, and I was worried about both him and my grandma.

I was 16, maybe 17 years old at this time, and every night my buddies and me would hang out all night on the downtown square in Troy. I started thinking that since we were out riding around all night, I'll just go get Grandpa and take him with me. So I got to hang out on Friday and Saturday night with my grandpa, and all my buddies.

Grandma would say, "Now, Jack, don't you take your grandpa out and get him one of those young girls, you know he's got a bad heart."

He would sit there on the square with us, and if we had to run somebody out of town, or go down to Vandalia to get a hamburger, we'd take him with us. He wasn't able to get out of the car much, so sometimes he'd sit in the car and laugh at the kids doing dumb kid things. It gave Grandma a break, and he didn't mind at all. When he got home after a night out with us, his butt was ready to hit the bed.

Later on, after Grandpa passed away, my grandma was going to have to move in somewhere. She asked me, "Why don't you move in with me?" I said, "Because I'm moving in with my girlfriend!" But we thought about it, and my girlfriend and I moved in with Grandma for about six months. Grandma had cataracts, and she could hardly see. One morning I woke up and looked down the hall, and there was Grandma, all alone, with the music on, dancing and singing. She was such a neat lady.

My dad was always my hero. He raced sprint cars, and man, I wanted to race. Eldora Speedway is not far from Troy, and I can remember when the pits were back in the number three corner, before they moved them to the infield. I have pictures from the time when there was no guardrail around the inside, and the outside had a steel guardrail. Up on top, that square piece of concrete, they used to have dances there. A company came in one time and had go-karts, and we would rent go-karts and race around that thing. One year the track promoter, Earl Baltes, had a car, a boat, a freezer, a TV, and a go-kart as give-away prizes. Each prize had a number; if they called your name, you got to reach into a jar and draw a number and you won that prize. I can still remember, number nine was the go-kart. They called my mom's name, and she pulled number nine. She told John and I, "Well, if I would have won the car, I would have bought both of you a go-kart!" We probably tore that thing up in a month, because we never let it rest. Oh, man.

I have to admit, we didn't have very good rules. John and I could just come and go, as we wanted, with no structure, no supervision. Our parents knew where we were, so they figured they could keep an eye on us. Well, they might have known where we were, but they sure couldn't keep an eye on us. One year John and I spent the entire summer living on an island on the Great Miami River, right behind the Kozy Kitchen.

Oh, I didn't tell you about the Kozy? Man, what a place. We moved to a big farmhouse near the river, very close to this little restaurant/bar, the Kozy Kitchen. Dad's best friend, Jeff Crawford, owned the place. My family adopted the Kozy as our second home. I had countless meals there, and my dad was all the time sitting at the bar, drinking coffee, or beer, and socializing.

The island was right behind the Kozy, and when we got hungry we'd just go the Kozy for a sandwich, or some fries. I can picture it in my mind, the lighting, the stools, the tables; the familiar faces all sitting around, like a family. It was a long time ago, but I have a lot of emotion in my heart when I think of it.

We had a tent on the island, and we stayed there rain or shine. We didn't have sleeping bags; we weren't in that category. We had blankets. The island was maybe an acre-and-a-half, not all that large. We had two swimming holes, and we'd swim all day long.

It's hard to believe we survived, we were so reckless. Dad was working for a company taking gravel out of the river, and they had blocked off the river for the mining operation. They placed a big round tile there-like a huge pipe-and the water roared through it, really fast.

We all wanted to go through the tile, in the water, just to see what it was like. We dropped all kinds of stuff in the tile, and watched it spring to the surface way out on the other end. Pop bottles, logs, whatever else we could find. My brother John is a big-time daredevil, and all of a sudden he jumped into the pipe and disappeared.

If there had been a grate at the other end, my brother would have drowned, because there was no possible way he could swim back through that length of tile against such a powerful current. It would have been like trying to swim through a water hose that's on full power. We held our breath, waiting, waiting, waiting, and all of a sudden John popped up on the surface at the other end, gasping for breath.

Instantly we jumped in the pipe, and took the ride to the other end, holding our breath, roaring through that cold, dark pipe, the water pounding you and shaking you all along the way. It was total darkness and suddenly you popped out the other end, and bobbed to the surface. Awesome.

That was a big deal, and looking back across my life it's probably the scariest moment I've ever experienced. We were stupid, no doubt; but there was something about the danger that was so appealing, so attractive, I just couldn't resist it.

Work was always a part of my life. When I was in seventh grade, I started babysitting so I could pay for my membership in a bowling league for kids; I bowled every Saturday morning. Not long after that I went to work for Junie Heffner at the H&H Truck Garage, cleaning the floors. My dad drove Junie's race car. Then I started working at Clark's department store, where I worked with Jody's mom. I worked there a couple of years.

A funny story about Clark's: When I was 16 I wanted to get a loan for a motorcycle. The bank said I needed a co-signer, but since my parents had never established any credit they couldn't sign for me. There was a girl working at Clark's who was four or five years older than me. Man, she had a body that wouldn't quit.

I told this girl that if she would co-sign for my loan, I would give her anything she wanted. Well, she signed, and I got my motorcycle. A few days later we were alone in the back room of the store, and she explained that she wanted "it," *right now!*

So we cleared a space in the storage room, and at exactly the wrong time her boss comes back there, looking for her. His timing was not very good. Oh, man, what a memory.

Here, hop in my truck and I'll drive you around Troy. It's a good town, with a lot of good people.

As I drive down these streets, everything is like one giant memory, all wrapped up into a package. I've traveled all over the country, but Troy will always be my home, and every time I drive through town I see things that make me remember things that have happened in my life.

Right there is the building where they make Hobart welders; another company bought them out but they still make the welders there. Welding has always been a big part of Troy's industry; matter-of-fact, we've got something here I'll bet you haven't seen before.

When you've got all these welders, how do you suppose they want to try and build a house? That's right, make it out of steel and weld it together. We have about six or eight steel houses built here, and they're still standing. There's one, right there! How could you heat a house made out of steel? But they sure look neat.

Hobart used to be the biggest employer here, but not any more. I don't know who is. Hobart Arena is still there, they have shows and different programs, it's a neat old place. When I was a kid they had a couple of TQ midget shows there. And ice skating. The Troy Bruins, a hockey team, used to play here. We also used to play basketball there, Troy High School, but I don't know if they still do. And right there is our new library.

This bridge here, the Adams Street Bridge, when I was six years old I fell into the river and almost drowned, right here. A guy came running out of that house over there, he saw me slip into the river and he ran out and saved me. Man, I got my ass whipped; I wasn't supposed to be close to the river. Actually, that's one of the only times I remember getting a whipping from my dad. He was so mad, but at the same time so happy I was alive.

That house over there, that's where my dad lived when he was a kid. They had a big family: there was Darrell, Dick, Don, Delmer, Della, Danny, Dorothy, and Dallas. They used to jump off this bridge right here into the river. The guy who lived in that house on that side, he would pay 'em a nickel or a dime to jump from the bridge. My uncle Delmer, he was the acrobat, and he got to doing a one-and-a-half gainer when he jumped. So the guy started paying him a quarter and wouldn't pay the other kids.

See that big bunch of trees? There is an island there, no, wait...the island is over here. That's where the boy scouts had a little camp, and when my dad was a kid he was a hoodlum, and the boy scouts came over to camp for the weekend. Instead of having a sleeping bag, Dad and his friends would make their own huts out of wood. Shanties. The boy scouts would come over to invade them, and Dad and his friends pushed them back by throwing rocks and things. They held them off for the whole weekend.

There is the old courthouse; it's a neat old building. They redid that, sandblasted it, it used to be an old funky green, now it's gray and it looks nice. There is Troy High School. *"Old Troy High, live on forever, forever and for I. We'll shout and cry, T-R-O-Y..."* I can still sing it. There's the old football stadium, right along this street here.

This river is the Great Miami River. My dad used to bet guys that he could swim the river from the Kozy to the town square faster than they could walk there. He damn sure did it, lots of times. The river starts up at Indian Lake, and winds all the way to Cincinnati. It cuts right through Troy, right by the downtown area. In a way, it cuts right through me, too, because so many of my memories here involve that great river.

Now we're getting out of town a little bit. That old farm house right there, back the lane, we lived there from my seventh grade to my 10th grade. A lot happened during that period. We could walk to the river from our house. And there is a little country lane that went all the way to I-75, my dad would get drunk and he'd have us behind the wheel of the car, going 70 mph across that field, ripping our ass if we let off the gas. We had a little Cushman scooter when we lived there, too.

This area here, right by the river, there used to be a line of old one-room cabins. When our house trailer burned, we got a new trailer and moved it here at the end of the cabins. My dad and the people who lived there, they used to joke that it was "Skid Row." Everybody living there hung out at the Kozy. All the old cabins are gone, and the Kozy burned down about eight years ago, so it all looks so different from when I was a kid.

Oh, yeah, I've got to tell you about that house on the corner right there, the one-story ranch house. My friend Rick Mohler lived there, and I moved in with him. There was a girl living two blocks down the street, and she and I had a thing going, and later on she got married. Problem was, she kept coming down to see me. Well, one night I was down at the pub with some other guys, and Rick came home. The girl's husband was there waiting, and he thought it was *Rick* she was fooling around with, and he started chasing him. There were some apartment buildings nearby, and Rick ran all the way around those buildings and back toward his house. He couldn't get a break to get inside, and the guy is chasing him all around the neighborhood because he thinks Rick is banging his wife, and Rick has no idea what this guy is sore about. Man, I can just picture that goofy son-of-a-gun running around that house, and I start laughing. It was hilarious.

There was a house standing right here, but they've torn it down. We lived here when I was a little kid, and we didn't have indoor plumbing. We had a pony, but it was too cold to stay outside, so my dad put the pony in the basement. Well, the thing died down there, and rigor mortis set in. Dad finally had to set a chain to it and drag her through the door.

My great-grandmother was visiting one day, and she gave John and I a silver dollar; I was maybe a first-grader, I think. We were walking down to the corner store, maybe six houses away, and a guy picked us up and dropped us off at the store. Can you imagine how scary that would be today, a stranger picking up two little boys in his car? We used to cut across the field here, and sneak through the cemetery. There was a big German shepherd dog that lived right there, and we would see how far we could get before the dog saw us and started barking and raising hell. Good memories.

Troy is like a lot of towns, and the stuff that goes on all around the country goes on here, too. We had a summer of racial trouble here, I think it was around 1970 or so. A gang of blacks was going through town closing down the white bars. The people who ran the Kozy locked the front door and told people that as soon as they finished their beer, they wanted everyone to go home so they could close. Well, Tommy Taylor went out the front door to leave, and he unlocked the door.

The gang of black kids was lined up across the entire door. When they came in, Mom said, "We don't want any trouble." One of 'em slapped Mom, and the fight was on. You've seen those fights in the movies, where they're throwing chairs and things? That's how it was, only it was real. Chairs, scales, equipment, it all ended up out the front door. Beer bottles were flying in every direction. The floor was covered with glass, tables were turned over, it was a bad fight. I took a cue ball and threw it as hard as I could and hit a kid in the head, and he just wilted. Pretty soon they were retreating outside, and Byron Mott, he had the last one inside, and he ran him out the front door.

But they were lined up across the front of the building like a firing squad. In a moment you could hear the gunshots, and the windows all blew out. You could see the bullets after they had ricocheted in the place.

My shirt was torn off, and I was holding my brother John on the floor, he was trying to get up to go attack them. When it was over we called the sheriff, but nobody was ever prosecuted. That just wasn't right.

As I was growing up, there was always a separation between blacks and whites. We just didn't mix. The world changes, though. Today, my cousin is married to a black preacher, Wesley McCoy. I think the world of Wesley; he went on one of our Canadian fishing trips, and you couldn't find a nicer, better person. But at the same time, I'm uncomfortable with my cousin being married to a black man. I wish I didn't feel that way, but I can't help it. I'm old fashioned, I guess.

As I grew older, my brother and I grew closer. We had each other, and that's about all we had. We had the same friends, did everything together, all through high school. John is 14 months younger than me. When I was 19, we had a huge blow-up that really strained our family's relationship.

John joined the Navy, and he was home on leave. I stopped by my house on the way to the Kozy, and Mom is crying up a storm. John is smokin' dope; drinkin'; throwing fits. He was married and had a little girl, Tonya, and they lived over by the river. John was driving a VW Beetle, and he went outside and the car wouldn't start. It made him so mad, he just hopped out and pushed the damned thing over the bank, into the river, which happened to be way up. Luckily the car got caught on a tree before it could roll all the way into the water.

He jumped into his wife's car, a '66 Nova, still all pissed off. There was a stump near their driveway, and he ran over that stump and wiped out the oil pan. But he kept driving, until he blew the engine up. So he's getting madder by the second.

By the time I got to the Kozy a little while later, Dad is sitting at the bar, drunk; John's little girl Tonya is crying, Mom and John's wife are sitting at the bar crying, and John is standing there screaming at 'em. Well, the one thing you don't do is mess with my mom. I told John, "Now look, you do a lot of shit, but you're gonna leave Mom alone." I know lots of brothers fight, but in my entire life I've only hit John with my fist on two occasions. Oh, I beat him up a bunch, wrestling around, but I never tried to hurt him.

But we got into it right then, and I had him down on the ground, and Mom yells, "Don, the boys are fightin'!" Dad, drunk, runs over and tackles me. Johnny jumped up and kicked me in the ribs as hard as he could. Luckily, my buddy Nick Gwin was with me, and he grabbed Johnny and got him down on the ground, just holding him. I finally got away from Dad, and I kicked John as hard as I could. Then, Dad is back into it, and all four of us are on the floor in a big ball, fighting.

Didn't I tell ya' that the Kozy was a fun place to hang around?

Johnny jumped up and swung at me with a cue stick, but I ducked and he hit the light over the pool table, and glass went everywhere. The fight kind of broke up a little bit, and I thought it was over. But John and I locked up again, and I had him down on the little bowling machine. He's pinching me, trying to stick his thumb in my eye, and I had finally had enough, and I drilled him. He just kind of went silent on me.

Well, Dad was standing there, and he hauled off and hit me right in the mouth. Well, that just broke my heart. Just snatched my heart right out of my chest. He was just drunk, and...man, I was always scared of my dad, I just knew he was the meanest son-of-a-gun in the world. I jumped up and threw him on the pool table, and I said, "Look, until I'm 50 years old you can beat my ass, because that's your job as a parent. But if you ever hit me with your fist again, you're going to regret it."

Then I left, but the damage had already been done. It wasn't that he hurt me with a punch in the mouth; it's that he tore my heart out. I moved out for two weeks and moved in with Nick and Bruce Rehmert. My dad was never the kind of guy who would say, "I'm sorry," he always figured things would get better as time goes by. It must have, because I ended up moving back home.

We never talked about that day again. Maybe that was best.

Talking about Jack...

Jack Hewitt is a person who enjoys having fun. He has a smile on his face and a positive attitude.

He was like that in high school. Jack was part of our occupational work co-op program, which was developed to help kids who were at risk of not finishing school. Most of his daily contact was with one teacher. That meant Jack and I spent a lot of time together. This program was the opportunity for the students to get into a job, work with an employer, and still earn the core credits they needed to graduate. It was a different kind of curriculum, but very practical.

We had to have signatures from each student's parents, and agreements that they would support the program, so I had an opportunity to meet Jack's parents. Jack was a big follower of his dad in racing, so when he would go on trips and help his dad, Jack would tell us all about it when he returned.

Jack talked early on about someday being a race driver, like his dad. Before he graduated, he was already starting to get involved in the sport. He was very proud of the fact that his dad was a winner in racing.

Jack has turned out to be very successful with his life. He has succeeded in his goals, and excelled at what he chose to follow. I read with interest when he raced in the Indianapolis 500. That was quite an accomplishment. That takes somebody with guts, motivation, and great dedication. Jack has all those things.

Dale Hershey
Troy High School (ret)
Troy, Ohio

2

UNCLE SAM

If you graduated from high school in 1970 like I did, there was a pretty good chance Uncle Sam had plans for you.

Vietnam was still going strong, so guys my age knew there was a fair likelihood we were going to the military. I didn't want to go; what I really wanted was to start my racing career. So I talked with every branch of the service -army, navy, and so on- and told them I'd sign up for as many years as they wanted if they would give me my summers off so I could race. They weren't interested in that deal, so I waited to see if I'd get drafted.

They had a lottery at that time based on your birthday. My number was 67 -a pretty low number- so I figured I was screwed. There was nothing I could do but ride it out and see what happened. I knew I wasn't college material, and I damned sure wasn't going to get married just to stay out of the service. Besides, that didn't work anyway; my cousin Jimmy had already been drafted even though he had a wife and a baby boy.

Jimmy and I were very close. He was about six months older than me, and when he got his draft notice we teased him something fierce. At that time Merle Haggard had a song out about a soldier writing a letter home. *"I'm writin' this letter in the trenches, Mom, and don't scold if the writing ain't too neat..."* When Jimmy would walk into the bar at the Kozy, we'd run over to the jukebox and play that song. Jimmy was a tough dude; I didn't realize it at the time, but he was scared, because he didn't want to go to Vietnam.

It was the spring of 1971, and one Saturday I worked early in the day carrying hod for Clarence Zeller. I finished work and went home to clean up and take a nap, to prepare for the Saturday night scene. Jimmy called me.

"Hey, I want you to hear this song," he said. "I'm gonna dedicate it to you."

He held the phone up, and there was that song: *"I'm writin' this letter in the trenches..."*

I said, "Jimmy, you got it all wrong, big boy. That's *your* song. You're the one who got drafted."

"Huh-uh, big boy, you got your draft notice today. Your mom and your girlfriend are down here at the Kozy right now, drinkin' and cryin'."

Smart-ass.

He was right, though. I was the last to hear about it, but it was true: I had been drafted.

My induction date was May 10, 1971. I reported to Cincinnati, flew to St. Louis, and took a bus to Fort Leonard Wood, Missouri.

That was my second time on an airplane; let me tell you a funny story about my first airplane trip, a few months after my high school graduation.

My buddy Steve Victor -everybody called him Virgil- joined the navy right after we graduated. Toward the end of his boot camp, he got out on a medical discharge (he had broken his neck when he was younger, and it was giving him problems). Another kid, from Syracuse, New York, was discharged at the same time as Virgil, so they hooked up together to make the trip home, hitchhiking.

By the time they got to Troy, they had a plan: this kid's dad owned a company in Syracuse -a newspaper, a printing company, something like that- and Virgil was going to Syracuse to get a job with this kid at his dad's business. They asked me if I wanted to come along. I had always wanted to go somewhere, so why not?

We were going to go out into the world to seek our fortune. However, I had a grand total of $2.40 in my pocket, and they weren't any better off than I was. We bummed a ride with two girls from Weirton, West Virginia, and they took us all the way to the west side of Pittsburgh before they had to turn south. We started walking east, and we walked all the way across Pittsburgh. It was the middle of the night, and we couldn't get a ride.

All of a sudden, my fortune didn't seem quite so important; I was cold and hungry and ready to get my ass back to the house. At two o'clock in the morning we went into a little bar, and ordered three cokes and a bag of potato chips. We counted our remaining coins and realized we had enough to take a bus to the Pittsburgh airport. We decided that the kid from Syracuse would call his parents and they would wire him a plane ticket, and once he got home he would send us tickets, too. That was the plan.

Two days later, Virgil and I were still hanging around the airport, and it was obvious we weren't going to hear from that kid again. We're both gettin' awfully hungry; you can only drink so much water, it doesn't fill that growling deal. Finally I got to where...I'm not a thief, but I had to eat something. I was going to steal me a candy bar. I went into one of those little airport gift shops, and there was this guy there in a green suit. Everywhere I went, he followed me. I thought, "Shit, this is a security cop." This guy was watching me, I must have looked hungry. I walked out of the store, my conscience was bothering me and I hadn't even done anything. I'm standing out in front of the shop just looking around, and the guy walked up and stood right beside me.

The guy was no security cop; he was gay, and he offered me $15 if I would meet him in the upstairs restroom in 30 minutes. I was somewhere between laughing my butt off and being totally grossed out.

I walked back to where Virgil and I were sitting, and I've got my head down on my suitcase, and I'm crackin' up. I mean, I'm just hysterical. I told Virgil what happened, and we both laughed. You might know, it's 35 minutes later and Virgil is getting those hunger pains, so he's going to walk across the terminal to get a drink of water. He hadn't got halfway across the way, and the gay guy is standing right behind me.

He says, "You couldn't do 'er, huh?"

I said, "No, it's just not me, I really can't do that kind of stuff."

He said, "Well, what about your buddy?"

Now, I'm thinking, that $15 would sure come in handy. So I said, 'Aw, man, he just got out of eight weeks of boot camp! They did that stuff all the time!"

So the guy left again, and Virgil came back. I said, "Virgil, we've got to do this. I'll tell you what, we'll do it this way: You get paid in advance, and I'll give you enough time to just get started, and then I'll come in the bathroom and scare him off."

Virgil stared at me, and his eyes narrowed. He paused for a second, then finally said, "Naw, I don't trust you." Can you imagine, him thinking I would leave him hanging like that? (That's just an expression, by the way.)

So neither one of us went upstairs, and pretty soon the guy came back over and sat down. We started talking, and we told him what had happened. He said, "I'll tell you boys what I'll do. I can't change my plane ticket; but if you'll fly with me to Erie, Pennsylvania, I'll buy you the biggest steak you want. You can spend the night with me, and in the morning I'll buy you both a plane ticket back to Dayton." Well, we couldn't do that, either. So he started to leave, and he gave us a dollar out of kindness. Virgil and I each bought a 50-cent chocolate ice cream cone; that thing was huge. The next day I called my girlfriend and she sent me some money so I could get home. Once I got home I contacted Virgil's parents and they got him home, too.

This time, the plane trip would be different. Uncle Sam, after all, was paying the fare.

Jimmy had shipped out a few days ahead of me, and he was also at Fort Leonard Wood. We were there for a long time before we saw each other. I was doing an obstacle course one day, and Jimmy was walking down the road nearby, and he could hear everybody yelling, "Run, Hewitt, run!" And he's looking around, ready to take off running, not sure what's going on. That's how we found each other, and found out which barracks we were in.

The army was all right, but it's kind of a cult deal. You're a kid, and they brainwash you, telling you, "Charge up that hill...go up that hill, and die!" They brainwash you enough, and scare you enough, that you'll do what they tell you. For me, I was a grizzly bear, but what they held over my head was a dishonorable discharge. That would have embarrassed my mom and dad, and I wouldn't do anything like that. We all believed that a dishonorable discharge ruined your whole life. That was probably one of the worst things a person could have happen to them. So you went out and did your job.

Part of the problem was that I was 19 years old at the time, and I wasn't used to people telling me what to do. I mean, I had been my own boss ever since I was a little kid. I just wasn't used to people shouting orders, telling me I had to get a haircut, or to shine my shoes, stuff like that.

I didn't really like the army, but when I look back now I know it was good for me. It helped me become a man, in a man's world.

I was certain at the time that I was going to Vietnam. There was no doubt in my mind. And I really didn't think all that much about it...I was kind of resigned to it. I wasn't worried about dying or anything like that, but I just didn't know...I hadn't been through any of this before. They had you so scared and paranoid, when I got off the bus, they started yelling and screaming, those drill sergeants. They asked you right off the bat, where do you want to be stationed, and what would you like to do? I don't remember what I put down for wanting to do, maybe nothing, but I told them I wanted Fort Knox and Vietnam. That way I could at least be home on weekends to race while I was at Fort Knox. I figured if I picked the worst, then I had a chance of getting the best when I got home. Every time they asked me that, that's what I told 'em.

The first few days we spent taking care of paperwork and stuff. They asked me who I wanted to list as a life insurance beneficiary. You could buy $5,000 for $1 per month, $10,000 for $2, and $15,000 for $3 per month.

"I don't need any life insurance," I told 'em.

"Why not?"

"Because I'm comin' home! I know I'm not getting killed. Wherever you send me, I'm coming back."

"You've got to take something."

"Whaddya mean, I've got to take something?"

"You can't get out of here without taking something."

"Okay, then, gimme the $5,000."

During basic training, I had the biggest mouth out there. Every night I'd be hoarse from the singing and cadence. There were three platoons in our company, and you could hear me over all of 'em, because I was wailin'. I was in the first squad, second platoon. I had a red-haired drill sergeant, Sgt. Blaisdale. My head drill sergeant was Drill Sgt. Gardner.

While I was in boot camp, a lot of bad stuff happened at home. Grandpa Wesco died, and two weeks later my Uncle Delmer was shot and killed. A guy in a wheelchair was beating his dog, and my uncle went over to his yard and confronted him about being mean to the dog. Well, the guy in the wheelchair had an attitude, and he just took out a gun and shot Uncle Delmer in the stomach. He died from the infection. And then, a week after that, Dad lost his eye in a racing accident.

My mom, bless her heart, she meant well, but she didn't call me and tell me any of this. I was calling Debbie, my high school girlfriend, and she said, "Jack, I've got some bad news." Well, it got to be where every time I called, I started asking, "Who died this week?" And she'd tell me.

A kid came up to me on a Wednesday night, and said, "What happened to your dad?" There was a bunch of guys in my company who were from the area around Eldora, and this kid had heard they had taken Dad out of Eldora in an ambulance. So I called home right away, and Mom said she didn't want to worry me. But by then, instead of not worrying, I didn't believe her. I was lying awake at night, worried about what I didn't know.

My dad was racing at Eldora, and a big rock came up and went right through his goggles, and he lost his right eye. I desperately wanted to come home to see him, and it led to my first confrontation in the army.

Sgt. Blaisdale really liked me. I was a lot smaller then, and I weighed maybe 160 pounds. Whatever we were doing, I would try to do as well as I could. When Dad lost his eye, the next day I had barracks guard, which is like guard duty. I made all the beds and cleaned the floors, and I had been awake half the night worried about my dad. I had just laid down on the bed when another drill sergeant walked in. That's an Article 15, immediately. Sleeping on guard duty. That's like a traffic violation, kind of minor deal. A misdemeanor.

Our barracks were these new three-story brick buildings, and we were standing in formation out front. There are a hundred guys in my company. Sgt. Gardner looked me right in the eye.

"Look, you got that Article 15, you were going to go home to see your dad, but now you can't go."

"Yes, I can go," I said. "I am going home to see my dad this weekend."

"No, you're not."

"Yes I am!"

I started to cry, because I was so mad. That's something I do; when I'm really, really pissed off, I cry. I just can't help it.

I told him, "Drill Sgt. Gardner, I'll tell you right now: I am going home this weekend."

He said, "I was going fishing this weekend, but if I have to stay here and handcuff you to the bed, that's what I'm going to do."

"Well, that might work, but the only thing I'll tell you is don't go to sleep. 'Cause if you go to sleep there's going to be problems."

I was crying, absolutely weeping, in front of the whole company.

"Just because I'm crying, don't think I'm not mad," I yelled. "I'll fight you or any of these sons-of-bitches out there right now. I'm not scared of any of 'em. Just because I'm crying, don't think I'm a pussy, because I will fight."

He said, "Hewitt, my wife went off and left me, and she took my two daughters. I've got a daughter I haven't even seen yet. And I haven't gone off chasing after them."

"Evidently you didn't love 'em," I said. "I love my dad and I'm going home."

By then he was just about mad enough to fight, but I didn't care. I was going for the jugular, too.

That was a Friday morning, and we went through the day doing our normal routine. That night Drill Sgt. Blaisdale told me he had talked to the captain. "With all you've been through," he said, "he's going to go ahead and let you go home."

It wasn't a half-hour later I saw Drill Sgt. Gardner going down the stairway. I said, "Drill Sgt. Gardner, can I talk to you for a minute?"

"Look, don't thank me...you thank Sgt. Blaisdale, because I didn't have anything to do with your going home."

"I wasn't going to thank you. I just wanted to apologize for some of the things I said this morning. I am sorry, and I didn't mean anything. But I was pretty messed up."

The next morning Drill Sgt. Blaisdale picked me up a little bit early, and he took me by Sgt. Gardner's house just to show me where he lived. The wind had blown the "ner" off the mailbox. It just said, "Gard.". I went home that weekend and saw Dad, and I felt a lot better. I came back Sunday night, and Monday morning I'm up early. Drill Sgt. Gardner came walking up, and I said, "Hello, Drill Sgt. Gard."

He said, "What?"

"I saw your name on your mailbox."

"Hewitt, before this eight weeks are up, you're going to know my name," he said. "Every time you see me, you drop down and give me 10 pushups. Whatever you're doing, wherever you are, you knock out 10 pushups. You're gonna remember my name."

Well, he didn't know what he was getting into. We would be out there in the morning and the senior drill sergeant would be up on the steps doing roll call, making sure nobody had gone AWOL that night. We're in the middle of these two brick buildings, and they're quite a ways apart. The other drill sergeants would come out to sit on the rail, listening to what was going on that day. Drill Sgt. Gardner got to where he couldn't come outside; every time he did, I'd immediately hit the ground, and do the pushups yelling the number as loud as I could. They finally told him to stop coming out because it would interrupt roll call. If I saw him pass in a car, I'd drop off the side of my group and do the pushups. To me it was a big joke, because I already got what I wanted: I got to go home and see Dad.

I had fire guard one night, and I went down to check in. Sgt. Gardner was the drill sergeant on duty. He said, "Hewitt, sit down here and talk to me." Instead of me walking the halls for a half-hour, I sat and talked to him. He said, "You're one crazy little son of a gun..." and we just bullshitted. We had a great old time. He really liked me, after all.

Not long after that they brought in these rookie guys, guys trying to learn how to be a drill sergeant. We had this old fat one, I can't remember his name. UGLY! He had a head like a pumpkin. Anyways, he said, "Hewitt, whenever I tell you to get down, you're not going to do pushups...I want you doin' sit-ups!" That went on for a while, and three or four days later we're in the chow line, and I'm talking (imagine that). He just screams, "HEWITT! Get down and knock out 30 sit-ups!" I had done about three, when he turned around to rip somebody else's ass. I'm just sitting up, looking at him. All of a sudden he turns back around and I said, "27!" real loud. He just scowled and said, "Get your ass back in line!"

Even though we were stuck in the army, I still had fun. And really, I didn't mind the physical stuff. They had a run-dodge-jump routine, where you had to take off running, go around a couple of small pylons, through these wide gates, jump a four-foot ditch with water in it, and go around a couple more pylons, then run back the same way. You had to do that within a certain amount of time. One day it rained, and everybody was just soaking wet. We were standing against the rail on the sidewalk, across from the ditch. There was a mud puddle there. I don't know who started it, but two or three of us, when somebody came by and splashed us from that puddle, we'd grab their ass and throw 'em into the ditch. It was a mudhole, but we had their ass in there, right now.

My birthday is July 8, and on that day our captain told us that instead of doing our afternoon training we could go swimming at the pool. I said, "Boys, I told 'em it was my birthday, so now we get to go swimming!" One of 'em yelled to the captain, "Is this because of a birthday, that we're here?" The captain just nodded, and didn't say any more. But my captain's birthday was July 8, too! Man, they thought I was a big shot after that.

On our last week of basic training, we were allowed to have people come down. My girlfriend Debbie, along with Jimmy's wife, Karen, drove down to see us. When I graduated, my mom and dad came down, along with Debbie and her sister and her parents. We spent some time at Six Flags before I had to get back.

After eight weeks of basic, they told me I was being assigned to surface-to-air missiles. It's strange how I got into the missile program; I truly have no idea. You've got to take an IQ test before you get into any of the programs, and I hate to read. I was evidently a really good guesser, because on the test I would read one question and answer three. But I apparently had a high enough IQ that I got into the missiles. They were

Chaparral missiles, used for shooting down airplanes, and they had them in Germany, Hawaii, Colorado, and Texas. The Chaparral was a mobile unit, mounted on a tank that ran on tracks on the ground.

Being assigned to the missile unit meant one thing for sure: I wasn't going to Vietnam, because they didn't have planes for us to shoot down. I just couldn't believe I wasn't going to Vietnam.

After Basic Training, I was shipped to Fort Bliss, Texas for Advanced Infantry Training, or AIT, and our training on the missile program. After 10 months in Texas I was shipped out to Colorado Springs, where I served out the rest of my hitch.

I never left the U.S. while in the army. The only foreign soil I saw was when I would tag with some of the other guys to go to Mexico to party on Friday and Saturday nights, at a place called the Chinese Palace.

I met a little girl down there named Patty Gierrtez. My buddies and I were sitting in a bar in Juarez, and she and her two sisters came walking in the front door. She was a secretary in Chihuahua, about 250 miles south, and they had come to Juarez to vacation. We were out there dancing, and a couple of guys from my unit were dancing with her sisters. We fooled with these sisters every night, all week. Dancing, having fun, it was great.

The only time we could ask them anything, or talk to 'em, was by using the waitress as an interpreter. It was neat. Here we are, talking all this nasty guy talk, because they can't understand us. Really nasty stuff. They were probably talking the same stuff; we had already tested them to make sure they really didn't speak English. Patty and her sisters were up there for two weekends.

Later on, Patty and I started writing back and forth. I don't know how she got hers translated; there was a Hispanic guy in our company, and he would help me read her letters. She called me, "Ciero Jack." "Ciero" means darling. We wrote each other for about six months. She was a hot tamale...she probably weighs about 240 now, I would imagine. But she sure was a cutie then.

My cousin Jimmy had gone to Fort Polk, Louisiana for AIT. He finished up, and was going to Vietnam. He was home on leave following AIT when he was out drinking, and while driving home he ran off the road near where we used to live. He got stuck in the mud, and he left the car running and he was asphyxiated. Jimmy's little boy was just nine months old when Jimmy died. That had been another reason I had signed up to go to Vietnam; I figured if I went, they wouldn't take Jimmy. But I guess it didn't really matter, because he didn't make it that long.

There were a few scuffles for me in the army. This guy named Huckleberry from California, he was one of those guys who...when I went in, you didn't have to get your head shaved, you just had to cut it real, real short; well, he shaved his head anyway. He was a hippie, a weightlifter, and he was about six feet tall, a giant compared to me. In our barracks, you used a butt can for your cigarette butts, and an ammo can for your personal items: deodorant, that kind of stuff. Well, one evening he just walked into our room, grabbed my ammo can, took my Right Guard deodorant, and walked back out. "Why...that sumbitch..." He wasn't even bunked in my room. I jumped out of my bunk, and by the time I got to his room -he was in a two-man room, I was in an eight-man room- he was spraying the deodorant around like an air freshener. I'm going to take it away from him. Right about this time, the goofy fat drill sergeant walks by. We're in there scuffling, I'm grabbing for the can of deodorant, and I'm loud because I'm cussing Huckleberry. The sergeant walks in the room to break it up, and he looks in the butt can, and he found a roach. Marijuana.

That's why Huckleberry wanted my Right Guard; they were in there smokin' dope and he wanted to cover up the smell. Well, the only two people the sergeant sees in the room were Huckleberry and me. This was eight o'clock at night, and they called the captain in. The captain was hot, because he was at home doing whatever, and he had to come in. He is not in a good mood. He was normally a good dude, but not at that moment. They were tearing down my locker; all your socks had to be folded just right, everything exactly in order. I never fooled much with that stuff, because I didn't want to have to keep folding it. I mean, they tore my locker plumb apart. I'm standing there in my underwear.

The captain said, "Hewitt..." I said, "Hey, sir, I don't suppose my word means anything right now?" Well, he really went off on me. "Don't you say another word...matter of fact, you stand at attention when I'm here!" Well, now I'm standing there with smoke coming out of my ears. I'm hot. So they sent us down to the day room. We got down there, and he said, "Now, Hewitt, what exactly is your word?" I said, "It's a little late now...first of all, I'll tell you this: I don't drink, I don't smoke, and I damned sure don't screw around with dope."

Well, he kind of paused, and then I told him what happened. Huckleberry was standing right there, and I never really did like Huckleberry much anyway. We had gotten into it one other time over some fatigues I found in the trash can, he thought he was going to take them away from me. I said, "You ain't takin' shit." He grabbed for 'em, and I threw my bayonet at him. He just grabbed the bayonet and slid it across the floor where I was cleaning my rifle. But I thought he slid it a little harder than he should have. Then I had him by the throat, and I'm wantin' to whip his ass, and the guys in our company finally broke us apart.

Now, here it was, a few months later on this deal with his dope.

Luckily, the captain believed me, and I didn't get into any trouble. Neither did Huckleberry, I guess those rookie drill sergeants couldn't prove anything so they just let it all drop.

I also had a scrap with another guy from California, a kid named Kaiser. He was a muscle-bound dude, too, but without the burr haircut. He was a big blond-haired boy.

Oh, did I tell you about the needles?

You have to understand, I'm scared to death of needles. I just couldn't take it, thinking about those vaccinations they were going to give us. I mean, I just couldn't take it. Every time, I got so scared...I would have fought anybody there, but those needles, that was different. I was petrified. We were all set to begin getting our shots, and we're standing in formation, getting ready to go into the medical building. The process was this: You would enter through a door in one end, get your shots, and exit at the other end. You had to take your shirt off before you went in, fold it up and lay it on the ground at your position in the squad.

The first platoon went through, getting their shots, and then came back around to get their shirts. Well, I'm in second platoon; I figured out that by the time we were supposed to start going through, the first couple of squads from first platoon were coming out, and getting their shirts back on. So I just stepped out of line a little bit, and slipped into the line with the first platoon. Then I'd act like I was putting on a shirt. When my squad came out from getting their shots, I'd slip back in line and put my shirt on. You're supposed to have a total of 20-some shots, and I avoided all but about seven.

When I went to AIT, I started doing the same thing, and it was working out perfectly. But my drill sergeant figured out that I was scared of needles.

"Jack, come with me and try it," he said. "If you can't do it I understand, but at least say you'll try."

"Okay, I'll try, but get me right in and out before I get a chance to get scared."

So we went down there, and if everything had been ready to go, I would have gotten my shot that morning. But a guy was putting the serum on that air gun they use for shots, and I saw him pull the trigger to test it. In an instant, the serum was dripping off the ceiling.

That's it. I'm outta here. Shit, I was already in a dead run. They weren't gonna hold me down, even if they tried. As I was going out the door this big ol' black guy, he was laughing at me. I said, as I was leaving, "I'll tell you what, I ain't got time at this moment, but if you think I'm scared of your big ass, you've got a lot of learnin' to do."

When I was ready to ship out, they told me to report with all my gear and my vaccination record which was a little booklet they stamp each time you get a shot. Problem was, my booklet was mostly empty. So I grabbed a couple of my buddies' records, and took them down to the office with me. "Hey, I've been here all this time with these guys, and I've taken every shot they have. But I lost my book during the shots..." The guy just said, "No problem," and he stamped my book full. What a system.

I did my job, but I'll admit I also tried to work things to my advantage. Sometimes it worked, and sometimes it didn't. During AIT we had these forced marches where you'd walk and run 2.5 miles to a stake in the ground, then turn around and come right back, as fast as you could.

I have flat feet, big-time (I had always heard that if you had flat feet or bad hearing, you're not eligible for the army; I've got both and they *still* took my ass). The forced marches were hard on my feet, and it was a problem. When I realized we were facing two fives, two 10s, and a 20-miler, after that I made sure I had a dentist appointment, a hearing appointment, or a foot appointment when the march was scheduled.

After the 20-mile forced march, my company came back to our barracks, and I was lying on my bunk. My buddy, Cline, he was all pissed off because I'm laying up there grinnin' at all of 'em. They're all hot and sweaty and mad, and now they're wantin' to fight. How a guy who just ran 20 miles wants to fight a guy who's been lying in bed all morning, I don't know. But we didn't fight, because Cline was my buddy, and he was just mad that I had outsmarted 'em.

I liked Colorado...but then again, I hated it. I was still in the army, and that wasn't at all where I wanted to be. I would probably have hated anywhere I went, just because of the circumstances. I didn't go skiing until two weeks before I got out, and I liked it so much I went every day after that.

My first "race" came out there, I guess you might say. My buddy Rick Willoughby and I each got a car, and we entered a demolition derby at a little quarter-mile track in Colorado Springs. We would also go up to Denver to watch races at a big half-mile paved track, and there was another paved quarter-mile up that way. We went to Continental Divide drag strip and watched Evel Knievel jump a bunch of cars. That was a cool deal.

My hitch called for two years of active duty, but they offered me the opportunity to get out three months early if I agreed to serve a year in the reserves. That was a mistake; I should have just done my last three months on active duty and been done with it.

At that time, the National Guard and the Army Reserve were kind of a joke. They *played* army. Nowadays they'll call those guys up for active duty, but at that time they didn't, so guys joined the Guard and the Reserve just to get out of going to Vietnam.

I had just finished almost two years on active duty, and here are these guys who would work at their job all week and once a month get away from their wife, and it was an excuse to get drunk. Or guys who were beat around all week by their wife, and they got to put a stripe on for the weekend and boss other people around. The whole deal just didn't go well with me.

I'll admit I was cocky about the whole thing. I mean, what were they going to do if I screwed up, send me back to active duty for three months? Hell, the paperwork would have taken that long.

Each year in the reserves, you go to camp for two weeks in the summer. They called it camp, but it's really a bunch of guys playing army. I was dreading the whole thing as it approached, but I shouldn't have. It turned out to be one wild-assed big-time adventure.

We left our center in Ohio, headed for camp in Virginia, and I somehow got thrown in with another company from Lorraine, Ohio. We had an overnight stop in Roanoke, Virginia to pick up some more equipment.

Being thrown in with the new company meant I didn't know anybody. I never was much of a drinker, but I took the jeep to go buy us some wine. I'm sitting at a red light, and a guy in a little red sports car pulls up next to me.

"Hey, where's the best place to buy some wine?" I hollered.

"Right here!" he said, pointing to a shop on the corner.

So I pulled into the liquor store parking lot with my jeep, complete with flashing lights and a giant "CONVOY AHEAD" sign.

Four or five hours later we're all standing on the street corner, drunk, yelling at the girls and carrying on. This same guy pulls up in his sports car, and he recognized me.

"Hey, did you get your wine?" he asked.

"Hell, yeah," I grinned. "I'm drunk! Where you goin'?"

He named some town about 20 miles away, where he was picking up his girl who worked at a Pizza Hut.

"You need a co-pilot?"

"Well, yeah," he laughed, and I hopped into his car.

Here I am with a bunch of guys I don't know, in the middle of Virginia, and I leave with a total stranger. I knew I had to be back by morning, but that was hours from now...no problem!

We got to this Pizza Hut, and sat down at a table with some friends of his. Three girls and two guys, us two, and his girlfriend. We got to shooting the breeze, and I left with the three girls and two guys. I didn't know their names, or what town I'm in, and I was getting farther and farther from my company. But it all seemed like such fun...

I woke up early in the morning in some fabulous cottage on a lake, just a wonderful deal. I've got me this little fat white girl laying next to me, I'm kind of looking over at her, with a massive hangover, just feeling like shit. I have no idea who this girl is, and the other people finally come out of their rooms, and I have no idea who they are, either. They could have really screwed me, but they took me clear back to the town where my company was staying. When we got there the guys were sleeping in the truck, and I can promise you I had a much better night than they did.

At the camp in Virginia we had fun. We weren't supposed to, but we had fun anyway. Somebody found this big black snake, that thing was as big around as your arm, I'm not kidding. They killed it, and that night after everybody was all drunked up we tore this guy's bed up and laid it down the length of his bed. Then we made the bed back. So here he comes a little while later to crawl into bed, and he's about half drunk. He pulled the covers up on him, and kind of rolled over against that snake. He went completely berserk, just wacko.

We had a black guy who was our platoon sergeant. He'd come in early in the morning and kick the trash can, yelling, playing army. So I got a bright idea: We took this snake and kind of coiled it up on a Frisbee, then left the door open a crack, and put the Frisbee up on the door. When he would kick that door open, the snake would drop right down on him. The next morning there was nobody asleep; we were all awake in our bunk, waiting on him to come in. Well, he kicked the door and came in and started raising hell, and he saw that everybody was already kind of awake. And we all busted out laughing. That damned snake was so big on the Frisbee, it bent it in the middle, and it was perfectly balanced on the top of the door. He looked up and saw that snake and he just roared back out the door. You talk about screaming and cussing, he was hot, man. He didn't trust us too much after that.

Maybe the problem was I didn't really respect most of those guys. I had a lieutenant tell me to get under the truck and check the hydraulic seal, and I had already checked it several times. I said, "I'm not getting under that truck." He said, "Why not?" I said, "For two reasons. One, you might think I like it here. The other reason is, I don't. I'm not gettin' under that truck."

I'm out in the field, and all I've got on is my fatigue pants, and they're rolled up like shorts. I've got my boots on, rolled down. socks rolled down, no shirt, no hat. When it got dark, here comes a captain and a lieutenant coming down the road in a jeep. There was no guard duty or anything, but I jumped out from behind the tree in front of their jeep.

"Halt! Who goes there? What's the password?"

They got to stuttering, it scared 'em. "Password!!?? Um....ah....uh...I don't know! What is it? What's happening?!"

I said, "Hell, I don't know! *You're* the boss...you're supposed to know!"

"Uh...uh....carry on!"

Sammy Mills, who lived in Roanoke, was in my company during my active duty. Our camp wasn't far from where he lived, so I called Sammy and got with his bunch of friends, and a couple of our guys came with me. We got to drinking Boones Farm again, and carrying on. They don't have beer joints there like they do in Ohio, so they took us up into the mountains to some bootlegging joint. It was an old school bus, with electric lights installed. There must have been 200 people up there. Next thing I know, some guy comes running out of the bus, spittin' teeth, with another guy right behind him, shooting a pistol. And I'm sitting on the front fender of a nearby car, half drunk. Sammy and all his guys are yelling, "Get down! Get down!" I'm the only dumb-ass still sitting on the hood of a car. I said, "Well, *I* didn't hit him, he ain't gonna shoot *me*."

We had a party at the camp that last weekend, and they took a big truck and filled the bed with ice and beer. Me and these two bruisers who lived over near Eldora, we'd stand by the truck and when somebody came over to get a beer, we'd grab their ass and throw 'em in the tank of ice water. That was fun.

When we were coming back from Virginia, we stopped at Charleston, West Virginia at a buffet for dinner. Earlier that day, we had stopped on the highway because somebody broke down. We jumped out of our tanker truck, and the Warrant Officer came up and started ripping our ass because we didn't have our shirt on, and no hat. He made us look bad. That night when we were stopped for dinner, the whole corner of the block was a parking lot at this buffet, filled with army trucks and soldiers. We're standing around on the corner, whistling at the girls, yelling at everybody.

That Warrant Officer comes out after paying the bill, and he cuts across the corner in his jeep to get to our truck. Well, get this: He didn't have his hat on. I jumped right up in his face, and said, "Sir!" everybody looked around, of course. "I don't want to bring this up right now, sir, and I know it's not something you want to talk about, but I believe I got my ass chewed out earlier for this same damned deal!"

He didn't come around my truck the rest of the trip. I think if I had walked around completely naked he probably wouldn't have said squat to me.

The army probably would have been a lot more enjoyable except for one thing: I was missing an opportunity to go racing. By the end of my hitch, I was really impatient.

I needed to race; I wanted to race; I was ready to race. Army days were over, and racing days were just around the corner.

Talking about Jack...

The first thing you've got to know about Jack Hewitt is that he'll fight at the drop of a hat, and he'll cry at the drop of a hat. He can go either way. He's tough and he'll fight, but this is a guy who cries at movies.

He thrives on people. Just being around them, giving them autographs, meeting them, laughing, joking, he's in his element. And he's just great with kids. If there's a kid who is a little bit bashful, standing in the background, too shy to ask for an autograph, Hewitt will find that kid.

There was a guy who lived near us named Roger Rice, and he developed an incurable crippling disease and was in a wheelchair. Most people were uncomfortable being around Roger because they didn't know what to say, or how to deal with the situation. So nobody would go see him. But Jack would go over and pick him up, haul him to the races, no matter how much work it was. It wasn't like Roger and Jack were best friends; they were really just acquaintances. But Jack took it upon himself to make sure Roger had some happiness and fun during his last years.

When Jack started racing, I never saw anybody pass him. He didn't make it too many laps, because he usually crashed, but he was super aggressive. Maybe the most aggressive driver I've ever seen. And he is a really determined guy, a guy who just won't give up.

How can I best describe Jack Hewitt? Like this: Go to almost any race, and afterward see who has the biggest crowd at their pit. Chances are, it's Hewitt. You look at the guy who won the race, and maybe he's got three people down there, and Hewitt maybe finished 22nd and he's got a crowd. That says it.

Bobby Snead
Ludlow Falls, Ohio

3

FIRST RACES

Getting drafted into the army cost me two years out of my racing career, as far as I'm concerned. You look around at racing today, and racers start out when they're still kids. They race quarter-midgets when they're real little, and by the time they're 16 or 17, they're racing midgets and sprint cars.

When I started racing in the summer of 1973, I was already 22 years old. That wasn't all that unusual at that time, because a 17-year-old kid in a sprint car wouldn't have been allowed at most tracks in 1973.

When I was 16, Junie Heffner allowed me to hot-lap his race car at Lima, Ohio a couple of times. I also wrecked the Nickles Brothers car at Eldora, so I had almost no experience in racing. Still, I was pretty much eaten up with the racing bug, and I knew it was what I was gonna do. After all those years of sitting in the stands watching Dad race, it seemed natural for me to be a race driver.

My deal with Junie had been pretty simple: I helped work on the car all year, and in return he would allow me to hot-lap the car a couple of times. That was my pay. Not only was I learning about race cars, I got to hot-lap the car! I wasn't complaining.

When I got home from the army's summer camp trip in Virginia, I was helping Pete Whetsel. Pete thought the only kind of racing was AAA or USAC. He and Spider Webb, who had been a great racer in the 1930s and '40s, they used to get drunk and have fun together. Pete started coming by the Kozy Kitchen, and he met Dad, and Dad started telling him about other races in the area.

I would go with Pete to Chicago every week, picking up VW Beetles at auctions. I helped Pete by driving one of the cars back to Ohio. Plus, I helped him around the shop. He kind of adopted me. Pete was a really neat guy. He didn't have any kids, so I was his adopted son.

One day Pete told me, "Hey, if you see a car at the auction you'd like for yourself, go ahead and buy it and you can pay me back. If it's a Corvette, whatever, just go ahead and get it."

I told Dad that Pete was willing to help me get a car, and Dad said, "See if he'll loan you the money for a race car, instead." Pete thought that was okay, so my buddy Frog (Mike Laughman) and I became partners and borrowed $4,000 from Pete. Our deal was to pay him back a little bit every week. This would have been mid-summer, 1973.

The car we bought was definitely an entry-level car. It had some age on it, for sure. Junie Heffner had bought the car from Ray Smith, and my dad drove the car for several years. Junie sold it to Ray Fontaine in Toledo, and he ran it for a couple of seasons and parked it. That's when Frog and I bought the car. Eventually we sold it to some kid in South Dakota.

When we bought the car from Ray Fontaine, he threw in a lot of stuff which helped us get going. We got the car, a trailer, motor, all kinds of spares, gears, a bunch of stuff. It was a pretty neat deal. We were excited.

Money was just not something I worried about at that time. I didn't care about being rich; I just wanted to have fun. I was drawing $68 every week in unemployment, and I wanted to draw that for a while before I worried about getting a job. Eventually I started driving a truck at the Ludlow Stone Quarry, and I focused on keeping the race car going.

My first race came at Eldora Speedway. Eldora is a fast, tough track, and a lot of guys are kind of scared of the place, because of the speed and the high banks. But I had watched races there forever, and it seemed natural to start out there.

Man, it was tough competition at that time. Jimmy and Freddy Linder, Doc Dawson, Dick Gaines, Bubby Jones, Rick Ferkel, and Sheldon Kinser were there a lot. Greg Leffler was starting out the same year as me his dad Paul was a famous mechanic on USAC cars. Greg had nicer equipment than me, but we were both learning. We were in a lot of races together, we ran the B-mains for a while.

I didn't make the show my first night; I spun out a bunch of times. Our car was an old rail-frame, spring-front car, and by that time there were lots of four-bar cars out there. Our car was old compared to what everybody else had, but it didn't make any difference. I just needed laps. I know I spun out a million times that first season. It wasn't pretty. But we were still out there, getting laps.

I was brave. I mean, I truly had no fear at all of getting hurt, no fear whatever. And when you're that brave...I thought I had a big "S" on my chest. I guess when you're young it's normal to be that dumb, to not realize how bad you can hurt yourself.

When I was 16, not long after I got my driver's license, I was flying along on Halloween night, and I ran off the road and rolled the car over. It pitched me out, and the car rolled over and landed right on top of me. We had just gotten a big rain, and the ground was so soft the car just mashed me into the mud. That's the only thing that saved my ass. Only my head was sticking out from under the car, and they just rolled the car off me and I didn't have a scratch.

So I thought I was invincible. Nothing could hurt me! And I just knew I was already a great race driver...no shortage of confidence on my part.

Even though I'd only been racing a few weeks, I wanted to travel. I was kind of restless, looking for something fun, something exciting. We took our old car to Granite City, Illinois, even though we knew it would be tough to make the show. Not only were we inexperienced, it was a bigger event that would attract a lot of good cars.

I had become friendly with Johnny Beaber, even though Johnny stole my dad's ride in the Nickel Brothers car. Beaber was younger than me, but he had already been racing for several years. When we went to Granite City, we pitted near Beaber.

Rick Ferkel was Beaber's buddy, and we had already met Ferkel at Eldora. He came walking by our pit at Granite City, and he said, "What are you guys doing clear down here?" Everybody else had a stack of tires and a four-bar spaced-framed car, and we have this old rail-frame, spring-front car. "Aw," Ferkel said, grinning at us, "I forgot...you boys want to race."

Damn right, we want to race.

Later that same year we went to Williams Grove to run the National Open, and our first day we were parked between Kenny Weld and Jan Opperman. We missed the show, though, and came on home.

Racing against guys like that made me better. You're only as good as the guys you race against. You see lots of guys who can be track champion 10 out of 15 years, but then when they go someplace else they miss the show. It's because they don't get any better, racing against the same guys every week. You don't have to get better, because you've lost that extra drive, you're already winning. Why not start venturing out to other tracks?

If you can chase the best racers in the world and you start to beat them, all of a sudden you're a better racer. Donny Schatz is a perfect example today; he runs with the World of Outlaws here in the U.S. and it's tough, then he goes to Australia and kicks their butts.

We were a little short on cash, so we couldn't travel all that much in the beginning. We ran Lima every Friday night, and Eldora on Saturday. Eventually Pete Whetsel gave us some more money to help us out, like our sponsor. We got through my first season, and when we started the 1974 season I wanted to travel more.

My dad had always traveled some...I remember as a small kid going with Dad to Heidelburg, Pennsylvania; Lakeside Speedway in Kansas City, Kansas; and also the Knoxville Nationals in Iowa. I was in the third grade when we went to Knoxville, and I remember it very clearly. We were sitting in the grandstand, and a car shot into the infield and hit a guy standing there, and pinned him against a light pole, cutting off his leg. He was lying one place, and his leg was a few feet away. That's a vivid sight, especially for a third-grade kid.

In 1974 I didn't follow any particular circuit, just traveled some to different tracks, and ran a lot around home at Eldora and Lima. We went to run the dirt mile at Springfield, Illinois, and I had never been on a big track like that before. We drove down the straightaway and down into the corner, and everybody backed off. Why are these guys slowing down, I didn't see a yellow flag...so I stayed in the gas. I didn't realize that on the mile you're really hauling ass, and that corner comes up in a hurry. Next thing I knew I'm up against the fence, but luckily I kept the car off the wall and kept going. It got my attention; now I knew why those guys were backing off so early for the corner.

One of the neatest things I did in my first full season came at Eldora, like the third race of the year. A week earlier my dad had quick time of 17.6 seconds, and he said afterward that was the quickest he had gotten around Eldora. The following week I went out and did a lap of 17.53 seconds. All those years Dad raced, and I went out with less than a year's experience and set quick time. I've never been a good qualifier, not ever. But we had it together that night. However, we didn't do squat in the feature.

My first few years racing, it's kind of like how it would be if my son Cody started racing today: I wasn't Jack Hewitt: I was Don Hewitt's boy. Even though my dad didn't really get that involved and help me all that much, and I wasn't anything like him with my driving style, they still looked at me as Don Hewitt's boy.

I'll admit, I was exciting, right off the bat. To go to Eldora and have quick time against Freddy and Jim Linder, Dick Gaines and all those guys, it was pretty amazing. I guess people knew who we were. They watched me a lot because I crashed a lot. I was fun to watch until I couldn't go any more.

By then Pete Whetsel had helped me even more, and was now my car owner so we could keep it going. Dad was also still driving for Pete, he and Dad would go drink beer at the Cozy. They were good buddies. Dad and I were teammates, whatever that's worth. Not much, obviously. One night Dad started behind me in the feature, and after following me for a couple of laps he bumped me into the wall. It was one of those, "I ain't got time to wait on you, I got to go..." type hits. Well, when the race was over, when we were all back at the Cozy, Pete fired Dad.

Dad's drunk, and at the bar he's saying to Pete, real loud, "Well, don't think I need you..." Then they got to arguing. But he was already fired, because he wasn't supposed to be messing with his kid. But as the week went on, and a couple more drinking sessions with Pete, he and Pete were back together.

By the middle of the year Pete had bought a better car for me; it was a Steve Stapp car, purchased from Ray Smith, and it still had No. 98 on it. I finally crashed that car, and Pete bought the car from Ralph DePalma that my dad and Junie Heffner were working on. That was the first time I drove a car with power steering, and man, what a lesson.

We towed the car to Eldora, and went out to run the track in. They weren't even hot-lapping yet, just running the grease off the top of the track, and they had both sprint cars and stock cars on the track. I went down the back straightaway, and a stock car spun out in front of me. I turned the wheel back and forth, and with that greasy track, I ran right into that damned stock car. Bent the frame and all, right off the bat. We fixed it, and we ran that car for quite a while.

Sometimes we ran down at K-C Raceway in Chillicothe, Ohio, and in the middle of the summer that's where I won the first feature of my career. It was a good, good race; I beat George Harbor at his home track, and a full field of good cars. George was driving the Reno Auto Parts car, No. 99. It was a killer car and George was the local ass-kicker at the time. It was neat, because we *won* the race. We earned it. That was probably the ice-breaker; after that first one, I can't even tell you when the second one came, because I don't remember.

Let me back up a little bit: I did win a race my first season, but I felt like it didn't count. At the end of the year they had a race at Findlay,

Ohio, and it was spitting snow that day. Dean Benjamin was there in his car, a really nice Edmunds car that Dad used to drive when the Nickles Brothers owned it. Dean bought two cars like that, one for him and one for Johnny Beaber. Dean's car was yellow with a black ribbon painted as a stripe, and Beaber's car was black with a yellow ribbon. That day at Findlay, they only had six or seven cars, it was so late in the year. The promoter came to us and explained that there was enough money to pay the insurance, and that was it. If we wanted to race, our purse would be a hot dog for the dash, and a trophy for the feature. No money. We raced anyway, and Dean spun off the end of the track and I won. That was my first win, officially, but because of the circumstances I just didn't feel like it was legitimate, something to brag about.

By that time I had begun to figure it out just a little bit. When I started slowing down, I got a lot better. That was always my problem: I was always too brave, instead of smart. You look at great racers like Sammy Swindell, Steve Kinser, Doug Wolfgang, they were smart race drivers. Steve and Sammy were as brave as they come, but they were also very smart race drivers. It took me a long, long time to become a smart racer. I was always so brave, and...yes, people know who you are and they remember you if you're spectacular, but that kept me from winning a lot of races. We crashed quite a bit. That's what brave gets you, instead of smart.

In 1976 I wanted to race with USAC. Was I ready for USAC? Probably not, because it was a very, very tough deal. Kids starting out today might think they've got it hard, but let me tell you about USAC in 1976: Tom Bigelow, Pancho Carter, Sheldon Kinser, Rollie Beale, Jan Opperman, all those badass boys were there at that time. The best of the best of the best. Bruce Walkup, Johnny Parsons, George Snider, it was a helluva bunch. We ran with them for maybe the first half of the season, and didn't do very well. Se we went back to running closer to home, trying to get better.

If you ran USAC then, you had to run exclusively with USAC. It wasn't a hit-and-miss deal; you couldn't run anywhere else if you wanted to keep your USAC license. I missed the show at Eldora by just one car, maybe two, so I was close. At Winchester Speedway in Indiana, I had a shot to make the feature in my very first pavement start. when Bruce Walkup -he was in either the Longhorn car or the Siebert car, I don't remember which- banged my front end and knocked me out of a transfer spot. He basically knocked me out of the way for the position, and that was the only pavement show I was in a position to make.

Why was I beating my head against the wall, running against those guys? Because I wanted to get to the Indianapolis Motor Speedway, and at that time you got to Indy through USAC. Larry Dickson, Gary Bettenhausen, those guys were good in sprint cars and they got to Indy. Bubby Jones, he got there after they did. So that's where I wanted to go. There was no World of Outlaws yet; everybody went to USAC. If you made the show, that was like winning a feature somewhere else. I figured if I could kick their ass, I could make it to Indy. That was my thought process.

Pancho Carter, he was definitely my hero, even though he was only a year or so older than me. I always heard you had to be smooth on the pavement, and watching him at a place like Winchester, man, he was awesome. He would manhandle the car...he was smooth when he had to be, but he was not afraid to throw 'er sideways to get that position. And at that time he drove Steve Stapp's car, the prettiest race car in the world. It was robin's-egg-blue No. 4, it was just beautiful.

Now, there was a tough combination: Steve Stapp and Pancho Carter. Damn, they were good.

One of my problems was my long hair and beard. And I was still just learning to be a race driver. To start racing in 1973 and go to USAC in 1976, well, that's just too quick. Maybe some guys could do it, but with the car we had, that first half of the year wasn't the best. I learned things, but the wrong way. Later on I would have to go back and learn a little bit better. When I got into a four-bar car, for example, I had to learn things all over again. The whole thing was a good learning experience, but it was tough.

I'm sure I got discouraged. Maybe that's why we went back home and started running around home again. We thought that might be easier. And I'm not complaining, because taking another route -not through USAC- I got to go to California, and later Australia. If I had stuck with USAC exclusively, I wouldn't have been able to do all those other deals. So I don't regret quitting USAC that first time.

As it turned out, staying with USAC probably wouldn't have helped me get to Indy, anyway. I would have had to really pick up the pace to get there before CART took over Indy Car racing in the early 1980's. There were a lot of guys better than me at the time who didn't make it to Indy, so looking back it's unlikely I had much of a shot.

When I began running closer to home again, that was a little bit easier on me because I also had a job. Hell, nobody could make a living in sprint cars at that time. The only guys who could race for a living were Indy Car guys. And I was nowhere near their league. So I had to work to pay my bills.

When I was still with USAC, I had two separate flips on the Indy Fairgrounds mile, just a few weeks apart. The first came in June, in the first of two features. I ended up in the B-main, and finished fourth for a transfer, but had lost my brakes. We just had a minute or two to get ready for the feature, and we tried to get the brakes going, but couldn't. So I said, "I'll just start the race with no brakes and take it easy."

Problem was, I got up to 12th place, and I was chasing Rollie Beale. I'll never forget it, we went into turn one, and I slipped out of the groove a little bit and lost ground on Rollie. So I wanted to make up that ground in turn three, right? I really hauled 'er in there. Not being very smart, I had forgotten about the brakes. Oh, shit. Next thing I know I'm up on the fence, flipping my butt off.

We got the car repaired, and took it back to the Indy mile for the USAC triple-feature event in July. Steve Chassey and I were racing, and we got together, and I flipped again, in turn three. I still hurt the car pretty bad, but it didn't ring my bell nearly as much as the first one had. But it made Bobby Snead really mad, he went down and blamed poor Billy Engelhart. Bobby took a big wrench down there ready to kill Billy. And it wasn't even Billy's fault, it was just that his car was the same color as Steve's and Bobby had the wrong guy.

It's not a good thing, crashing a sprint car at the mile. You're really flying there, and when you get in trouble the car just really beats you up. At the time I was driving a truck at the Ludlow Stone Quarry, and I went to work Monday morning after my first big crash at Indy. I was still sore and a little gimpy, but I made it to work. Those big ol' trucks -they called 'em UTEs- didn't have much for brakes, and I was about halfway up a big hill and the engine died. It rolled backward and turned over, and started rolling toward the pit, the gigantic, deep hole where they carve the rock out of the ground. One more roll and it would have been over the side into the big hole, and I would have been history.

I was knocked out when the thing was rolling over, and when I came to, my arm was laying out the window, on the roof of the truck; if it hadn't had a cab guard, I would have lost my arm, for sure. I crawled out of the truck and was looking around, about half goofy from the blow to the head, trying to figure out where I was. I saw all the guys at the gravel pit running toward me, and I thought, "Holy shit, I've done somethin' now, and they're about to whip my ass!"

So I took off running across this gravel pit, running for my life. When I got to my car and started to get in, I began to regain my marbles a little bit, and started to realize what had happened. I got the rest of the day off, which was nice; but it probably wasn't a good deal, ringing my bell twice within a two-day period.

Not long after that I took a job with Yates Builders in West Milton, not far from Troy. They built houses, and I really learned to like carpentry work.

Pretty soon, though, I was doing better as a race driver. I finally started making more money in one night of racing than I made as a carpenter for the whole week, so I thought it was stupid to work with the full-time job.

That was 1978, which was an important year for sprint car racing. Ted Johnson formed the World of Outlaws, and all of a sudden there was an opportunity to travel all over the country, racing sprint cars. Hey, guys could make a living at this!

By then lots had changed for me as far as a car owner. Pete Whetsel sold his stuff to Ralph Johnson and Bobby and Larry Snead. Then Ralph sold out and Larry Farno and Verlin Adams bought in and helped out as our pit crew. When I left that car, I started driving for the Nickles Brothers.

Doug Trost also had a car that Karl Busson had driven, as well as Roger Rager, a Ronnie Ward car (my friend Don Smith now has that car in his showplace in Terre Haute, Indiana). Doug Trost always believed in me, and I also drove his Tognotti car for a while. I ran pretty well at Eldora for him one night, and finished fourth.

Doug actually let me take the car to Winchester. He thought I was that good, but I really wasn't. I don't know, I've just never caught on to the pavement. Doug had really good race cars, but running well on pavement is something that comes from doing it for a while, I think. At least it did for me; I just wasn't very good.

After that I drove for Harold "Flake" Kemenah, the 3x car that Johnny Beaber and Freddy Linder had driven. Harold had four kids: Laurie, Amy, Chad, and Brian, but we called the boys "Warhead" and "Wimpy." Warhead was Chad, who is a good racer today. Brian, he went everywhere with us, he was only 14 or so. Nick Gwin was still my mechanic, and he and I took Brian all over the place with us.

The first year with the Outlaws, 1978, I finished 10th in points. Right then was when things started changing for me; I was traveling all the time, making more money than I ever had made before, and people started noticing us and talking about us a little bit.

My first really long trip had come in 1976 when I went to California, and that turned out to be a really important warm-up out there. We went to the Gold Cup at West Capital in Sacramento, Ferkel talked me into making the trip. Rick was driving his own No. 0, and Jim Brandy and Dick Gillespie, who had two cars, offered him one of their cars as a backup. Rick said, "Well, I don't really need a backup car, but I'll tell you what...we've got this little driver coming here from Ohio with me, and he's looking for a ride." Hell, I ended up running fourth in the Gold Cup, just about the biggest race of the year out West. Ferkel had a tough week out there, and I made some money.

From there I picked up a ride at San Jose and Santa Clara in an old Grant King car from Idaho. So it was a pretty good trip in terms of racing.

The deal with Brandy and Gillespie opened some important doors. They were tied in with Don Tognotti, a highly respected car builder. Mike Andrietta worked for Tognotti, and in late '78 Mike was planning on going to Australia to run Tognotti's car down there. But Mike hurt his back right before he was supposed to go. I had already purchased a plane ticket and a visa to Australia, hoping I could find some way to go, and they knew me from running so well at the Gold Cup. So they made me the offer to drive the car in Australia, which was an awesome deal for me.

When I got to Australia something just clicked. My driving style was so different than the guys down there, all of a sudden everybody was talking about this American guy who drove way out on the outside, and that turned out to be my ticket back to Australia year after year after year. Everybody was playing follow-the-leader on the bottom, and I wasn't smart enough to know that. I was clear out by the fence, and I'd drive by 'em on the top.

I wasn't out there because I knew what I was doing; I was out there because that's the only place I knew how to drive the car.

Running the top groove was always more comfortable for me, partly because I had always heard people talking about my dad running the outside. Louie Mann once told me about leading a race at Eldora.

"I knew I had that baby won," he said, "I was running up against the fence, had a good line, just really doin' good. Next thing I knew, your dad drove by me on the outside. And I thought I was running out on the fence!"

I had always heard those stories, and I was definitely braver than I was smart. I think you have to be a smart racer, with more patience, to run the bottom. I wasn't smart or patient, so my style was to run the top. Now, today, I can run the bottom, but I hate it. If I can win three features on the bottom or one feature on the top, I'd choose winning the one on the top. Because it's just neat to get everybody excited, and they get really turned on by it. A perfect example was Lee Osborne, he had as much talent as anybody, but the majority of his wins came on the bottom. Freddy Linder, Bobby Allen, and Johnny Beaber, they were the same way. Johnny Beaber has probably won more races than I have, but it's nowhere near as exciting. The fans don't remember you as long.

When you're running right out against that fence, and you're either gonna win it or wear it, the fans remember that. It's the excitement, the thrill that makes it different. If you're wanting to make a name for yourself, running the top will get your name out there quicker than winning a few features. You'll get more fans by running the top. I didn't know that at the time...but if you could run both, you're starting out as a really smart racer who knows when to go where. I just didn't have that gift, so I ran the top, regardless.

Later on the announcer at Eldora, Terry Baltes, he noticed how high on the track I ran. When he introduced me, he would yell into the microphone, *"He rides it high cause he ain't afraid to die...from Troy, Ohio, JACK HEWITT!!!!"*

Now, how they gonna yell like that about a guy runnin' the boring old bottom?

I rest my case.

Talking about Jack...

Jack Hewitt is probably the bravest, most strong-willed person I know. Nothing scares him, and there isn't a challenge he wouldn't face.

He's a guy who has fulfilled his lifelong dream. When he was a little kid he said he wanted to be a race driver, and that's exactly what he did. Not many people can say that.

He's one tough son of a gun, all around. When he gets something in his head he's right no matter what. It's very hard to convince him any different.

It was meant to be that Jack was going to be a race driver. Every obstacle in front of him, he climbed right over. In the beginning he had no money to race, but still got it done. He's a very determined guy. Early on he struggled sometimes because he was so headstrong that he knew the best setup for the race car, even if there might be a better way. Bob Hampshire probably changed him as much as anybody, because Bob showed him that it's good to have an open mind and listen.

When Jack walked into a room, everybody knew he was there. There's been nobody in racing more devoted to the fans than him. Even on his worse day, he had time for the fans.

Jack could really burn you out on racing! He'd race 100 percent of the time if he could, and he'd always give the car a good, hard ride. I saw him get into cars that nobody had ever made go fast, and win in them. As a crew member it was tough to keep up with him, because he'd wear you out.

I wouldn't change the things we did for anything. We went around the world, literally. We spent a lot of time together, and we created a lifelong bond. I'm proud that he's my friend.

Nick Gwin
Troy, Ohio

4

ON THE ROAD

Through all the fun periods I've had in racing, nothing tops the late 1970's and early 1980's, when I was a traveling racer.

Having fun was something that came very easily for me: I was never very serious about stuff; I had a big mouth; I love people (especially girls); and I was a little bit rowdy.

Well, okay, maybe more than a little bit rowdy. Maybe a *lot* rowdy.

When the World of Outlaws started in 1978, it was a great opportunity for me to see the country and make a living as a race driver. I had made other trips out West and elsewhere, before the Outlaws, but racing with them week-in and week-out took me to a lot of different tracks.

I didn't have much money then. That was okay, because money wasn't what I was after. I was looking for fun. I must have been successful, because I can't think of very many days in that period when I wasn't happy and laughing with-or at-my friends.

One of the keys to having fun during that period was my friend Nick Gwin. Nick and I grew up together and were good friends in elementary school, but we kind of drifted apart when he went to college. But after I got out of the army, Nick and I hooked back up and spent a lot of time together.

I was driving Harold Kemenah's car a lot just before I started racing with the Outlaws, and Nick came on as my mechanic. I helped him learn quickly; he got to repair all the parts I bent up. So he got a lot of experience, especially in repairs, in a hurry.

There were a bunch of guys from Troy who were good friends, and we raised a lot of hell. I was living with my friend Rick Mohler for a while in his apartment. One night I brought a girl home, and she and I were getting it on in my room. She's screeching like hell, and of course the walls were paper thin. I'm trying to quiet her down. Shhh! "The guy in the next room has to get up real early! Quiet down!" The next week I'm lying in bed, and I hear this very familiar screeching sound. After I had been so considerate a week earlier, do you think that dog Rick would keep her quiet so I could sleep? Hell, no! They were raising the roof!

Nick was dating Cathy Dietrich, and I dated Cathy's best friend, Julie Snyder. They made a bet with Nick one night that he couldn't get 50 pieces of bubble gum in his mouth. Well, he had to do it in 25-piece sections, and I mean...believe it or not, he did it. That gum wad was huge. He got it all in his mouth to make it official, but when he took it out, instead of throwing it out he laid it up on Steve (Virgil) Victor's dash. When Virgil came out the next morning, there was this monster wad of gum, it had all ran down on the dash, it was gross. Man, we laughed our ass off at poor ol' Virgil.

When the WoO started, I didn't go to their first race at the Devil's Bowl in Mesquite, Texas. But we were there when they got to Eldora a week or so later. That first year we ran with them quite a bit. I was in a lot of different cars, sometimes I'd run a car for just one night, and really didn't even know the guys name who owned the car. I ran a lot for Doug and Joanne Howell, and I had some success with them. I won at Santa Maria, California, and Butler, Michigan with them. The first one I won was with Dwayne Starr, up at Skagit. We won a prelim at Knoxville, and won another prelim somewhere else.

Sometimes the car I drove already had a mechanic, but Nick just stayed around to help me out. We'd ride from race to race together.

We went to Phenix City, Alabama, and I didn't have a ride. Ted Johnson asked if Nick and I would help out a little bit, so we helped at the pit gate. Everybody did okay coming in...then we started checking people as they came *out*. M.A. Brown and Bruce Cogle, they started to walk past and we stopped them, "Whoa, whoa, whoa, we've got to see your pit pass." They started showing us, then realized we were screwing with them, and they just grinned and said, "Get outta here!"

It wasn't just Nick and I; hell, it seemed like everybody out on the tour was up for having fun. I got along with everybody, but I guess there were a few guys who didn't associate much with others. Some of the guys, like Steve Kinser, he was a helluva racer and a partier, too. I like to party; Steve and I got along really well. I wasn't all that interested in getting drunk, not that kind of partying, but just going out and goofing off, raising a little hell.

My first trip out West came in 1976, two years before the WoO started. Nick went with me, and it was Tube, Jim Darley, Rick Ferkel, Nick and I staying at Earl Kelly's house in San Jose. We were playing putt-putt, we were golfing, ping-pong, whatever we were doing, it was fun. When we played ping-pong at Earl's, you would have thought it was a million-dollar tournament. Ferkel is so competitive, and such a bad loser, if you could beat him at anything it just tore him up.

Nick is about Ferkel's size, and Nick could get a bowling ball down the lane without touching the wood. I mean, he can hit the pins. And there is Ferkel, trying to throw the ball as hard as Nick, just to prove he could do it.

We had Johnny Beaber so mad out there one year, playing putt-putt, he threw his clubs in the pond. Then he went up to the office and told the guy that a little kid threw them in. Johnny just stomped out to his truck and drove off, never even finished the game. We were raggin' on him, big-time. We'd get into a guy's head and get him all screwed up. They couldn't take it. They were just serious racers, and they didn't know how to have fun.

We had a big bowling tournament one year at the Knoxville Nationals, and everybody was down there. We celebrated Nick's birthday at a little bar downtown, a strip bar, called Dishonest John's, or something like that. In downtown Knoxville, if you can believe it. Dick Gaines was in there drinking beer, I remember.

I had a '66 Chevy Nova, six-cylinder, three-speed on the column, and I took the back seat out and carpeted it so I'd have a place to sleep. I went to Shreveport, Louisiana, and then to Dallas, and from there I went to Hutchison, Kansas, and LaVern Nance got me a ride in one of those supermodifieds. I don't remember the car owner's name; we just called him "Old Sparky." We drove that car at Hutchison, and made the dash. The car was one of those 100-inch cars with a coupe body, they were pretty cool.

I left Kansas, and picked Nick up in Denver, and then we went on up to Wyoming and shot across I-80 into Sacramento, California. We were out there for a month or so, and we'd keep going with the money we'd win. By the time we got to Ascot Raceway in Los Angeles, I think we had 20 cents left, literally. I hadn't been racing at Phoenix and Ascot, so between Nick and I we had 20 cents. Ferkel said, "I'll buy your car from you!" It wasn't that he wanted the car, he just wanted Nick and I to stay out there with him, because he was having so much fun with us!

There was another race out there a few days later, but we headed for home, buying gas on Nick's credit card. We got to Colorado and started up one of those big mountains west of Denver, and burned some valves in the motor. Shoot, that old thing...when you got off the interstate to get gas, you'd think it wasn't going to make it, but once you got up a head of steam it was fine. We made it all the way home, and about the time I got home it broke a rod. It put a hole in the oil pan a little ways from the bottom, and I gave the car to my brother. He would back the car up on a little stone pile so it could get going, and he drove it like that for another week, busted rod and all.

I thought California was great. Really, what else could you think? The weather was sunny, and everything seemed so exciting. I remember on that first trip in 1976, Bill Simpson had just made his first set of arm restraints, the two-inch wide ones. He made 20 sets, and gave away 19 of 'em to guys running at the Pacific Coast Nationals at Ascot. He couldn't give the last pair away, so I bought 'em. Turns out I bought the first pair of arm restraints from Bill Simpson. Pretty cool.

I didn't get to run the Pacific Coast Nationals in '76, but it was still neat. The driving style of the California Racing Assn. (CRA) was the same as today, back 'em in. People just didn't drive like that back home. I never did do very well out there, believe it or not, without the wing. I didn't run it a lot, but then we went out there for a WoO show with Darryl Saucier, and passed Steve and Sammy -or maybe it was Bobby Allen and Steve- with five or six laps to go and ended up winning the feature on a preliminary qualifying night. I think we finished fourth on the final night.

One night in Phoenix at Manzanita Raceway, Ron Shuman had checked out, but he broke pretty quick and I led it up till six or seven laps to go and broke a ring-and-pinion gear. Tim Green won, and Steve Kinser was second. We were ahead of 'em, and would have had to mess up bad for them to beat us. We eventually did win a main event there, though.

I don't know if it helped me to travel. It might have, because I was enjoying it more. People got to know us, and that helped me in the long run. If I had stayed around home and ran Eldora my whole life, maybe I could have won every week, but there are only going to be a certain amount of people who know you, who read about you. When you travel all over, people know you. To this day people say, "Man, it's neat to finally get to meet you." I think they're just young. If they'd have come to the races before now, they would have met me a long time ago.

We went back out West in '77. I met this girl, Lisa, in San Jose. She kept hanging around with us, and we're trying to race. Women are for after the races; other than that we didn't have time for 'em. I'm getting in the car one night and she's hanging all over me, kissing me, wishing me luck, and Nick finally said, "Would you leave him alone??!! We're gonna have to jerk him off just to get the seat belt fastened!"

"Getting there" was way, way fun. And there was a great bunch of guys we were racing with, Lenard McCarl, Sammy Swindell, Steve Kinser, Ferkel, Jimmy Boyd, Dub May, Bobby Marshall, Jimmy Sills, Danny Smith, Ron Shuman, a bunch of neat guys.

Our maintenance program probably wasn't up to Karl Kinser's level, but we had time to have fun. We didn't fall out of many races, even though we were screwing off a lot. Some of the guys were pretty serious: Karl, Tommy Sanders, and at the race track, Ferkel and Steve Kinser.

Ferkel was a guy I really looked up to. It was so funny, when he'd play any kind of game, he was intense, and if he got beat he'd just clench his teeth and say, "You sucker, you!" But once he got to know us, he loved us. In early '76 we talked at the races and stuff, but when he took us to California, that's when we hung out together. And we had a ball. Of course, he never asked us any racing questions, you didn't have to worry about that. And he didn't give away any secrets, either. Oh, no. But then again, we didn't ask him to.

He was a guy who had done it all, from the bottom to the top. He ate it, lived it, slept it, drank it; he was racing all the time. He was a competitor, a guy who had that edge; he wanted to win. He was one of the first guys from Ohio who traveled like a gypsy, and made it big in sprint car racing. He came along at the right time, and his lifestyle -the traveling deal- fit what the sport was coming to. The two biggest travelers at that time were Ferkel and Bubby Jones, more than anybody. Where there was $1,000 to win, that's where they'd show up. Jan Opperman did it first, but Ferkel and Bubby kind of perfected it. A memorable trip for them was Ascot, when they had the big humper tires and rolled in and just blew everybody away. The humper tires were actually big drag racing tires, grooved for dirt track racing. The people laughed at them when they showed up; they didn't laugh very long.

In the late '70s Ferkel was really coming into his own. He had started late, when he was maybe 27, 28 years old. He learned his trade and he learned it well. He didn't really have the killer motors, but he was one of the most weight-conscious guys out there. He was beating everybody with weight in the early days. Ferkel was truly ahead of his time.

He was a thinker, too, and he focused on things the rest of us didn't pay any attention to. He would unhook the shocks on his car when they were hauling it down the road so he wouldn't wear 'em out. When he'd load the car, he'd change to old tires first, and block the frame to keep it from bouncing when they traveled. Everybody else would just roll their car up on the trailer when they were done, but not Rick. It was unreal, his attention to detail.

Ferkel wasn't a drinker; maybe one beer, socially. He never fought much, either. Of course, who wanted to fight him? He had such long arms, and he was really built. Just from his looks, most guys wouldn't want to fight with him. One time Johnny Beaber got all ruffled up and hit Ferkel, and Ferkel put Beaber's lights out. Beaber was a feisty little dude, and he hit Ferkel in the mouth. Ferkel had no choice but to beat him up. Beaber said later, "I knew that. But at least I got one in!" Beaber would fight at the drop of the hat, too.

Believe it or not, Earl Baltes threw Ferkel out of Eldora once. And Bucky Bonds, too. Barred him! Bucky said, "Earl, you can't throw *Ferkel* out!" "Not only can I throw him out," said Earl, "but you're leavin', too!" Ferkel had been down in the pits early, changing a motor, and he wasn't supposed to be in there that soon.

On one of our later California trips, Jac Haudenschild rode with Nick and me. Oh, shit, we had a ball. Poor ol' Haud, we just tormented him something fierce. He was still just a kid, and I was taking him under my wing like Rick Ferkel had done for me a few years earlier.

We ran out of gas one night near Reno, Nevada, within walking distance of the Mustang Ranch. It was totally dark at night in the desert, and since I was driving, I had to walk to get the gas. Haud is panicked, he's scared because it's so dark and spooky out there.

"What are you gonna do?" Haud asked.

"Well, I got to go to town."

"IN THE DARK???!!!!"

"Yeah, we're out of gas."

"Aw, ain't no way..."

Now, Nick is a big boy, he comes in around 210. I kept trying to tell Haud there was no problem since Nick was there with him, but boy, he didn't like being stuck out in that desert.

One time we were driving out West on the northern route, and Haud got to drinking. He wiped himself out on a fifth of Boone's Farm wine. The traveling deal was, you drive a tank full, and if there are four people, you get three tanks off. Nick was driving, and Haud started drinking. When Haud's turn came up, he was drunk. So I drove, and I had to put up with him. We're riding along, and all of a sudden Haud puffed out his chest.

"I'm a helluva man, ain't I Hewitt?"

"You sure are, Haud, but why are you sayin' that?"

"'Cause I drank this whole fifth of wine and I'm not even drunk!"

"Yeah, you're a helluva man, Haud."

Finally when my tank was over, I turned to him and said, "Your turn."

"I can't drive, I'm drinkin'!"

Luckily, our buddy Loffy (Larry Laughman) was with us, and he took Jac's turn. Jac just crawled in the back to sleep it off. Shithead.

On that return trip Haud told us he was itching real bad, like he had a rash.

"I don't understand...I itch real bad from here up," he said, pointing to his crotch. "And I've got these little scabs. Come see if you know what it is."

I went in there and looked at it, and I started laughing. "Jac, those are crabs."

"What are crabs?"

"You get 'em from sex, they're like little bugs and they bite."

Man, we were hard on him. We made him sleep on the floor, he had to shower last, he had no options. He went to the drug store, and he told Nick, "Man, I can't go get that medicine...I'm too embarrassed." So Nick went into the drugstore with him. Nick walked over to the shelf and yelled across the whole store, "Hey, Haud! I found that crab medicine!" He had to put the medicine on and 20 minutes later take a shower, and he was in the shower for a long time. Nick was yelling, "Haud, you ain't gonna drown 'em! Stop usin' all the hot water!"

Ol' Haud was something else. He traveled with us a lot then. In the race car he was on the gas, all the time, just like he is now.

When he first started riding with us, we really pissed him off. Nick and I would stop to eat just once a day, and Haud was a guy who liked three meals. We just about starved him to death. But he wouldn't say anything. Well...maybe he did, and we wouldn't stop.

He got sick up at Fremont one time, and one of the girls took him to get something to eat. They were like his mother.

We'd tell him things, and he'd believe every word. Nick could tell him stories that were out of this world, and Haud would swallow it hook, line, and sinker. He was a neat, neat kid.

We were down in Australia one year and somebody asked me, "Where you from?" "Troy, Ohio." And they asked Haud, "Where you from?" He said, "I'm from Millersburg, Ohio, but I don't sound like him," pointing at me.

He was braver than dirt. I had met him when he first started, but nobody really noticed him until he drove that No. 75 car at Eldora, and just about won a race. He ran second, I think, and the car had no power steering, and here this little kid just about won it at a bad-ass place like Eldora. After that, they knew who Jac Haudenschild was.

The first year of the Outlaws was when Steve Kinser was coming into his own, too. We had a good time, hanging out with Steve. He would win races, drink beer, and chase women. Sometimes people talk about Steve being mean, but I never saw it, not once. He was always a good time around me, there were no problems at all.

One night we were drinking, and we had these two sisters lined up. Right before the bar closed, Steve changed his strategy, and started hitting on another girl at the bar. When it came time to leave, he waved goodbye, and I had the two sisters all to myself. What a night.

One night in Phoenix, after the races, Steve came running up to Nick and handed him a bag that contained $5,000 in cash. "Man, I'm leaving," he said real quickly, "Karl's madder than hell at me...here, take this, man, I've gotta hurry up." He had his uniform in his hands, and then he was gone. The next day, Nick walked up to Steve with his money and said, "You missing something?" "Aw, man, I knew I gave somebody some money, but I couldn't remember who it was! Thank you! Thank you very much!"

Once Steve got to the races, he wouldn't socialize much with anybody. He was really serious. Oh, man, he was always nervous.

Richard Tharp owned a race car during that time, and Steve was telling me one day that Tharp was getting on his nerves.

"Well, punch him out," I told him. "You should be able to handle him."

In a millisecond, Steve grabbed me and had me in a headlock. "I think I could handle you, too," he said, then he let me go. He just grinned and said, "But I'm not ready to find out."

We did come close to fireworks one night. It was New Bremen Speedway in Ohio for a WoO show, on a hard, dry-slick track. I was leading, Steve was second, and he stuck me coming out of the turn, and I crashed.

After the race he had to walk past us to get to the window. "What are you doing?" I asked him. He swelled up for second, and he saw the fire in my eyes, and he just ducked his head and walked away. We were fixin' to fight, but we didn't.

I told Steve he and I could have made $2,000 anywhere in the country just putting on the boxing gloves on the front straightaway. Because of what we had for a reputation, we could have picked up some spending money.

One thing I really liked about the Outlaws those first few years was the races were split about 50/50 in terms of wings or non-wings. I still like that deal better than anything; that was the ultimate. I didn't like it later on when USAC put the wings on, that was kind of a bad deal. Today, I think for safety purposes they maybe should use the wings, but they should take the sideboards off. It wouldn't look good, I know, but if they say the wing is there for safety reasons, they ought to trim 'em back to where they aren't doing as much.

We didn't just travel out West, of course. One year Bobby Snead, Larry Laughman and I took Dad's car and Harley Haynes' car to West Memphis, Arkansas to run during Thanksgiving weekend. If we did any good, we were going to go on to the Devil's Bowl. We got to West Memphis, and we're haulin' ass, running third with four laps to go, when we blew a motor. After the races, Bobby Davis, Sr. invited us to come over to his place for Thanksgiving dinner. Sammy Swindell and Tommy Sanders were working for Bobby at that time, running the black No. 71 car. So we went over and had dinner with Bobby's family. Sammy came over, Tommy Sanders came over, Bobby Davis, Jr. was just a little boy then. We had Thanksgiving with them, plates full of food, and we sat and talked for a long time afterward. We had a really good time. You talk about a great guy, that's Bobby Davis. He didn't know a stranger.

We left our car and trailer at Shorty Chambliss' house in Memphis, and went to Devil's Bowl. It was snowing during the races, it was so cold. Coming back, we weren't quite to West Memphis and we're broke. We've got nothing. I'm with Snead and Laughman. Now, I was used to being broke; but they weren't. Bobby had $10 left. He knew his $10 wasn't going to be enough to get us home, so he said to hell with it, and he bought a 12-pack of beer. Now we've got *no* money. I told 'em we'd probably have to find a place to work in the morning to get enough money for gas. "Oh, we can't do that!" "Boys, I've got no money," I told 'em. Finally, after two hours of sitting there, Larry had to dig deep and he came up with $100 to get us home. Boy, he wasn't wanting to get up off that $100. But I had nowhere to dig, because I was flat broke.

Another time at West Memphis we went to the dog races in the afternoon, and out to Riverside Speedway that night. Sammy was running the sprint car and a late model, and he was really leaning and shoving on those guys. We're sitting on our open trailer, watching it all. We're parked right close to him. Riverside is known for fighting; Sammy pulled in after the race and Nick told him, "Sammy, you ought to get up on this trailer with us." "What?" "You'd better get up here with us." Within two seconds Sammy was sitting up there between us. And in a minute or so, here came a big group of guys, madder than hell, yelling, cussing, hollering, looking for Sammy. He had shoved and knocked them out of the way and they didn't like it. He was rough back then. So I can honestly say I saved his ass as much as I've tried to kill him.

That was an awesome time, chasing the Outlaws all over the country. But in the early 1980s, I started staying close to home. But that didn't mean I couldn't have fun; not by a long shot.

Talking about Jack...

Jack Hewitt first caught my attention as somebody who had great anticipation on race restarts. In those early years they were inverting the whole field, and I was starting in the back a lot. Jack was maybe a couple of rows ahead of me, and I could see how well he would restart, almost every time. He either had great instincts for it, or he was a heckuva jumper, depending on how you look at it!

The easiest description I can give of Jack is that he's an easy guy to meet. Very easy to talk to. There are no strangers around him. He'll voice his opinion and he won't hold anything back, right or wrong.

Man, he loved to race. He stood on the gas, and he'd race anything. He could hop from one car to the next and not even give it a thought, without a moment's hesitation. Not too many guys can do that, because they start thinking about the setup and worrying about all the details. Not Jack. He felt like he could carry the car, so he just jumped in and gave it his best shot.

When I think about those early years...aw, yeah, that was a fun time. We had a ball. When Jack was around, there was always something going on. We just had a good time.

I don't think that period will ever be duplicated, because I'm not sure you could have the camaraderie today that we had back then. Jack was always right in the middle, and he's one of the guys who made it really special just to hang out together. I definitely have good memories of those times.

Rick Ferkel
Tiffin, Ohio

5

BACK TO THE MIDWEST

As a racer, there aren't many places better to grow up than the Midwest. Within just a few hours of my house, there are a ton of great race tracks: Eldora, Lima, Findlay, Bloomington, Terre Haute, Fremont, Kokomo, and a whole bunch more.

By the early 1980s I began to have more success as a race driver. It's funny how it works; the better you get going, the better rides you get, and you win more races. I guess they call that a breakthrough, when you're finally able to get that right combination of confidence and a good car to drive.

It was only natural that over time I would begin to race more with USAC, because there were a lot in my area. Although it was still a tough series, things had changed since I raced with them in 1976. At that time I was really just learning the basics, but by the early 1980s I had improved. I went from missing most of the shows to being a contender to win races.

USAC had also changed, too. In 1976 you had to buy a USAC license, and with that license you agreed not to race anywhere else. By the early 1980s USAC relaxed that rule, and you could race on a Temporary Permit (everybody called 'em a 'TP'), allowing you to also race with other series. That suited me, very much. When USAC was racing on pavement, I could go race somewhere else.

I still held out hope that racing with USAC would help me get to the Indianapolis 500. That was still my dream. Plus, some better races cropped up in my area for USAC. In 1981 Johnny Vance introduced the 4-Crown Nationals at Eldora, and big races like that made it more attractive to stay closer to home.

So much of what a driver does is dictated by the car owner. It wasn't that I didn't want to race with the World of Outlaws; it's just that I didn't have a ride there. I could have chased some hit-and-miss events, but it wasn't solid enough to give up the rides I had around the Midwest. And I crashed a lot, so maybe I didn't suit the car owners very well. I don't know. Racing with the Outlaws as a career just wasn't meant to be, I guess.

In 1980 or so I began driving the Radar Racing car out of Pleasant Hill, right around the corner from me (everybody around here just calls the town P-Hill). We picked up the USAC schedule in 1981 and ran many races, and we were doing okay, running in the top 10 pretty consistently. When I wasn't running the Radar Racing car, I raced a good bit with the Nickles Bros. car out of Lima. I won several All Stars races in Ohio with them in 1980 and '81.

One All Stars victory that stands out in my mind was in September 1981 at Lincoln Park Speedway in Indiana. That was a weird race, because I ran off the track and had to go to the tail for the restart. I had to come all the way back from the tail to beat Brad Doty for the win, which was no small feat.

Let me tell you about the Nickles Brothers. Throughout my career, no matter what happened, it seemed like they always had a car for me to drive when I needed it. There are several brothers in the family, but Harold and Don are the ones primarily involved in racing.

If you knew those guys, you would laugh, just thinking about being around them. They are characters, I'm telling you. They're also just about the greatest guys in the world.

The Nickles are from Lima, not far from Limaland Speedway. The first time Dad went to Limaland with Junie Heffner, Don Nickles came down to their pit, and he was a cocky little dude. He walked up to Junie and said, "How much do you want for that car? I think I could stick my driver in that car and make a winner out of it." Dad went out and won the dash, his heat, and the feature, and then he told Junie, "Fuck that greasy little hillbilly!"

After that they all became really good friends. Don was a hell-raiser of the first order. When Dad started driving for Harold and Don later on, they had an old CAE-built car. He'd spend a lot of time up in Lima with them.

I had gone into the army by this time, and right after basic I bought them each a hat at Six Flags, and had their names stitched on it. Don's nickname is "Scritchy," so I had 'em sew "Scritchy" and "Hurald" on their hat. Yeah, I know, that's not how you spell "Harold." But I honestly didn't know any better because everybody-and I mean everybody-called him "Hurald."

Later on I started driving for them, and I've been in and out of their car more times than I can count. They're so much fun to work with, although sometimes it doesn't seem quite like fun. One night at Limaland I was the last car to qualify and set quick time, which is very difficult to do. Now, you have to understand, Don and Harold weren't the most delicate, highly technical, mechanics. For example, Don used to adjust the fuel injection with a pair of Vice-Grips. Nothing delicate as far as he was concerned!

I no sooner pulled into the pits and they're changing the car all around. Don jerks the hood from the car and starts adjusting the fuel injectors. Harold starts jacking weight in the car. My dad was parked right next to us, and he and his mechanic jacked my car up and started changing the stagger. All this, after I had gone out last and set quick time. Man, I was hot. I told 'em, "You guys drive it!"

They kept you in stitches, all the time. They had a trailer with a big metal tray underneath, where they stowed all their spare gears and other parts. But if it rained, water would fill the tray, and it was a mess. Down in Florida one year their van was broken into, and Harold said, "I lost a suit and a half!" The thieves had taken two T-shirts and a pair of pants.

The thieves also stole their tools, and you couldn't help but laugh at that thought. If you'd ever seen their toolbox, you would have figured you needed a tetanus shot just to reach in and grab a screwdriver. They just said afterward, "Aw, them poor people really needed those tools..."

They'd give you the shirt off their back; they're just those kind of people. And so full of shit! They'd lie to you when the truth is easier, just to screw with you. That's where I learned to bullshit, and I got pretty good at it. It wasn't that I wanted to lie; with those guys, it was self-defense. Survival. Actually, over time I think I got even better at it than them. I would call them on the phone from my house, "Come out on the interstate and pick me up, my car broke down!" They always had a brand new tow truck, and they're running up and down the interstate, looking for me, and I'm sitting at home laughing my ass off. Then they'd figure out I was messing with them, and they'd get hot. It was so much fun.

For a while in 1981 I drove for Merle Thomason, he owned the B&L Electric car Jeff Swindell later ran for a while. He was from Clinton, Missouri, and everybody called him Crockett. Our initial conversation went something like this:

"Would you like to drive my race car?" he asked.

"Sure!"

"It's a done deal, then," he said. "You'll be my driver. But I'm going to tell you this right now: If you think you're going to lie in bed till noon, you're mistaken. And if you get up at 9 a.m. and think you're going to go out there and stand around while the other guys work on the race car, you're mistaken again."

I got to laughing, and I said, "Crockett, I'll tell you what...I don't know you very well, and you don't know me, and right now we kind of like each other. But I can see right now that I don't want to drive your race car."

"Why not?"

"What are you paying me?" I asked.

"Forty percent to drive it," he said.

"You just hit it right on the head. I drive for 40 percent. I don't do a damned thing I don't want to do for that 40 percent."

You know what's funny? I ended up driving for him, keeping the car at my house, and doing *ALL* the work for my 40 percent. Showed him, didn't I?

The point was that was my choice. I didn't want anybody giving me a rash of shit about how hard I was working, what I was doing, all that. Man, I'd get a *job* if that's what I wanted. But if I chose to work my butt off for that 40 percent, that's fine. As long as it's my choice.

Crockett was a really neat guy, and we used to joke a lot about that 40-percent deal. I raced on the road with him quite a bit, hitting all kinds of races around the country. I quit him at Fremont, Ohio in July to run C.K. Spurlock's Gambler house car, not realizing that was only a one-night deal. I screwed up when I quit Crockett, and that's one thing I look back on with regret.

Not long after I quit Crockett I got a major break when Johnny Vance called and asked if I'd be interested in running his car at an unsanctioned 150-lap race at Paragon Speedway in Indiana. Johnny had one of the best cars on the USAC circuit, and Rich Vogler was his driver at that time. But Rich didn't want to run anything other than USAC, so that opened the seat for one night at Paragon. We won the race, but Vogler was back in the car for the USAC races.

A funny story about that night at Paragon: Bobby Kinser (Steve Kinser's dad) was leading, and I was running second when Bobby got taken out by a lapped car. I went on to win, and Bobby was so mad he was spitting nails. He went down to the kid who spun him out, and the kid looked at him and said, "Mr. Kinser, I'm real sorry I bumped into you...I've admired you ever since I was a little boy, and I'm so sorry I cost you that race." Well, what can you do when a kid says that to you? You can't just haul off and hit him, it wouldn't be right. So Bob just walked away. Problem was, he still had this real good mad worked up. So he walked into my pit, and started to give me hell. I saw him put his beer in his pocket, and I knew he was fixin' to take a poke at me. I said, "Now Bob, if you swing at me, we're going to fight. There ain't going to be one punch, we're really going to fight. So don't swing at me. Besides, you've got no bitch with me...you're just mad because you let that kid get to you." He looked kind of surprised, and then he had this great big grin on his face, and he took his beer out of his pocket and we were friends again. Just a little diplomacy, you know.

By that time I was running a little bit of everything. A lot of car owners called me if they were looking for a driver, and other drivers were calling me because I knew where the open cars were. I was the middleman; I should have worked on a commission! It wasn't that I didn't want to stick with one car; I just bounced around a lot, in terms of the series. All Stars, USAC, World of Outlaws, whatever it took to go racing at the time.

My one-off deal with Vance in 1981 paid good dividends, however. That winter he came to me and said, "Look, you can drive my race car, but you've got to cut your hair." No problem, I said. Johnny was promoting his company, Aristocrat Products, and I understood he was conscious of the image of his driver. So I cut my hair, no big deal. Driving that car was kind of special for me because Johnny and his company are located in Dayton, right down the road from Troy.

I'm not sure what happened with him and Vogler. I don't know if Rich left, got fired, got hurt, I just don't know. But it damn sure opened up a good ride for me; one where I knew could win races. I had no idea how quickly I'd find out.

We started out at Eldora in April for the USAC opener. The race was televised on ABC's *Wide World of Sports*, a big deal. I qualified fifth-quick, looking for a good transfer to the feature in my heat race.

During this time Weld Wheels had introduced some new wheels, steel wheels with magnesium centers. But there was a problem. The taper on the wing nuts that held the wheel in place weren't exactly the same as the wheel, and they wouldn't stay tight. I'm flying around Eldora and my left rear wheel came off. I absolutely flipped my butt off, and bent the car all to hell.

They towed it back to the pits, and we're all depressed. Jim McQueen, who was the mechanic on Vance's car, was all set to load the thing up and call it a day. I was looking at the car and I finally said, "Look, Jim, we've got to put it on its wheels to load it, so let's do that before we make a decision." We thrashed around, replaced the axle, and fixed the bolt-on stuff that was broken. But the frame was busted up near the radiator, on the bottom of the car. Joe Saldana came walking by and saw us fixing the car, and said, "You're not going to let that boy race the car like that, are you?" Jim just kind of shrugged.

I had been running on Hoosier Tires, but Duke Cook talked Vance into trying a set of Firestones. I guess they figured they couldn't hurt anything. Jim cranked as much weight in the car as he could, and he finally said, "Jack, I can't do any more to help it. It's probably got 150 pounds of weight in the left rear, and there isn't a thing I can do about it." Then I climbed in and rolled onto the track for the B-main.

Amazingly enough, that bent-up race car was really hooked up. I won the B-main, which gave me an outside front row starting spot for the feature. Johnny came to me right after the race and he was just tickled to death that we had come back to win the B-main. He said, "Jack, I'll tell you what...I know this car has been bent pretty bad, and if you're not comfortable racing it, you just say so, and we'll park it. You've already made my day...you go ahead and do what you think is right."

"Well," I told him, "now we're gonna win the feature."

We did, and we were all on cloud nine. We didn't just win; we beat Vogler and Sheldon Kinser by a half-lap, and they were the nearest guys to us. I can't explain why that car worked so well, but it did. I came up to lap Gary Gray going into three, and I dropped down to put a big slider on him, and that ol' car just stuck so hard...I could go anywhere on the race track and I was fast.

The Hoosier Tire guys were so excited and they came running, but they were sure surprised to see I was on Firestones. It wouldn't have made any difference; that car was gonna win that day, no matter which tire we were on. It was just our day.

I've thought of something else about the Nickles Bros: They are fashion trendsetters. Really! You know the fashion for kids today, to wear their pants way down so that their underwear and butt crack is showing all the time? Well, Harold and Don Nickles have worn their pants like that for years.

Trendsetters!

Vance was the kind of car owner a race driver is always looking for: He's always willing to buy whatever it took to win races. Having Jim McQueen for a mechanic was a big, big bonus, too, because Jim was one of the best guys with a wrench I've ever worked with.

Jim set the car up to win races. Not how you drove; but what it took to win races. It was up to you to adjust. The race car was always tight; Jim always had tight race cars. That's why we did so well on slick tracks, but on the other side we struggled some when the track was wet and heavy. It just seemed too tight for the way I drove.

With Jim, everything had to be meticulous. Even him personally; his hair seldom out of place, his clothes always clean and neat. He always had a couple of guys working with him, and he ran those guys to death. But that race car was ready to go when the time came, you could count on it.

Jim's wife Helen had several children from a previous marriage, and one day I spotted Helen's daughter Dana. She was laying out by the pool in her bathing suit, and she was absolutely a living doll. Naturally, I was very interested. She was going to Indiana University, and I said, "Yeah, you probably go out with doctors and stuff." She said, "No, I like racing people, that's who I was brought up around." Not long after that Dana started dating Steve Kinser, and the next thing you know they're getting married.

Am I surprised Steve got married? Not when he could marry Dana. That's a catch of a lifetime, and I think Steve was smart enough to see that.

Some years later Jim and Helen split up, and he was back to being a ladies' man, playing the field. But it never changed his racing deal. He was good to learn from, just a good guy all around. He is still involved as a racing mechanic, and I still see him at the races. He didn't used to have a job outside racing, but today he works for Roadway Express, loading trucks. And he loves it. Still, he takes no shit from anybody. He just doesn't. That's why he's moved around some through the years, from race car to race car. But it's always on his terms. I admire that. Without a doubt he's pretty sharp on making the car go.

By the middle of the year, though, I could see I wasn't getting the job done for Vance. Sure, we had won some races, but after such a good start it was disappointing that it hadn't gone better. We were getting along just fine; we just didn't have enough success on the race track. Eventually, later in the summer, Vance fired me.

We had a good parting. We never had hard words, ever. We weren't getting the job done for each other, so we both moved on. And that's how we left it. No hard feelings at all. It was just time to try something different. I don't remember how it was said, but I can tell you that it's not easy quitting or getting fired. I don't enjoy it at all. But there is nobody I've ever split with where I've felt we left problems on the table. We've always managed to be civil and positive about everything.

I become friends with people way, way too much to have lots of hard feelings. It's not that I couldn't handle being fired; it's just that I wasn't going to be with the friends I had made. You always leave a little bit behind. Then you have to start things all over again. It's part of racing, and you understand that. It's not like a regular job. If you get mad and quit because you don't think the car is capable of winning, or you're not winning in the car whatever the reason might be; then you really can't get upset when you get fired, because they think it's the driver. Now, maybe it's a little of both; maybe it's neither, and it's a little bit of luck. But whatever the reason, it's not an easy deal to change.

Later on that summer, Vance called and asked me to run his car at Bloomington Speedway in Indiana. It was only a one-race deal because I had already committed to travel to North Dakota to drive Doug and Joanne Howell's car. Jim McQueen had Vance's car set up tight as usual, and I went out to qualify and just crashed the shit out of the car. It was way tight, and I drove 'er into the corner and bicycled, and I just couldn't catch it. It just wasted the car, and I felt terrible. Johnny wasn't sore about it; he knew I didn't crash it on purpose. That was the last time in my career I drove for Johnny, and to this day I wish I'd had a chance to get in the car again sometime down the line, just to do well for him. I still like him, very much.

Like I said before: He and Jim McQueen were associates that first night only. After that, they were my friends.

I'm thinking now of a day at DuQuoin, Illinois, and I'm standing there talking with Johnny. He had just bought a new Ferrari, and he was telling me all about his new car.

"Jack, it's just an awesome car, you've got to come down and take it for a drive."

"Oh, John, I can't drive that car."

"Why not?"

"Because if I wrecked it, I'd feel just terrible."

He paused for a moment.

"Hell," he said, "it didn't bother you to crash my *race* car! What's the difference?"

Good point.

In early 1983 I hooked up with Bill King and Bill Powers, from Evansville, Indiana. They had a nice race car, and I had good success in that car. They had a guy named Doc as their mechanic, I never knew his last name. Just Doc. I actually drove the car on a one-off basis at the Terre Haute Action Track in '82, where we finished second to Sheldon Kinser driving Ben Leyba's car.

I was in the King & Powers car in early May for the Tony Hulman Classic, and we won it. That was a big race to win, there are some heavy hitters on the list of winners of that event. Jan Opperman, Pancho Carter, Gary Bettenhausen, George Snider...I was proud to win that race.

I don't know why, but I soon quit the car and went somewhere else. In the meantime they hired Rich Vogler, and won the summer USAC race at Terre Haute. A few weeks later I was back in the car, and in late August we won again at Terre Haute with them. The King & Powers car won all three races that year at Terre Haute, between Vogler and I. It was a really good race car, it worked very well.

When they hired Vogler, they asked him how he wanted the car set up.

He said, "You know how you had it for Hewitt?"

"Yeah?"

"I want it just the opposite."

Vogler liked a lot of left-rear weight, and I liked right-rear weight. He liked to go into the corner and throw the car sideways, and then he's on the gas all the time to keep the car driving forward. I've got to stay on the gas to keep my car from spinning.

I like my car to go in tight on the right rear, where today most everybody likes their car loose on the right rear. Kids today run the right rear way out, with more air pressure in the tire. They're so brave they can haul it in really hard, and you can see how hard they drive today without flipping. Years ago we couldn't do that, because we would have flipped over. They're fearless now because they've got the right rear way out there, and they're trying to get the left rear to drive forward so they can come off the corner really hard. They're making the cars work like that, and usually they're fast. But when you get the tracks dry-slick, you see guys struggle who are usually unstoppable. Tracy Hines is a perfect example, and so is Derek Davidson. They can't get their cars hooked up tight enough when it's slick. They won't move their right rear in and lower the air pressure because they're paranoid about flipping over. They just won't. They'll try to do it in other ways, but there are times when that doesn't get the job done.

One of my wins in the King & Powers car came in early August, at the expense of Sheldon Kinser. USAC implemented a rule that season requiring every car have no less than 12 pounds of air pressure in the right-rear tire, and they checked the winner after each event.

Sheldon was leading the feature that day in Ben Leyba's car, and Jack Steck was his mechanic. I was running second and Kenny Schrader was third. There were two red flags, and each time Jack would come out on the race track to check his car over and make adjustments, like all the other mechanics. At each red flag, they apparently didn't check the air pressure.

One of the problems with racing tires is that as they heat up, the air pressure increases which really changes the setup on the car. To remedy that we use "bleeder" valves, which we can set at a certain pressure and it "bleeds" anything greater than that. Sometimes, they stick closed, or they leak, and that's what got Sheldon and his team that day. Their bleeder was apparently leaking, allowing the pressure to slowly drop in the tire.

I was absolutely driving my ass off to try and catch him, running just inches from the wall, balls out. But Sheldon was just too fast, and I finished second. After the race Schrader told me, "Jack, if you would have taken it into the corner just a little bit harder, I think you could have caught him." That damned Schrader loved to be cute.

We were pitted right next to Sheldon, and all of a sudden USAC officials came over to check our tire pressure. "Looks like you won," they said. "Sheldon's been disqualified for low air pressure in his tire."

Man, Sheldon was hot. "We didn't even check it!" he screamed, insisting that the low air pressure was an accident. Finally he got so pissed off he grabbed one of their tools and threw it on the ground, busting it into pieces.

But he didn't raise hell with *me*, which was a good thing. A very good thing. I had long ago decided that I didn't want that big boy mad at me, not ever. He was so physically strong, with huge hands, and you didn't have to be a genius to realize he wouldn't be much fun to tussle with.

We just kept our mouth shut and took the money and went home.

Sheldon was a neat guy. He liked to laugh and clown around and have fun. One time we were flying home from California together on a red-eye flight, seated right next to each other. He wasn't all that much older than me, but the flight attendant took his drink order, nodded at me, and then asked him, "And what would your son like?"

He just went crazy. "Lady!" he yelled. "How old do you think I am??!! He is NOT my son."

Aw, come on Dad. Lighten up.

Sheldon died of cancer some years ago, but not before showing us all that he was one tough sumbitch. He had surgery and cancer treatments, and he still came back to race. He had a hole in his throat from the surgery, and when he raced he taped a little air filter on his throat to keep the dirt and dust out of the hole.

Now *that's* a guy who wants to race. I loved ol' Sheldon. He was my buddy.

A few days after my August win at Terre Haute, I left the King & Powers car to drive for Fenton Gingrich out of Kokomo, Indiana, in the McGonigal Buick car. Fenton was a really cool guy, he had absolutely the scratchiest voice I've ever heard. Very distinctive. It was a good situation because Jim McQueen had moved from the Vance car to work for Fenton, so I felt right at home. Bobby Adkins was also helping on the car.

One night at Kokomo we were leading the feature when there was a red flag. My radius rod had broken off where it mounts on the birdcage on the right-rear suspension. Jim looked at it and said, "Well, we better bring it in." I said, "Oh, Jim, wait a minute, now...I've been running it that way for a few laps, and we're leading this thing. Let me just go back out there and ride around on the bottom, and see if I can finish. At least let's see what it's going to do."

He finally agreed, partly because there were only four or five laps to go. We restarted, and I drove to the bottom, and that car was so absolutely nasty bad down there, I took that sumbitch right back to the fence and we ran up there. We won the feature with no right-rear radius rod, which was pretty cool.

I also won the sprint car feature at the 4-Crown in September in Fenton's car, which was my first 4-Crown win. Later on we were going out to Phoenix, and I remember a funny story from that trip.

It was late at night, out in the middle of the desert. Tony Elliott was driving our tow rig, a Chevy Suburban, with the race car trailer on the back. Tony was traveling with us to Phoenix, to run somebody's car out there, and he was taking his turn driving. Fenton was riding shotgun, and I'm sprawled across the back seat, asleep. Andy Hillenburg (Indiana Andy) was asleep in the back of the Suburban.

All of a sudden, Tony is slowing down, saying, "What the hell is this guy's deal?"

I sat up in the back seat, and we could see this goofy sumbitch standing by the side of the road, wearing a stupid-looking old leather aviator's helmet from the 1920s, and goggles. When we got closer he walked right out in the road in front of us. Tony swung the truck to the left to miss him.

Well, the whole thing just pissed me off. What's this guy doing, waking me up like that? I leaned over the top of Tony from the back seat, grabbed the wheel, and swerved back toward the guy.

"Hit that goofy sumbitch!" I yelled.

Poor ol' Tony probably figured he was about to die, with the trailer whipping around behind us, and he's wrestling me for the wheel. We miss the guy, and by then I'm really hot. "Stop!" "Stop!" I'm yelling. "I'm gonna kill that sumbitch! Let me out!"

Fenton sat over there so calm and cool, not the least bit excited, and he looked at Tony and said in that raspy, coarse voice, "Tony, just keep going. Don't stop. If Jack kills that guy, we'll be all night taking care of the paperwork. We've got to get to Phoenix. Keep going."

During the winter of 1983 I hooked up with Dick Briscoe out of Mitchell, Indiana, for the 1984 season. Richard had been running a heavy old Mitchell car with Randy Kinser driving, but he got a Gambler chassis and it looked like it was going to be a pretty good race car. Daryl Tate was the mechanic.

Dick was a good guy. Just like he is now, he didn't say much then. If you won he was happy, if you didn't win he didn't say anything. His boy, Kevin, was just a little kid then, but today he's a good race driver. I had a good year in '84 with Dick; we would race all over the place, sometimes with the wing and sometimes without.

We won a couple of USAC races that season, at Kokomo and Eldora. We also won five All Stars races, including one at Little Springfield in Illinois. Probably the neatest race of the year, though, came at one of the last All Stars races, at Avilla, Indiana.

Avilla was an asphalt track, but they put dirt on it that season. We had a helluva race that night. We came from way in the back, and on the last couple of laps we passed Kenny Jacobs and Jac Haudenschild. Haud, who was in Bob Hampshire's car, hauler 'er in on the high side on the last corner and passed me back, or tried to pass me. When we hit the finish line, I felt like I was in front. Instead of just pulling up and stopping the next time around, I took another lap. When I came back to the front stretch, my buddy Haud was climbing out of the car, and they're getting ready to present him with the trophy.

I stood on the gas and roared up there, and jumped out of my car. "Hey, whoa, wait a minute, this ain't the deal," I said. They said, "Well, we think Haud won." Nobody was completely sure, and Jerry Clum had his video camera in the number two corner, so we all looked at his tape. When you looked at it from that angle, it looked like Haud smoked by me in the last five feet and won the race.

But before we had looked at the tape, I told Hampshire, "Before they go to all this trouble, let's just put first-place and second-place money together, and split it." Hamp said, "Hell no, I won!" I said, "No, you didn't, Hamp." Haud didn't say anything, he was just standing there smiling.

Jerry Clum's wife was taking videos right behind the flag stand, and they went to get her tape. When they looked at the tape, it showed that I had beaten Haud by less than a foot. They gave us the trophy, and man, was Hamp mad. I said, "See, you greedy bastard, that's just what you get!" I really rubbed it in. Ol' Briscoe was pretty tickled.

Little did I know that I had a big, big season coming, right around the corner. And who would be my partner? Bob Hampshire, of course. It was the beginning of a beautiful relationship.

Talking about Jack...

I still have a lot of fun at the race track, but during the period when I raced with Jack Hewitt, Sheldon Kinser, Tom Bigelow, and Rich Vogler, that was a fun group to be around.

Jack is a throwback to another time. His personality would have really fit well with the racers and the times of the past. He got into some fights at the race track, but I don't think he went looking for it. But he's the wrong guy to mouth off to, I believe. You could screw up and crash Jack, and you could go over and do the beg-for-mercy thing and you're okay. But you didn't want to plead innocent if you were guilty. We never had a problem, though, because both of us always raced each other clean.

You could race hard with Jack, and never have a problem. He had a lot of love for the sport, and even while he was having fun, he took it seriously. This is our livelihood, so you've got to take it seriously, but at the same time Jack was happy to be there, and was always having fun at the race track.

My wife Ann will tell you that Jack was her boyfriend, the cutest guy at the race track. As soon as we got to the track, she had to hurry over and get a hug from Jack.

Jack and I raced each other in a match race in modifieds at Findlay in 1994, when he still had the patch on his eye from his Eldora crash. He came down before the match race and said, "Listen, I still can't see real good, and I'll try to leave you lots of room, but remember that I can't see much!" You know, a guy has to be pretty stout to come down and tell you something that honest. Later on that night I won the modified feature, after I accidentally bumped Jack into the fence. But he was okay about it, because it was an accident on my part.

Jack is a guy who has spent his life doing what he loved. I think that's really cool. I consider him a good friend, very much so.

Ken Schrader
Concord, N.C.

6

HAMP

I first met Bob Hampshire in the fall of 1983. Kenny Schrader drove Hamp's car for the first day of a two-day winged show at Eldora, but Kenny was venturing into stock cars and he wasn't able to be there for the second night. I didn't have a ride, and Hamp approached me about driving his car that night.

I knew Hamp only paid his driver 30 percent, instead of the 40 percent I normally asked for. But I didn't mind the difference for just one night. We had a chance to win the race, but I ended up sticking the car in the fence. We were hauling ass before we crashed, though.

Bob must have seen something he liked, because after the race he asked if I would be interested in driving his race car on a regular basis. But I said no.

"Bob, you've got a bad-ass race car, and I'd like to drive for you," I told him. "But my dad would beat me to death if I drove for anything less than 40 percent. I just can't. I'm not saying I'd never drive your car, but not on a regular basis for 30 percent."

So we parted on a friendly note, and Hamp hired Jac Haudenschild for the 1984 season. I got hooked up with Dick Briscoe, and at the end of the '84 season Hamp called and asked if I'd run his car for 1985.

"I found out the only way I can get the better drivers is to pay 'em a little more money," he told me. So I was set with Hamp at 40 percent. Life was good.

I didn't know it at the time, but Bob Hampshire would be a very special car owner and friend, someone who would have a big impact on my career. I don't know how many years we have been together, off and on, but he is by far the guy I've raced with the most. We discovered a special bond there, a really tight friendship and working relationship that made us both better. It was a really good situation.

In 1985 McCreary Tires were really starting to come into their own in sprint car racing. Whether we realized it or not, Hamp and I found ourselves right in the middle of their progress, because we were both loyal McCreary customers.

Let me give you some background on the tire situation. In 1980 I drove a late model using a Hoosier tire. It was a 100-inch tire. We took the late model tire to Iowa for the Knoxville Nationals. We qualified pretty well, and it was a good outing for us. The feature event that year was moved from Saturday night to Sunday afternoon due to fog. Had we ran on Saturday night, we had the right tire: the Hoosier. It was 13 inches wide, compared to the Firestone "humper" tires everybody else used. We were the first sprint car racer to use a Hoosier. I know we were, because they didn't build a sprint car tire, but they were supplying tires for late models.

The following season, Hoosier started building sprint car tires. I was on a deal that allowed me to buy tires at dealer's cost. I kept using the late model tire; it was an 803 (I still remember that number 20-some years later). Everybody else was using a bigger tire, but the 803 suited my driving style better. I abuse a right rear tire, and the 803 would heat up faster, which I liked.

The several years I ran Hoosier tires, I never once asked for a free tire. In 1984, when I was with Briscoe, I saw Hoosier President Bob Newton at Eldora at the season opener.

"Bob, am I still on my dealer's cost deal for this year?" I asked him.

"Aw," he said, "I can't do that deal any more. You'll have to talk to Ben Leyba or Shirley Kears (dealers)."

Well, that pissed me off so bad, I went right down to Dave Dayton at the McCreary trailer and asked about running McCreary tires. They said, "Sure, we'll put you on a dealer's cost deal."

Later on I talked with Ben Leyba and Shirley, and they both said, "Wish you would have come to see me, because we would have offered you the dealer cost deal." But by then I was so mad, it was too late. I had been there the entire time, using Hoosiers, and by then they started picking up some of the other drivers. But when Bob shit-canned me that was that. We won some races on McCreary in '84 with Briscoe, but over the next three seasons we won a TON of races with Hamp. I guarantee you that Bob Hampshire and Jack Hewitt cost Bob Newton a lot of money.

Don't get me wrong, I don't dislike Bob Newton, not one bit. I really like Irish Saunders of Hoosier; he started with them about the time this was going on, he and Dennis Sherman. They felt bad when this happened, and it wasn't their fault. But Bob made a business decision, and they had to live by it. So I made my decision, too. I've been with McCreary-they're now called American Racer-ever since.

Hamp and I really got it going. We ran USAC, the All Stars, the World of Outlaws, whatever was the best money within a reasonable tow. In late June we hit the Ohio Speedweek, a series of seven All Stars races over seven nights at different tracks in Ohio. Obviously, it was right in our backyard, so we planned on running 'em all.

I fractured my shoulder June 16 when I flipped over the wall at Millstream Motor Speedway in Findlay, so I was kind of sore. Still, we were going so good, it helped the pain go away.

Bob and I had a great Ohio Speedweek, winning three races and finishing in the top three every night. We always did well on dry, slick race tracks; that was our strength, where we shined. Up on the cushion; that was our deal. The third night of Speedweek it had rained at K-C Raceway. The track was just the opposite of what we liked: wet, and heavy. But we were so much in the zone it didn't matter. Doug Wolfgang and Kenny Jacobs were having a heckuva race up front, and I snuck into their battle. Wolfie was holding me up a little bit and I finally got around him, and I passed Kenny, too. Man, we were running awfully good.

When the week was over we looked at the All Stars standings and we were leading the points. Even though the season was already half over, we decided to focus on the All Stars and run for the championship. Points had never played on my mind before, and really, even when we were chasing the title I didn't think about points. We just tried to win every race, and hope that was good enough. Truthfully, I don't like running for points. Maybe you'll run a show for $2,000 that's a six-hour tow, because of the points, and pass up a $3,000-to-win show just down the road. I just don't like chasing points.

Still, it turned out to be worth it, because we won the All Stars title by a pretty close margin over Kelly Kinser in Butch Smith's car. The race came down to the final event at Dixie Speedway in Georgia in November, but we won it and settled the issue. That was our 12th All Stars victory of the year, so it had been a pretty good season.

We crashed a lot that first season with Bob, but we were always going fast. Then again, we ran the entire season with the same frame, so it couldn't have been all that rough. That was an ass-kicking race car, a chassis built by Gary Stanton out in Phoenix. We called the car "Betsy."

Hamp always had a really tight race car, and Betsy was no different. Once I got used to that and got going, we were fine. If we were close on the setup, Hamp was an expert at fine-tuning it from there. After racing together for a little while, we got to where we could almost read each other's mind, before words were even spoken.

For example, we were coming back from Sharon Speedway in eastern Ohio one Friday night, and I was getting ready to crawl up in the bunk and go to sleep. Hamp always had the car so tight that I could never use the wing slider to pull the wing back, because the car was already so tight. I was lying in the bunk, thinking, and I leaned my head out of the bunk.

"Hamp, what would happen if we'd change the wing slider so that instead of moving the wing back, we would move the wing up and down?" This would allow us hook the car up a little better with more forward bite.

"That might work," he said, staring through the windshield. Sharon was four hours from Hamp's shop in Findlay, so I went to sleep. By the time we got off the turnpike at Fremont, I woke up and crawled down into the cab with Hamp. By that time, he had already figured out how we were going to change the wing slider.

That was how Hamp was...he could come up with almost any solution if you gave him some time to think about it. We changed it the next day, and we started winning more races. I mean, we were kicking butt. I was really surprised that nobody else tried that, moving the wing up and down. But it suited us perfectly.

With Hamp, I got into a zone where I was just so confident, I could do no wrong. No matter what happened, I figured we were going to win. Period. During the Ohio Speedweek, for example, we raced at Fremont. We broke a rear end in Hamp's car during our heat, and hopped into Todd Kane's car to try and transfer from the C-main. But I clipped an infield tire and broke the front end, and we were done.

Well, no, we weren't. The Nickles Bros. put me in their car, and I started on the tail of the feature. I drove my ass off and caught up with Doug Wolfgang on the last lap, and finished second. Wolfie was in the Weikert car; they were also a great team in '85.

The All Stars were very tough during this period. If you look at a list of winners there from that season, it's a bad-ass list of racers. Steve Kinser, Wolfgang, Bobby Davis, Jr., Rick Ferkel, Bobby Allen, Kenny Jacobs, they all ran a lot with the All Stars at that time.

I liked the All Stars. Bert Emick, who was the lead guy during most of its history, is a good guy. I'm sure there were some decisions he made that I didn't agree with, probably like with any organization, but overall Bert was fair. I've always had a lot of respect for Bert, I know he would never intentionally screw anybody. They made a set of rules and stuck by 'em; I knew the rules and I knew how far I could go with them. The All Stars were good for me; there's no doubt about it.

Today the All Stars, and the World of Outlaws, run only with a wing. I liked it better when they ran both with and without the wing. I didn't mind running with the wing, as long as we also ran some without the wing as well. It helps keep you sharp for both forms of racing. If you go run Eldora for a few races with the wing, then take it off, it's like racing in slow motion. It changes everything, the attitude of the race car, everything. It's surprising, backing off a little bit you wouldn't think would change that much, but it does. It seems like you're going faster, but you're actually slower. It's amazing how that works.

Hamp and I won a lot of races together throughout the late 1980s. Did we have a leg up on the competition, in terms of the race car? Yeah, but there was something else, too: Hamp and I worked so well together, we didn't have to have a superior car. We could beat 'em on confidence alone, I think. Don't get me wrong, we did have some advantages: for example, almost nobody else was running McCreary tires. That worked in our favor.

I'd also be remiss if I didn't point out Lee and Jeff Barfield, who were our sponsors for many of those seasons. They didn't just sponsor us; they were a big part of our team, offering encouragement, elbow grease, whatever it took.

Hamp was a misunderstood guy, I think. A lot of people judged him to be a grouch, and some thought he was arrogant. They were wrong on both counts, because the truth is Hamp is just quiet. After he was around me for a while, he figured out that he was going to have to open up and be more vocal, just to survive. We spent so many hours together, riding down the road in his truck, towing the race car, we became lifelong friends. It was kind of eerie, we got to be so close it was almost like we were brothers.

We're both left-handed, we wore the same size clothes, and we even got to thinking alike. No kidding, there were times I would think about suggesting something, and before I could even get the words out Hamp was telling me exactly what I was thinking. It was cool.

Sometimes guys would ask Hamp about setups, or tires, stuff like that. He would never lie to 'em; not ever. But he also didn't offer a lot of information. If somebody asked him something he'd rather not have them know, he wouldn't lie about it, he just wouldn't tell 'em anything. Some of the other car owners weren't sure about him, I suppose they figured he acted like he knew everything. He really didn't, it's just that he didn't say much.

Hamp is such a detail guy, with a great memory. Too great, really. He operates an auto repair shop in Findlay, and he can tell you from memory the part number for a throw-out bearing on a '63 Rambler. Why would a guy clutter his mind with such stuff? That's just how bad Bob has got it, that he keeps things on his mind. He used to get so upset sometimes he'd have stomach problems, and I'd get on his ass about taking things too seriously.

"No wonder you have stomach problems, worrying about all that stuff," I'd tell him, "Why clutter up your mind worrying about all those little things?"

Bob's wife, June (I called her June-bug) and their daughter Tracy were with us a lot. We'd haul over to Chillicothe and if they got rained out, we might wind up in Fremont, or Paragon, Indiana. We just kept at it until we found a race. Todd Griffith was a mechanic with us, and we were all pretty happy, winning races and traveling around.

That's how it is when you're winning. It's easy to be happy.

Talking about Jack...

I'm not sure I could really describe Jack Hewitt. One day you might hate him, and the next day you love him. He's one of a kind.

As tough as he likes to act, deep down inside he's pretty soft. He has a lot of feelings for people, and he really does care what people think. He might not come across that way, but he does.

His desire was always huge when it came to racing. I've seen him with his leg cut so badly that the blood soaked through his driving uniform, but he still won the race. He's raced with broken bones, when we had to lift him in and out of the car. He just wouldn't let anything stop him from racing.

He never gives up until the checkered flag waves. Last corner, last lap, he's still trying to win the race. That's what's made him really good. His first lap might not show what's there, and that's why he hasn't been a great qualifier, but as the race goes on, he gets more and more out of the race car.

If you were to cross him, he's as tough as anybody. But if you're a friend, he's a real friend, for the duration. There isn't anything he wouldn't do for you.

Bob Hampshire
Findlay, Ohio

7

GUSSIE

Sometimes in a guy's career, he'll get to drive a perfect car, a car that is just so special he gets all mushy when he talks about it years later. That's how it is for me and Gussie.

I loved Gussie.

First, let me tell you about USAC Silver Crown racing. They're probably the neatest cars in the world, and the most traditional. It's racing with class, that's what it is. If you look at racing history, those cars have always been the prettiest, coolest cars out there. It's been that way for a long, long time.

The first time I saw a Silver Crown race, I was hooked. It was August 1973, and I was just starting my driving career. Ralph DePalma owned a race car and Junie Heffner was his mechanic, and Ralph invited Junie, Dad and me to ride with him to Springfield, Illinois, for a USAC Dirt Car event.

That's what it was called, then: Dirt Car, or Champ Dirt cars. USAC had split the series off from the old Championship division two years earlier. They didn't start calling it Silver Crown until 1981.

They might have changed the name, but they didn't change the cars. That's the most important thing: those big ol' Silver Crown cars, you've just got to love 'em.

Ralph owned a Champ Dirt car, and he had several different guys in his car back then: Rollie Beale, Bill Puterbaugh, some good racers. Later on, Dave Blaney won the Silver Crown championship with Ralph.

Ralph kept his car in Junie's Heffner's garage, where I worked. I'd look at that thing sitting there...it was long, and racy-looking. Just beautiful.

Those cars ran on the big one-mile dirt tracks, and that was part of my attraction to them. Those miles really turned me on; I wanted to run 'em in those cars. It would be a while before I got the shot, but eventually they became a big part of my career. And they were just as neat as I had always imagined they would be. Eventually I drove Ralph's car, which was really cool since he's the guy who introduced me to Silver Crown racing.

On that first visit to Springfield as a spectator with Dad, Junie and Ralph, I must have been like a little kid at Christmas. That beautiful mile track at Springfield, great-looking cars, and a 100-mile race on a summer afternoon. Great! There were big stars there, too: Mario Andretti won the race, and the lineup had guys like Al Unser, Johnny Rutherford, A.J. Foyt, Jim McElreath, Pancho Carter, Bill Vukovich, Jr., Sam Sessions, and Joe Saldana.

My deal at that time was to find a way to get to the Indianapolis 500, and those guys all raced at Indy. So in the back of my mind I figured if I could get into those cars and do well, maybe that would open the right doors. But even if they didn't get me to Indy, these cars were still awesome.

If it sounds like I'm gushing about these cars, I am. Of all the racing I've done, Silver Crown racing is far and away my favorite. Those good-looking cars, the big tracks, a little bit of nostalgia in the air, it's great.

I got my first shot at Silver Crown racing in 1978, when I ran the POB Sealants car at the Hoosier Hundred on the Indiana State Fairgrounds mile. I made the show and finished 15th, which is kind of amazing when you realize at that time they took just the top qualifiers, that was it. No B-main, no last-chance race, nothing. The grease plug fell out of the rear end, and I pulled in. We weren't winning by any means, but we were hanging in there.

Silver Crown racing was, and is, a big departure from sprint car racing. You figure out right away that you've got to finesse the car more, and save the tires for the end of the race. You can't just go out there and blast around. Today, it's getting to where you have to race harder earlier in the race, but it's still a matter of staying smart and not using up the car too early.

My second time out I did really well. It was an overcast day on the mile at Springfield, a fast track with a big cushion. I qualified seventh-quick, and Jimmy DePalma (Ralph's brother) said, "Look, just follow Pancho (Carter) and Bettenhausen and those guys. Don't do anything stupid, just follow 'em and learn."

I followed them for maybe 15 laps, and they're all running around the bottom, and there is that beautiful cushion up there. That's like putting a naked woman in front of me and telling me not to touch; it's only a matter of time. Finally I couldn't take it anymore, and I shot the car to the cushion. I ended up taking the lead, but we blew a motor. Pancho won it, but it felt great to have such a good showing in just my second start.

I ran Johnny Vance's Silver Crown car some, and crashed it at Springfield in May 1982. I ran fourth a few days later on the Indy mile. I also drove for Bill King in the Brake-O car, and ran fourth in John Haduck's car at the Hoosier Hundred, an older J&J car.

I was getting better, and I felt like it was only a matter of time before I won a Silver Crown race.

Let me tell you about Gussie. Gussie was a very special race car, a car that in my opinion changed the direction of Silver Crown racing. I loved 'ol Gussie. And Gussie loved me. Very much.

When I hooked up with Bob Hampshire he was running chassis built by Gary Stanton out in Phoenix. In 1985, Stanton sold his chassis business to Challenger Chassis in Iowa, and he was cleaning out his Phoenix shop. Hamp went to Phoenix to buy a used truck and trailer from Stanton. Gary just about had everything cleaned out of the shop, and sitting in the back, all by herself and all lonely and everything, was Gussie.

It was a bare Silver Crown frame, and Stanton told Hamp, "Look, I know Hewitt likes those champ cars, and I've got this spare frame just sitting here. You just take it back home with you."

And that's how we met Gussie. I loved Gussie. Did I already say that?

Hamp and I had already been together for a year, and we had already clicked. We were still primarily sprint car racers, but Hamp told me he was going to put the Silver Crown car together for the '86 season, and we'd run those races in addition to our sprint-car schedule.

As usual, Hamp waited until the last minute to get the car finished. We were scheduled to race in the Silver Crown opener on the Indy mile on May 23, and I think Hamp was still finishing up the car when they were loading it in the trailer that morning. We got to Indianapolis, and the car had a new Ram clutch, and there was no way to get it centered exactly on the crank. I went out for warm-ups and the thing vibrated something awful, because it was off-center on the crankshaft. Hell, it shook so bad I couldn't see, and I pulled in. Hamp is immediately trying to fix it, standing on his head, never having worked on something like that before. He had to eyeball it to get it centered, and I went out and qualified on the third row. But everything went great from there and I was leading by lap 26. We eventually won, leading Billy Engelhart and Rich Vogler the rest of the way for my first Silver Crown victory.

Next came a 100-lap race in June at the half-mile Hagerstown Speedway in Maryland. We just spanked their ass that day; I mean, spanked their ass. I sat on the pole and lapped every car in the field.

Gussie was looking mighty sweet to Hampshire and me.

We were on the pavement at Indianapolis Raceway Park next, for a mid-July race. Pavement is not something I enjoy; I've never figured out how to do well on pavement. I didn't qualify very well, and started 21st. But Gussie and I finished sixth which I think surprised some people.

A week later the Silver Crown cars headed for Oklahoma City, but Hamp and I skipped that race to run the All Stars show at Findlay. We won, so I guess it was the right decision.

Gussie was back in action in mid-August on the mile at Springfield. We qualified tenth, but by lap 29 we were leading and we held off Chuck Gurney to win. Gurney was really good at Springfield in Junior Kurtz's Plastic Express car, and beating him there was a feat.

Next was DuQuoin on September 1. We started 11th and took the lead just past the halfway point, and lapped everybody but second and third (Steve Butler and George Snider, respectively) to win it.

Two weeks later, we returned to the Indiana State Fairgrounds mile in Indy for the Hoosier Hundred. We started fourth but had the lead on the first lap, and lapped everybody but Larry Rice, who finished second.

The finale was set for the Eldora 4-Crown Nationals on September 28. Hmmm, you've got me and Hamp, already fired up, with our girl Gussie, who was an ass-kickin' race car, going to my favorite race track. You'd figure it would be easy; it wasn't.

The 4-Crown race was a dogfight. I started seventh, and Sheldon Kinser, Vogler, and Kenny Jacobs and I were fighting hard for the lead. With 15 laps to go, I spun in turn four. With just a couple of laps left I caught Jacobs, who was leading by himself in Galen Fox's Genesee Beer car.

I tried to get under him, but I couldn't hold Gussie on the bottom and we slid up into him. It wasn't a hard hit; but it was a bad deal because it flattened his left rear tire. I slowed down to let him back by; that's how bad a pass it was on my part. But he stalled and didn't finish.

After taking the checkered I pulled up on the front straightaway and stopped. The crowd was booing me something awful, really loud. At Eldora! I don't like being booed; it doesn't feel good, especially when you know you've got it coming.

They interviewed me over the PA and I told the crowd I was going to pay Kenny the difference between first place and second-place money. I meant it, too. You always want to win, but not like that. That makes it hollow, empty. I just felt sick inside because I felt so bad for Kenny. He's a good racer and a good guy. I went to his pit and told him I wanted to pay him for first place. But he told me, "It's not the money. I don't want your money. That's not what I'm here for." He was pretty glum, and I can't blame him for feeling that way. I'd probably feel the same way under the circumstances. All I could do was apologize and walk away. It was a rotten feeling.

Despite what happened in the finale, we were pretty happy with our 1986 season. We won six of the eight Silver Crown races, and won the title by a big margin. Gussie was our girl, and we had the other guys in the series scratching their heads about what it was going to take to beat us.

What was our secret? There was no secret. Oh, sure, we were doing some things differently, but we didn't have anything trick. We just approached the Silver Crown setup a lot like we did a sprint car setup, and it worked. With Hamp and I, we went everywhere believing we had a shot to win. I had so much confidence in what he did to my race car, he could have switched the right rear wheel with the left front, and that would have been fine with me.

If Hamp missed a little bit on the setup, I would drive harder to overcome it. If I wasn't quite on my drive on a particular night, Hamp would have the car extra-nice, to where I could still win the race. Now, if we were *both* on, sorry about their luck. Because when we were both 100 percent, there wasn't any chance for the other boys.

At that time everybody in Silver Crown cars ran left-rear weight, four-wheel brakes, very conventional things like that. Gussie never did have four-wheel brakes, except when we went to pavement. I ran three-wheel brakes, right-rear weight, four inches of stagger, all the things nobody did with a Silver Crown car. Our McCreary tires were also a big advantage, and our Stanton race car was really a good one. Plus, Bob Hampshire was doing the setups. If you've got all those things working for you, you're going to be good.

When we won that first one, at the Indy mile, people said we were lucky. When we spanked 'em at Hagerstown, they said we were cheating. When we won the third one, at Springfield, that's when they started looking at us to see what we were doing.

Rich Vogler's wife, Emily, figured it out as quickly as anybody. In our second season with Gussie Emily was standing in the infield during a race when she heard somebody nearby say, "Man, that Hewitt just keeps getting faster and faster as the race goes on." Emily always kept two stopwatches, one for Rich and one for anybody else who was fast. She told the guys nearby, "You guys don't pay attention. Whatever speed he qualifies, he'll run 100 laps at that speed. Everybody else just backs up to him." She was right; ol' Gussie never slowed down, even late in the race.

And Gussie was so forgiving! You could do almost anything with that car. At the Hulman Hundred in Indy I almost spun 'er out; with all that right rear weight, she got plumb sideways, and normally the car will come right around in that situation. But if you stayed off the gas and the brake, and just let 'er slide and slide, the front end would start dragging back around and you could keep going. Awesome!

Did I tell you that I loved Gussie?

It does a lot for your confidence when you have a year like that. You just feel like you can't lose...like you've got a big "S" on your chest, you think you're Superman. You know when you pull into the pits you've got 'em beat a little bit mentally, and you've got to play upon that. It builds your confidence up and takes a little of theirs away. As you win more races, it grows even more. It's kind of weird, but that's the way it happens. It feeds on itself. In your mind you think you're gonna beat 'em; in their mind they think you're gonna beat 'em. So it plays right into your hands.

Of course, being in "the zone" doesn't last forever. Hamp and I had Gussie ready for the '87 season, but I'll have to admit that the other guys were starting to catch up with us a little bit. They were looking at us, adopting some of the things we were doing. Also, our luck wasn't as good in '87. We broke in a couple of the races, so that was a setback. Still, there weren't very many days we weren't in the hunt with ol' Gussie.

We were leading the opener at Tampa in February when we blew a right-rear tire, but we came back to finish second to Jeff Swindell in the Hulman Hundred in May. We had the race won on the IRP pavement in July, but our magneto quit on the last lap and I couldn't get the car out of gear to coast to the line. I'm sitting there helplessly, watching Jeff Bloom pass me twice to win. I still finished second, even though I didn't cross the finish line.

I got my revenge on Bloom a few weeks later at Springfield, beating him and setting a speed record for 100 miles to win the Tony Bettenhausen Memorial. We won at DuQuoin a few days later, then finished third in the Hoosier Hundred. We were fourth at Eldora at the 4-Crown.

The season finale came on the paved mile track at Phoenix in November, and we blew an engine with just seven laps to go. Still, we clinched our second-straight Silver Crown championship, and Hamp and I were really happy.

Silver Crown racing was one of the most special parts of my career. Eventually, I won more Silver Crown races than any other driver in history, and when you look at the quality of guys who ran that series, I'm really proud of my record there.

Sometimes young guys ask my advice about Silver Crown racing. I tell 'em, "Go to a bar and find you a big ol' fat girl, and you'll find you have to treat her a little different than a queen. You've got to respect her, and know she's not like a skinny little girl. If you treat her with respect, things will work a lot better."

That's what I tell 'em. And I mean it.

I ran Gussie for Hamp until I quit him a few years later, and he hired Robbie Stanley. We were at the Indy Fairgrounds, and after hot laps Robbie came down and shook his head. "Jack," he said, "how do you run that race car? It's terrible!" So there is Gussie, the greatest race car in the world, and Robbie misses the show.

Not long after, Bob hired Rusty McClure, and he crashed Gussie. After that Hamp parked 'er, and said, "That's it...nobody else is gonna drive this car." He put another car together and Gussie was officially retired.

It's not that Gussie was a perfect car; it's just that she was perfect for me. I loved Gussie.

INTERLUDE
August 14, 2002
5:30 p.m.
Indianapolis, Indiana

It has been three weeks since my crash, and I'm getting better. The bad news is that the crash at North Vernon broke my neck, and once again I've been fitted with an orthopedic halo.

I'm just barely able to move my right arm, and walking is very difficult because my right leg isn't working right, either.

It's all in how you look at it: I could bitch that I've got to endure a halo once again, but at the same time I've got to admit I'm pretty lucky to be alive, having broken my neck for the second time. Plus, I could easily be paralyzed, but the doctors tell me my right arm and leg will probably come back over time. The feeling is there, it's just that there was some nerve damage, which takes a long time to heal.

They kept me in Methodist Hospital for a couple of weeks where they did surgery on my neck to fuse a couple of the vertebra. They tell me my body isn't going to be the same as before. So what else is new? I'll deal with it, whatever it is.

Jody has been right there with me, once again. Damn, I feel bad I've put her through this, but she doesn't complain. I guess she's like me: We'll just deal with it and go on.

No matter what shape you're in, you can always find somebody worse. They've transferred me to a place called Rehabilitation Hospital of Indiana (RHI), and you can look around and see some really tough situations.

There is a black girl here named Nicole who is paralyzed from the neck down. Her friend shot her in the neck over $100. The bullet hit her spine and that was that. She's just a kid, 21, maybe 22 years old. She has the prettiest smile of anybody you've ever seen.

We were sitting in the reception area here the other day, and I had a bunch of people here to visit me. That's been nice; all the people who are pulling for me to get better. We were all laughing and having a great time. When everyone started to leave, I looked over across the way and there was Nicole, lying there all alone, with nobody here to see her. I told her, "Next time, you have them wheel you over to where we are, and you can join us."

I'm sharing a room with an 18-year-old kid named David who is paralyzed from a car wreck. It's tough to sit here and listen to him yell at his family; he's a know-it-all teenager who is mad at the world. I hope he gets over it, because his family is all he's got.

It's very sad here. I had only been out of ICU a couple of days when they transferred me here. It all seems to be going very fast, and I don't know what to expect from day to day. I had just gotten used to my hospital room when I was transferred.

The ambulance ride was very tough, because it bounced me around. They hit every bump in the road, I think, and with my halo I can't lie down very well. I should have been sitting up, maybe that would have been less painful.

But my room is nice, and the bed is comfortable. I'm beginning to feel calmer, like things are going to be all right. I don't know if I'll ever recover from this crash, but somehow I feel like it's all going to be okay.

That first night Jody wasn't able to stay here, and I didn't like that. That's the first time she had left my side since my accident. That night I got all tangled up in my sheets, and I'm not able to use my arms enough to free myself. A nurse had to come help me. I got depressed after that, and I don't know why. I wasn't sleeping much, and I just felt down in the dumps.

Right outside my window is a small pond. I stare at that pond, and I want so much to be free from this, to be able to go outside and go fishing. There are two things I love: racing and fishing. Now I can't do either. It's a bummer and I'm having a hard time adjusting to it.

Yesterday was kind of a breakthrough for me, at least mentally. They asked me what I'd like to do, and I told 'em I really wanted to go fishing. They got me a cheap fishing rig, and took me out to the pond. My left arm works great (I'm left-handed), so I could cast without any trouble. I was trying to figure out how to work my reel, and I was thinking of Brad Doty. He's the toughest guy in the world, and I thought about what he might do in this situation.

He's in a wheelchair from a racing crash, but he didn't let his situation slow him down. So I decided I wasn't going to slow down, either. I learned how to hold the fishing rod between my knees and crank it with my left hand. It wasn't pretty, but I got it done.

And I caught a fish! I was so proud. I also caught a turtle, and that was fun. Once I found out I could do it, I started feeling better.

I'm still all messed up physically, and my thoughts are just swirling around in my head. I don't know what the future is. I don't like to admit this, but it's true: I'm kind of scared.

8

FAMILY MAN

Life was pretty good for Jack Hewitt in 1988. I had a great ride with Bob Hampshire, and we won a lot of races together. My dad was able to travel with me a lot, and he and I were as close as any father and son could be.

Also, I was married. Yep, Jack Hewitt, ladies' man, settled down and got married.

It was around 1980 when Nick Gwin and I were hanging out one night at The Pub, a popular nightspot in Troy. The Pub was the place to look for girls; that's where you went if you were looking to meet someone. I sure did meet someone, but I can honestly say I didn't expect it would lead to me becoming a family man.

Nick and I would sit toward the back of the place, not far from the ladies' room. We figured if we sat there, it was only a matter of time before every girl in the place would be parading past us. That way, we could bullshit with all of 'em at one time or another.

I asked a girl to dance, and as I'm walking past the jukebox I noticed a pretty girl and her friend standing there. Naturally, I said hello. After I had passed, the girl turned to her friend and said, "That's the guy I'm going to marry, right there."

Her name was Jody Cobaugh, and she lived in Troy. We didn't go out for a long time, but I remembered who she was. I was dating other girls, but Jody and I began to date more and more. She had an apartment, and I had bought a house out on Greenlee Road, west of town.

We had been dating for a while when she got pregnant. It was a shock, really; I was kind of strolling through my life, without a care in the world, and all of a sudden she's going to have a baby. Our son Cody arrived on March 24, 1984.

She still had her place in town, and I had my house, which was way too big for one person. I thought it was kind of silly, us living separately, so I asked Jody to move out in the country with me.

We lived together for a couple of years before we got married. I think Cody was maybe two years old. I couldn't have people sneaking around thinking his name was Cody Cobaugh, when his name was Cody Hewitt. That wouldn't be fair to society; they needed fair warning that this kid was a Hewitt.

Settling down was an adjustment, I'll admit. It isn't easy for a woman to be married to a race driver. We have people hanging around all the time, and some of 'em are pretty girls. My mom told me one time (this was before Jody came along), "I'm sure glad you were born a boy, because you're nothing but a little whore." I laughed when she said that, and said, "Aw, Mom, you don't mean that, do you?" She just smiled a little bit and shook her head.

By the time Jody came along I had grown up some, I was in my early 30s. Still, it's an adjustment for a single guy to get married, because you've been living such a carefree lifestyle.

It didn't feel different to have a child. Not really. I tried to do things that Dad didn't do with me, but I still wasn't a role model as a father. Not by a long shot. Cody didn't play sports much, but I did go and watch him play indoor soccer one time. That was something my dad never did; come to watch my ball games or school activities.

Cody didn't have a lot of school activities. He wasn't in band, or choir, stuff like that. Maybe some of it was our lifestyle as racers; we were always on the go, traveling, and maybe that made it difficult for him to do those things at school. Whenever we traveled, Cody was right there with us.

When he was two years old I bought him a four-wheeler, and when he was three he was riding it everywhere. We did lots of roughhouse stuff like that together. I don't know if Cody ever really had a chance to be a kid, because he's been around adults his entire life. When he was 12 or 13 years old, I remember us going to a banquet in Terre Haute. Cody spent the evening talking with Larry Rice and his wife Bev. He wasn't around kids a lot, but he was always comfortable around adults.

Then he got older and turned into a teenager. At that point we didn't get along very well; he's 18 now, and we still struggle to get along sometimes. The worse thing he can tell me is, "I know..." "No, you don't know, that's why I'm telling you." I'll blow up when I'm trying to tell him something, and it's, "I know, I know..."

Cody raced go-karts as a kid, and Jody would videotape his races and we'd watch them when I got home from my racing. He might have won the feature, but I'm still pointing out his mistakes. Rather than tell him how good he did, I was critical, telling him how he could do it better. That would piss Jody off.

Hey, I've never been a Ward Cleaver. I was never very patient at anything; parenting was no different. I suppose that isn't good for a parent, to have so little patience. Dads are probably harder on the kids, and moms are more lenient, more understanding. Hopefully the kid picks it up somewhere down the middle and turns out okay.

I did try to do a better job than Dad did in some areas. We took Cody to Disneyland when he was young, and we spent a lot of time together. But it's hard; you can't be a good dad if you don't know how to be a good dad. By today's standards I probably wasn't very good. When he did wrong, I was whipping his ass. I never did anything to abuse him, but I whipped his ass when he needed it. I insisted he have good manners, things like taking his hat off when he walks into a building. He's really a polite kid, so I guess we did some things right.

In 1988 Hamp and I had a big blowup that led to us splitting up. Our friendship endured, and we would race together on and off for many years after. Still, it was a difficult period in our relationship.

We were set to run the Kings Royal at Eldora in July. That week, Hamp decided to put together a second car for our backup. With all the racing we were doing, that made sense. But Hamp didn't have a lot of help in the shop, and he was putting the car together himself.

The Kings Royal was a two-day show, over a Friday and Saturday night. I showed up on Friday looking for Hamp, but couldn't find his pit. I waited for him to arrive, wondering what was going on. When it came to crunch time I suited up, and I looked stupid as the entire show went on with me standing around in my uniform with no car to drive.

What happened was that Hamp hadn't finished the second car, and he was back at his shop, thrashing. But since he didn't call, I had no way of knowing that. As far as I knew, he just changed his mind and didn't show up. I went back to Eldora Saturday afternoon, after having all Friday night to think about it. I was mad and upset.

Bob showed up at Eldora on Saturday with two cars. He had no idea I was upset; I suppose he should have known I would be, because if I hadn't shown up *he* would have been mad. I just walked up to him and said, "Bob, I quit." That's the first thing I said. I asked him, "Where were you?" "Putting this car together." Then I walked away. You could tell he was mad; he just loaded everything back into the trailer and left.

The truth is, I was acting like a little kid, pouting. I should have been more patient. Hamp was doing what he thought was right, putting together that second car. You can't really fault him for that. Sure, he should have called, but I shouldn't have overreacted like I did.

I was a spectator for the rest of the night at Eldora. Billy Anderson approached me; he was the mechanic on Stan Shoff's race car. They had just parted with Rocky Hodges and they needed a driver. After three-and-a-half seasons with Hamp, I was with a new car owner.

The Shoff car was a good experience for me; I won a lot of races with 'em through the rest of 1988 and most of 1989, and I really liked Stan and Barbara Shoff. Still, it was hard to compare anything to what I had with Hamp, because I've never been as close to anyone in my career as we had been. We were like brothers, and when you're that close with your car owner, everything else seems to fall short.

In 1985 Hamp and I won something like 31, 32 features, and the All Stars title. In '86 and '87 we won the USAC Silver Crown title, and a bunch of races. So when we changed partners, we both had a tough standard to measure up to.

It was a little strained the next couple of times Hamp and I saw each other. After a week or two had passed and we had both cooled down, we talked about what had happened and tried to figure out what to do. I still wanted to drive Gussie, his Silver Crown car, and Hamp was happy with that. He hired a new sprint car driver, and I was still his Silver Crown guy. So we moved on and tried to put our Eldora squabble behind us.

I had a good tenure in the Shoff car, with Billy Anderson turning the wrenches. We were together for about a year and we won 30 races together, most of 'em winged races.

Stan owns a manufacturing and machining business near Peoria, Illinois, and he's a pretty wealthy guy. Stan has a great business, with his sons working for him and his dad stopping in regularly to check on him. It's a neat deal. Stan is a good guy to work for because he cares about people. Really cares about them, and wants them to be happy. Stan loves racing, but he didn't like non-wing sprint car racing much. He liked the speed of winged races. I didn't really care for skipping all those USAC races in our area, but that was part of the deal. Actually, USAC was running some winged races during that period, so we'd still run with them some.

Billy Anderson was a good mechanic, with a great history in the sport. He had been with Bubby Jones when I started racing, then later on with Joe Saldana. I got along real well with Billy, but by the time I left the car in late 1989 we were kind of strained. I felt like we weren't going forward, that the team wasn't working very well, so I quit.

I thought Billy was lazy, to be honest. That got under my skin, I'll admit. But after I left, I began to see what was really going on. That happens sometimes; when you're racing you're just too close to the situation to analyze what's wrong. Billy wasn't lazy; he was burned out. He had been traveling and working for so many years, he just didn't have the fire you've got to have to compete. Winning wasn't as much fun for him as it used to be, and losing was probably worse. It was just a job to him. You can't fake it; you've either got the fire or you don't.

We should have gotten more help on the team, to take some of the maintenance load off Billy so he could be more of a team manager, and not be working himself sick. But that's hindsight. To this day, I think a lot of Billy. He's a good man, and a great mechanic, one of the guys I'm proud to have worked with.

After I quit, Stan hired Jeff Gordon. He raced with them only for a little while, and he got fired, if I remember correctly. Not long after they hired Frankie Kerr, who had a tremendous career with Stan. I think Frankie and Stan had the kind of relationship that I had with Bob Hampshire, something special that just comes along once in your life. Maybe it was destiny that I quit Stan, so he and Frankie could hook up.

After I left Stan Shoff, I was back in the bouncing around mode. I ran Chuck Merrill's car some, and we won five winged races and one non-winged race with him. I drove Jack Nowling's sprint car a few times, and ran a few times for Lenard McCarl. Plus, a few races with the Nickles Bros.

Eventually I got back together with Hamp. I heard he needed a driver, and he heard I was looking, so we were back in business. When we got back together, it was almost like nothing had ever happened. We were still very close, and we raced really well together. I guess that's how it is with a true friendship; it takes a lot more than a race car to break it up.

Talking about Jack...

Jack Hewitt is a very caring, giving person who usually puts other people ahead of himself. That probably seems kind of unusual, because being a race driver you have to be aggressive and be for yourself. But if somebody needs something, Jack will give up what he has in order to give it to them, even if he needs it.

He's a lot of fun, and he cares about people. That's what drew me to him, made me fall in love with him.

Jack is very sincere with what he says. If he tells you he's going to do something, you can count on it. With him, everything is right up front: If he's happy, or sad, or mad, you're going to know about it right away. He doesn't hide his feelings; he's very expressive with his emotions.

A lot of people have no idea what he's really like. They see this gruff, tough old bear who would fight in a heartbeat. But there are lots of times when we're watching television, and if it's just a little bit sad he'll start to sniffle and reach for his hankie.

I have to chuckle a little bit when I see that. Tough guy Hewitt, crying over a silly TV show. But that's the real Jack Hewitt.

Jody Hewitt
Troy, Ohio

9

MR. HUNT

If you look around in racing, you'll see lots of sponsors. There are famous ones and rich ones and good ones and bad ones. But there was only one J.W. Hunt.

He was a big guy, a strawberry broker from Florida. That might not sound like much, but Mr. Hunt was a wealthy man with a ton of love in his heart, a love for life and living.

During some of my best years in this sport, Mr. Hunt was right there with me. I know I've worn you out telling you that my car owners and sponsors become friends after that first night out, but I'm sincere when I say Mr. Hunt was one of the best friends I've ever had.

He was from Plant City, Florida, and he loved racing. Before I met him he was involved with Charlie Swartz, Bobby Allison, Jack Ingram, Rodney Combs, and maybe a few others. Mr. Hunt loved the attention and fun that came with racing, and he thrived in that environment. He had a reputation as a guy who would throw money around like wild, adding hundreds of dollars to the night's purse. He had a really successful business distributing strawberries, and that was the source of his money.

He was an older guy when I met him, but even with our age difference we became best friends. A guy can't have too many friends.

I first got acquainted with Mr. Hunt at Eldora when I ran Charlie Swartz's late model. Mr. Hunt had a son, Jimmy, who was my age, and both Jimmy and I had long hair and a beard at that time. Mr. Hunt didn't think much of long hair; he had to put up with it on Jimmy, but not me. So he kept his distance.

But he liked the way I drove, so we started warming up to each other. Still, I didn't know him all that well, when all of a sudden in 1985 he dropped into my life like a 275-pound strawberry.

It was early on a Friday morning, and Bob Hampshire and I were in Pennsylvania for a World of Outlaws show at Williams Grove. The weather was ominous, with rain pouring down. Our plans were to run Williams Grove that night, then hustle back to Eldora for a Saturday night USAC show.

I told Bob, "Hey, we know it's going to rain out tonight here at the Grove; why not head toward home, and at least tomorrow we won't have that far to drive? Plus, we can stop and run Lernerville (Pennsylvania) tonight on the way if it isn't raining there."

Bob agreed, so we hit the highway. We got to Lernerville by noon; much earlier than we figured. That night's race paid $1,000 to the winner, the same as Lima, which was much closer to home. Bob and I looked at each other and got to thinking, and I said, "Bob, hell, we can make it to Limaland in time to run tonight, for the same money!"

So we left Lernerville, heading west, hustling to Lima. I called Jody back in Troy and told her we were headed for Ohio.

"That's good," she said. "Mr. Hunt called and said he was coming in for the weekend to stay with us."

I was puzzled, because we hardly knew Mr. Hunt.

"Whatcha mean, Mr. Hunt? He's staying with *us*?"

"Yes, he called and said he would be in today. I'll just bring him up to Lima."

We got to Lima and there he was, in a big Cadillac with Jody and Cody and a cooler full of booze.

Out of the blue, he wanted to go to the races with us. That was fine with me, but I really didn't know what to expect. He wasn't sponsoring Charlie any more, I don't think. That night at Lima he put up $500 for fast time, and Fred Linder won that. We were second-quick, and Mr. Hunt gave us $300. He put up some more money for the dash, and shortly after that he walked up to Hamp and said, "Could you have my name on the car by tomorrow?"

Hamp said that wouldn't be a problem, and Mr. Hunt handed him a wad of bills. A few minutes later Hamp whispered to me, "I think he gave me $1,000!" For us, that was a lot of money in terms of a sponsorship.

That night we won the feature, and it paid $1,000. Mr. Hunt came up on the straightaway, hugging me and carrying on, and he gave me a wad of money. I didn't quite know what to make of all this, but I stuck it in my uniform pocket. When I saw Hamp a moment or so later, I quietly handed him the money, and said, "Hamp, I think Mr. Hunt just gave me $2,000 for winning the feature!"

We got home from Lima late that night, and I'm just about ready to take a victory lap with Jody, if you know what I mean. The phone rang, and it was Hamp.

"Jack!" he said, all excited. "You know that $1,000 Mr. Hunt gave me?"

"Yeah?"

"Well, it was actually $2,000! And you know that $2,000 he gave you?"

"Yeah?"

"It was actually $5,000!"

Hamp could have kept that money, and maybe I would have never known it. But we had just won maybe $8,500 for winning a race that paid $1,000. To think we had been sitting in the rain early that morning at Williams Grove, and might have missed the whole thing.

Before you jump to conclusions, I want to make it clear that I loved Mr. Hunt, but not for his money. Sure, his support helped us a whole lot. But what I felt was more than that; he was so special because of his zest for life, his laughter, him just being such a blast to be around.

When the weekend was over I was taking Mr. Hunt to the airport on Monday morning. I'm driving along, and he reaches over and puts $1,000 in my pocket.

I looked at the money and said, "What's this for?"

"Bringing me to the airport," he said.

"Man, I'm not gonna come down and stay with *you*!"

He was shocked. "Why not?" he asked.

"Because I can't afford to have you take me to the airport."

"I wouldn't charge you for something like that!"

I looked at him and said, "And that's exactly what I charge," and I handed him his $1,000.

That was an important moment for Mr. Hunt and me. It wasn't just about money; I wanted to establish that it was about mutual respect. He realized I viewed him as not just somebody with money; I wasn't trying to take anything from him.

After that weekend we became really, really good friends. With our difference in age it was kind of amazing. With Dad and Mr. Hunt both being older than me, they were still my best friends.

Mr. Hunt loved people. That's what drew him to racing, because he could mingle and get close to all those people. He loved 'em. He also loved his wife, Mimi, and he respected her greatly. He might drink and carry on and party at the races, but when he was in Florida with Mimi he wouldn't touch a drop of liquor because she didn't care for it. He always kept a quiet, low profile around home.

People find it hard to believe, but Mr. Hunt was actually a shy, backward person. As big as he was, he had to drink a little bit to do things that would excite people. He couldn't just go and give you the money if he hadn't been drinking. He was too shy for that. Now, don't get me wrong: I'm not saying he had to be drunk to give you money; that's not true. It's just that he was more comfortable letting his hair down after he had a few drinks.

Was I shocked at how much money he had given Hamp and I on that first weekend? Absolutely I was shocked. So was Hamp, for sure. We had no idea what was going on, and what all this meant. Was this guy trying to buy us? Why was he throwing money around like that?

The thing to understand is this: Mr. Hunt was never trying to "buy" anything when he gave people money. In his eyes, he was just sharing his good fortune with others. He was a very giving person, deep down inside.

Still, watching all this develop, I got a glimpse of some of the bad qualities of people, and their bad attitudes. He was our sponsor, but he often put up money for fast time, the dash, and the feature, stuff like that. There were nights when he gave us $2,000 for winning the feature, and he gave everybody else $100 for starting the feature. You would not believe how many guys came up to me after the race and bitched because he only gave them $100! It was amazing.

After a couple of years I spoke up one day and told Mr. Hunt, "You know, there is only one thing you do this for, and that's these two little words: 'thank you.' If you don't get these words from guys, quit giving them money! I'm not wanting the money for me, but if they're not going to appreciate it, quit giving it to them!"

Eventually more and more people began to appreciate him for what he was giving to the sport. At charity functions, he was awesome. At the Chili Bowl, for example, he really helped get the ball rolling on the charity auction that still goes on there.

Later on, when I put together the two-seater and ran it at the Chili Bowl, helping raise money for charity, I was just carrying on Mr. Hunt's giving tradition.

Mr. Hunt also got involved with sponsoring Brent Kaeding, and I'm glad I had the chance to introduce them.

Brent is a good friend, a competitor with whom I built a great relationship a long time ago. Now his kids are grown, just like Cody, so I guess we have that in common, too.

I always had lots and lots of racers stay with me in my house, because I'm centrally located in the Midwest and I've got lots of room. The Hewitt Hotel, we used to call it. Brent and his crew stayed with us a lot in the early 1980s, when he came to the Midwest to race with us.

Brent is from California, and he's a great racer. They call him the King of California, and he's won so much he deserves that title. I first met him out in Chico in 1978 or '79 when I was driving for Dwayne Starr. Brent had walked out on the track and was fighting with another driver. He's a big guy, and at that time I figured he was nothing but a big bully. A year later we got to hang out together, and we really hit it off. Just right off the bat, we were friends immediately.

The following year he got hurt at Manzanita, so I went to Tucson to drive his car, and I drove it again at Manzanita. Ours was one of those "friendship forever" deals, we might not talk to each other for a few months but when we get on the phone, within seconds we're as close as we ever were. We still call each other all the time.

Later on when I got involved with Mr. Hunt, he started helping Brent, too, because we were so close. Brent was coming to the Midwest more and more, running some Silver Crown races, and Mr. Hunt would come with us. Sometimes he went out to California to stay with Brent. In later years he began spending more time with Brent because Brent and his guys partied and raised a lot more hell than I did. If there was one thing Mr. Hunt liked, it was partying and raising hell.

Brent and his family and crew stayed here a lot, and they would follow us in their tow rig, racing where we raced. We were in Hales Corners, Wisconsin, and I spotted this little decorative well for sale. It was $450, and I bought it for my yard. We loaded it in Hamp's trailer, and brought it home.

I sat it in the yard, and right before we left to go racing, Brent and his guys tossed in a quarter for good luck. Wouldn't you know it; they won the feature that next night. The next time we raced, Brent and his guys went to the well again and threw in more money. As soon as they turned their back, I went down there and dug all the money out of the well. No damned way I'm getting beat because of my own wishing well! So I was about $1.60 ahead on that deal.

Brent and his wife Joan had two little boys, Bud and Timmy. Both are good young racers today, but they were little brats when they were little. Oh, maybe they weren't brats, because they minded their mom and dad, but man...they were a handful.

Bud was maybe three years old, and he would point his middle finger at me, narrow up his eyes, and say, "I hate you, Jack Hewitt." They weren't bad kids, but when a little guy tells that to an adult, in my opinion that's cause for an ass whippin'.

One day Brent and Joan asked if I would baby-sit the boys while they went into Troy to run some errands. Why, sure! We were doing something out back a while later, and Bud, that little shithead, he did something wrong. I cracked him on the butt with my hand.

He got that finger pointed at me, with his face all tight and mean looking, and he hissed, "I hate you, Jack Hewitt!"

What!!!??? I grabbed him by the leg and held him out over the balcony of the porch, like I was going to drop him. He's screaming and crying, 'AAHHHHHH!" I look over at Timmy, and his eyes are big and wide. He immediately dropped to his knees, and yelled, "I love you Jack!"

We got along great after that.

I've just remembered a funny story from when Brent was traveling with us. We raced at Lernerville, and I crashed and broke my ankle. They took me to a local hospital, and they wanted to keep me overnight. I said no, and we headed down the road.

Brent was driving, and I'm lying in the back, with my ankle elevated. They wouldn't give me any pain medication to take with me, and their initial stuff was wearing off, so I'm really starting to hurt. My buddy Donnie Hewitt was riding shotgun up front with Brent.

Somebody had given me this little stuffed toy as a gag; it was called "The Final Word." When you bumped it a voice inside the toy said, real loud, "YOU'RE AN ASSHOLE!" We laughed about it for a few days, then tossed it in the console and forgot about it.

We're flying down the highway, and Brent is trying to get me back to Troy as soon as he can. All of a sudden, we have company; a cop is behind us with his lights on, pulling us over.

He came to the window, and Brent can't find the registration for the van. I'm agitated because I'm hurting, and I want to get home. I'm handing my license up there, telling the cop, "Look, just give *me* the ticket if you have to, but just let us get home!"

The cop asks Brent if the registration is in the console. Donnie, as innocent as a newborn, flips the console door open and roots around, looking for the registration.

The Final Word came alive. All of a sudden this voice booms through the van, "YOU'RE AN ASSHOLE! YOU'RE AN ASSHOLE! YOU'RE AN ASSHOLE!"

When we were on the road with Brent and lots of other guys, they would figure out pretty quickly that I love Wendy's hamburgers. I can't explain it, but that is by far my favorite place to eat.

My eating habits are funky, anyway. I'm a really picky eater, and I put Heinz ketchup on just about everything. Grilled cheese sandwiches, pizza, you name it. Sometimes guys make fun of me, but I always tell 'em, "Don't knock it till you've tried it."

I ate at the fourth Wendy's ever built, near its headquarters down in Columbus, Ohio, and I've been a loyal customer ever since. I knew this was *my* hamburger. There are tons of Wendy's in Ohio, but in other areas I have to search around to find one. And I will search; I'll drive 20 miles out of my way to eat at Wendy's.

There are probably few people who have worked there who've eaten more Wendy's than I have. I was flying out west one time and the guy seated next to me was a supervisor at Wendy's corporate headquarters. I told him, "So what's going to happen to those two Wendy's in Australia?" (I was going over there every year, and those two restaurants were important to me! They eventually did close 'em.) I think the guy was surprised at my questions. He said they were going to try to hang in there with the stores in Australia. Then I said, "Let me ask you another question: Why did you switch from Heinz Ketchup to Hunt's Ketchup? You've still got Heinz in the packets, but not in the main dispenser."

He looked at me kind of funny, and said, "Who told you that?"

"Nobody, I can tell the difference."

I think the guy thought I was weird. I'm not weird; I just love Heinz ketchup. On Wendy's hamburgers.

Something I forgot to mention about the Hewitt Hotel: We had a party downstairs one time and we had over 200 people here. Brad Doty, Jac Haudenschild, Kenny Jacobs, Kenny Woodruff, it was a helluva time. I have no idea how we parked all the cars, but somehow we managed.

My house in Troy wasn't just my house; it was *everybody's* house.

Through the years Mr. Hunt was right there beside me, but in the early 1990s his health began to fail. He was too heavy, he smoked too much, and he drank too much. He lived life wide open, but his body was beginning to pay the price.

My family just came to be a part of his family. We loved Mr. Hunt; we loved Mimi, their son Jimmy, and Jerry, Mr. Hunt's man Friday. One year we had Thanksgiving dinner with Jimmy's wife's family in Florida, along with all the Hunt family, and it became very close-knit. We would stay with them in Florida at their house, and we worked on our race cars in their shop at Plant City.

Mr. Hunt died on January 6, 1994, and that was a hard, hard deal. It was shortly after my big crash at Eldora a few months earlier, and I was all beat up, trying to recover from my injuries. It was a painful winter.

We went to Florida for the funeral, and I have to tell you a funny story. I don't mean any disrespect to Mr. Hunt in telling this story; hell, he'd laugh like crazy if he were here.

There we were at the funeral, broken-hearted and all. Jimmy Hunt was out front at the funeral home, greeting people. In Florida they don't have open-casket viewings like we do at home. It's closed-casket, and the day of the funeral they'll have an open-casket viewing for the family. Jimmy approached me and said, "Jack, would you and Jody and Cody like to go inside and say goodbye to Dad?"

I said yeah, that would be good. We went in there, and I cried and cried. I'm standing there crying, looking down at Mr. Hunt, and finally after I said my goodbyes I leaned over to kiss him on the cheek.

You know how when you've been crying a lot, your nose gets to running? Well, when I leaned over Mr. Hunt and gave him a kiss, my snot ran all down his cheek. True story. Well, you can't just wipe it off, because they've got all that makeup on him, so you just hurry up and get the hell out of there, you know? Luckily it was on the back side.

Jimmy was still out front greeting people, and I walked up to him and said, "Jimmy, I'm sorry." He said, "For what?" I said, "I just leaned over to give Mr. Hunt a kiss, and I got snot all down the side of his face."

Jimmy is standing there, his dad just died, and he's biting his lip trying not to laugh in front of all those people. He thinks I'm joking, but he really knows I'm serious. He's shaking his head, trying to look sad, and I'm telling him how I dripped snot down Mr. Hunt's face. It was hilarious.

You know one thing I've learned? You can't replace good friends. Oh, I have lots of friends, and I feel really blessed for that. But friends like Mr. Hunt are few and far between, and when they're gone all you can do is be grateful for the years you got to spend with 'em.

I'm still close with Mr. Hunt's family. Just a few weeks ago Jimmy lost his wife to cancer, and Jody and I went to be with him. They're very much our family.

I still think of Mr. Hunt all the time, when I see his picture, or when something triggers a memory of an adventure we had together. It's hard, him not being here, but I guess it's just a part of life, losing those you love.

Mr. J.W. Hunt. God bless you, my friend.

Talking about Jack...

There are so many different ways to describe Jack Hewitt...he's not complicated, not if you know him. He is a straightforward guy, very intense, very friendly, yet he also has a temper.

He has changed in many ways through the years, but as a person he hasn't changed a bit. He's still as determined as ever, at both life and racing. He's still passionate for the sport, and passionate about other people, and he always has something to say. And he's always funny. You're always laughing if you're around Jack Hewitt, even if you're laughing at yourself.

To a stranger, it wouldn't take but two or three minutes to get to know Jack. He's always got a grin on his face, and he's just an exceptional person. He's one of the most positive people in the world, and most of the time he'll be thinking about other people and what they need before he's thinking about himself.

As a racer, Jack was one of the greatest. He did the most with the least, and was even better than everybody said he was. He still is one of my heroes. Every night I raced with him, whether we were helping each other, or racing against each other, he always thought he had a chance to win. Even if I figured he didn't have a shot at coming out of the C-main, he had so much determination and desire he would never give up.

Everybody in this business is always looking for an excuse, and that's something Jack never did. He worked harder than most, and that's where his success came. He always got it done.

I've met a lot of people over the past 25 years, both here and overseas, and I have many friends. But with Jack there is a special friendship there. He's a special person. He's one of the best friends I have. I could cry talking about Jack Hewitt.

It doesn't matter what happens from here, Jack has had a wonderful life. He can still make you smile.

Brent Kaeding
Campbell, California.

10

DOWN UNDER

When you're growing up, you tend to look at the world directly around you and figure that's about all that's out there. I was no different, because as a young man I had no idea that beyond Ohio, beyond the United States, there is a great big world far outside of anything I could even dream.

Then I discovered Australia.

It's a great big place, full of friendly, funny people. I fell in love with the country, and from 1978 to 1993 it was my home for a couple of months each year.

I'm a racer, so obviously I tend to think of things from a racer's perspective. With that I'll say Australia has some great racing. However, and maybe more importantly, it's a very interesting place filled with people who are friendly, outgoing, and so hospitable you'll find yourself enjoying every moment you're there. At least I did.

Well, almost every moment. I didn't much care for the time I was getting my head kicked in. But more on that in a minute.

Geography isn't normally very interesting to racers; we don't usually study stuff like that. However, there is an important consideration: In the winter in America, we all but quit racing because of cold weather. While we're enduring winter, Australia is in its summer season. Some bright guy figured out many years ago that instead of sitting idle all winter, an American racer can travel to Australia during their summer and keep racing.

When I traveled to California in 1976, Rick Ferkel hooked me up with the car owner team of Dick Gillespie and Jim Brandy. They were connected to Don Tognotti, a major force in performance equipment at that time. Mike Adrietta was Don's primary driver, and they were planning on racing during the American winter in Australia. I had hoped to tag along, so I bought a plane ticket and a visa. I still remember, Tognotti had a flyer on his bulletin board, *"Australia - $848 round trip!"* Mike hurt his back at the last minute, so Tognotti was looking for a driver for Australia. They knew I already made arrangements for the trip, so I was at the right place at the right time.

It's hard for me to describe what a huge break that turned out to be. It was like a key to the world, because all of a sudden I saw a place so new, so different, it was a great eye-opener. I had a lot of success there on the race track, and that helped my confidence greatly as a race driver. Plus, it was in Australia where I learned to be comfortable in front of people, or on a microphone.

The first few years, I raced stock cars. They don't look anything like stock cars in America; they have a shorter wheelbase, and they use different engines, things like that. We raced primarily on dirt, with some pavement races mixed in.

After my first visit, I talked some of my friends into coming with me over the next few seasons. My buddies Nick Gwin and Larry Laughman came that second year, when Charlie Swartz and I drove for Tognotti, and the third year my brother John joined us. Eventually I met Brian Donaldson, whom everybody called "Scruff." I drove his cars for many years, and we built a really tight friendship. Scruff began traveling to the U.S. during our racing season, so he was a year-round buddy. He was a late model guy at first, but later switched to sprint cars. Friends for life, that's Scruff and me.

One of the unique things about Australia is they race in a team concept: Team USA versus Team Australia. At each track we visited, it was the four best Australians against Team USA. That first year, Team USA consisted of Ed Wilbur, Gene Welch, Johnny Pearson, and myself. The second year it was Welch, Wilbur, Charlie Swartz, and myself.

The first year I had a lot to learn. I didn't know the cars, the tracks, the other racers, nothing. I was very backward in front of a microphone, but they interviewed the Americans almost every night, so I had to learn how to interview better. It was almost like big-time wrestling over there, because it was always about getting up on stage and stirring people up. I've got a pretty ferocious lip anyway, so when I learned how to get 'em going on the microphone, man, it really took off from there.

Sometimes, all the hype got to be a little bit much, and things got out of hand. Like when I got my ass kicked; things were clearly out of hand. At least I thought so at the time.

The people there are funny; they'll go nuts cheering for the Aussies to beat the Americans, booing us and throwing stuff at us. But when the races were over, they'll come down to the pits and be completely friendly, like everything was peachy.

I've had empty beer cans thrown at me, full beer cans, anything people had handy. Chunks of ice, whatever. I've had little girls spitting on me, it was downright heated. But after the races, they're just as nice as they can be. They want an autograph, or maybe the fans will have a barbecue for everyone and it's a party. Sometimes we'd stay there all night long, just hanging out with the fans.

If they crashed me, though, I was still enough of a racer that I was ready to fight. It might have been show, but I took it seriously. I wanted to win, and I didn't want those guys screwing with me or my race car. Not on the track, anyway.

For the Aussie drivers, if you beat the Americans, or crashed the Americans, you're a hero. It all seemed to come to a head one night during the feature event at Claremont Speedway in Perth.

Perth is a big half-mile, with great big corners. Tony Giancola and I were racing off turn two, and instead of him trying to beat me off the corner, he just turned into me and drove me straight to the wall. It rang my bell pretty good, and I rolled to a stop in the infield.

I climbed out of my bent race car, and the scene was unreal. A piece of fiberglass from my car had blown back into Benny Ludlow's car, and he's driving around the track, waving it at the crowd like it was a trophy. The huge crowd is just roaring, cheering, like nothing you've ever heard before. I'm standing there with my head spinning, with a busted race car, and they've won. Ol' Benny was like Jack the Giant Killer.

For a short while.

Each night prior to the start of the races they would interview the top four Americans in front of the grandstand. Then the top four Australians are interviewed. When they did the interviews the following night, my mood was already pretty foul; a few minutes earlier I had punched Ben Ludlow. He came down to my pit, and I told him to leave. He wouldn't leave, so I drilled his ass.

I'm all pumped up for my interview. I stood up there, in front of the grandstand, and said the Aussie drivers were a bunch of assholes, no-drivin' assholes at that. Then I walked off the stage.

Tony Giancola happened to be the first Australian interviewed, and when he finished he walked back to where I was standing in the infield. I looked him right in the eye.

"If you think you're gonna do to me tonight what you did last night, you're mistaken," I told him.

He looked at me and sneered, "You don't know what happened."

I reached my fist way, way back, and brought it around and nailed him. He went to his knees, and I kicked him, and he was out like a light. This is all in the infield, in front of 20,000 people. He's sprawled in the dirt, and the Australians are hot, hot, hot.

I won the feature that night, and everybody was so upset I told Nick and the crew to load the car right away so we could haul ass. The promoters loved it; everybody was so wound up, we had just about guaranteed sellout crowds the rest of the way.

They fined me $5,000, and said I was banned from racing anywhere in the world. I told 'em to talk to Earl Baltes at Eldora, and ask if he would honor the suspension. "Banned worldwide." Yeah, right.

Apparently, when we left our hotel room to leave town the following morning, a bunch of guys followed us. We stopped to eat, it was Sunday and church was just letting out. The restaurant was packed, and we pulled around to the side. I got my food first and was sitting in the car with the door open.

The next thing I knew, somebody hit me in the face and broke my sunglasses right down the middle. For a moment I thought it was Nick, horsing around, playing a little rough. I jumped out of the car, pissed off, and there were a bunch of guys standing there.

They started beating on me, and got me down to one knee. I got away from them, and beat on the door of the restaurant. Nick came running over, but they were holding the door shut. He finally got the door open, improving the odds to maybe five to two. Nick was such a fool; it was like a couple of guys trying to help Custer. A lost cause.

I got one of 'em down on the ground, then two of 'em jumped me. One was pulling me by my hair, while another guy was putting P.F. Flyer (that's a tennis shoe, for kids too young to know) marks on my head. He was trying to kick me in the nuts, but he never got there. I finally got up, my shirt's ripped, my face is cut, and my knees are bleeding from where they dragged me on the cement.

We're all standing there looking at each other, and they said, "Hewitt, you ain't nothing but a girl...you get out of town, and don't you ever come back."

We were done racing in Perth; but these guys pissed us off so bad, we turned around and went back into town and stayed for several days. They might whip my ass, but they ain't running me out of town. No way, no how.

We heard later that a couple of the guys were brothers of Tony Giancola, but I don't know who they were.

That next year I saw Tony, and we were just standing around talking. I told him, "I'd like to meet your brothers, one at a time..."

"Just let it die, mate, just let it die," he told me.

My third season (1979-80) in Australia was one of the most awesome, exciting, successful periods of my career. So much happened on that trip, I'm not even sure where to begin.

In the fall of 1979, I was pretty much dead broke. I didn't have any money, and I didn't have a ride lined up for Australia. I had decided I was still going, no matter what. I finally figured out the only way to be sure of a ride was to buy a car when I got there, race it through the season, and sell it when the season was over.

Problem was, I had no money. I approached my buddy Loffy, and offered him this deal: if he would lend me $10,000, at the end of the Aussie season I'd pay him back $13,000. Plus, I'd buy his plane ticket to Australia and pay his travel expenses, and $100 per week for him to help on my pit crew. I also hired my brother John to help on my crew, as well.

Loffy agreed to lend me the money, and I bought the car from Don Tognotti. I also went to see Chuck and Shirley Kears at their speed shop in Tiffin, Ohio, and bought $1,500 worth of old tires. On credit, of course.

Mom and I took the tires to San Francisco, for shipment to Australia. It was a neat trip, just the two of us spending all that time together. We went out for the Pacific Coast Nationals, Manzanita, and Chico. We visited Las Vegas and I showed Mom the town. It was fun.

When I got to Australia, everything went just perfectly on the race track. I don't have any statistics or records from that period, but it seemed like I couldn't lose. Even though I was on the hook with my own money, I was paying my bills and still had lots of money left over.

The biggest race of the year for us was the Marlboro Grand National at Liverpool Speedway in New South Wales. I felt like I had been cheated out of it a year earlier, so I was out for revenge this time out. Rodney Combs, a great American racer, and I had a helluva race. There were several Aussies in the hunt, too, but Rodney and I were just back-and-forth in the lead. It was a 100-lap race, and at each restart, we started two-abreast. The guy on the outside had an advantage, so you might be running second before the caution flag but you're probably going to take the lead on the restart. After a couple of swaps like that, I kind of waved at Rodney, you know, just to get his attention, and the next time he flipped me off. So we were really motivating each other, and this is all in the first 30 laps of the race.

I finally got the lead, and I decided Rodney wasn't gonna pass me, no matter what. He's in a really good Ed Howe-built car, and I'm in a little old Baldwin car. His car had all the good stuff. I kept driving harder and harder, because I just knew Rodney was right there behind me, waiting for a chance to pass. It got to the last 10 laps, and now there is *no way* I can let him pass me. That would be embarrassing, to lose right at the end. I'm driving like a crazy man, just desperate. I came up on two lapped cars racing side by side. I tried to go up the middle to get past 'em, and I hit both of 'em! I mean, I ricocheted off one and hit the other. A grand slam. Luckily it didn't take either of 'em out.

I didn't realize it, but I had lapped up to second place. Rodney had dropped out on lap 40! So I had been driving like a fool for no reason at all.

After the race Rodney just shook his head and said, "Didn't you see me on the back straightaway, trying to slow your ass down?"

"Hell, no I didn't see you," I said. "Do you think I'd run into those guys for nothing? I was racing you all the way."

He just about flipped out, it was funny.

What a neat, neat race to win. First-place money was $8,600, including lap money, which was more than $10,000 U.S. I had already made well over $10,000 that month, so I was doing really well.

By the time I added it all up, I had enough to pay Loffy back for the loan, salary for him and John, our travel expenses, pay my bill with Chuck and Shirley Kears, and I still had over $30,000 profit. It was amazing.

We flew back to California, where my van was parked. I gave Loffy and John a $500 bonus, which was a mistake. Those bums immediately bought a one-way airline ticket to Dayton, leaving me to drive all the way home by myself!

So down the road I went, rolling along in my van with over $20,000 cash on me. I stopped in Reno, thinking this time I was going to be a high roller, a big-time winner. I did win $700 within the first two hours; but since I was by myself, it just wasn't any fun. So I got back in the van and headed east.

I got to the Wyoming/Nebraska state line, and there were two guys hitchhiking. I pulled to the side and they hopped in, and told me they were going to Detroit. I said, "I'll tell you what, boys. I'll make you a good deal. I'll not only go out of my way and take you to Detroit, but I'll let you do the driving and I'll furnish the gas.

"I only have two rules: if I hear anything but country music on that radio, you're walking; and if you light up a cigarette, please crack the window."

They drove all the way home, while I sprawled in the back seat and slept.

Thinking about it now it sounds pretty dumb, picking up hitchhikers when you're all alone and carrying $20,000 in cash. I don't know...it just seemed like the thing to do. And it worked out all right.

That was a helluva year.

The night I won the Marlboro Grand National, I couldn't get to a pay phone fast enough. I called home, looking for my mom and dad at the Kozy Kitchen. It was around 8 a.m. at home, and they got Dad on the phone.

"Dad! What are you doin'?"

"Nothing, just sitting here having some coffee."

"Well, you better have you a beer, because I just won the Marlboro Grand Nationals! It paid $8,600!"

"No shit! Okay, I'll switch to beer!"

When I got home, I had a $185 bar bill at the Kozy! Dad sat at the bar all day, and everybody who walked in heard, "Hey, come on in! Jack's buyin'! He just won the Marlboro Grand Nationals!"

I had bought drinks for the whole bar, on a Saturday. That was all right, though. Share the wealth.

I was just thinking about Rodney and Sue Combs and one of their trips Down Under. We all had to travel across the country from Adelaide to Perth, and they were going to fly. They asked Nick and me if we would bring their son, little Rodney, with us. We brought him, all right; we probably didn't get under 90 miles per hour the entire way across. Flyin' low. You had better get gas at every chance, by the way; there aren't many chances when you're going across the outback.

We arrived the next morning, and we're beating on the door at their hotel. They asked us how we got there so quick.

"Well, Nick ran over a kangaroo," I told 'em. "After a while the car got to stinkin' so bad, we had to go fast to blow the smell off!"

They laughed, but it was true.

One year we all stayed in a hotel where the rooms all looked alike, and it was very easy to walk into the wrong room. I was walking by the pool one day, and there was a British woman lying by the pool without a top to her bathing suit. Her titties were just right out there in the open! Well, I guess I was, uh, distracted, because I walked into my room, went to the table, and sat down, my head spinning. I looked around, and there are four people looking at me; people I had never seen before. "Aw, man, I've got the wrong room," I said, and walked back out. I didn't tell them why I had been so distracted; I'm sure they would have understood.

It wasn't always wonderful. In 1982-83 came one of the darkest periods of my life.

I've always been surrounded by friends. After I started racing, there were a bunch of my school buddies and friends from the Troy area who traveled with me, helped on the race car, and basically shared my life. Through thick and thin, they shared just about every aspect of my career.

We were all young guys, in our late 20s, and we didn't think much about death, or dying. Obviously, being a race driver had an unusual amount of risk, but nobody thought much about anything other than the things that filled our life from day to day: racing, chasing girls, partying, clowning around, traveling all over the country.

One of the guys in our circle of friends was Ted Moore. He was from Troy, and he worked at BFGoodrich. We were out at Knoxville in August 1982 for the Nationals, and we're all partying in my hotel room. Ted is lying on my bed, drunk.

"Aw, man, I got a knot in my gut," he said.

"Don't worry about it," I said. "It's just cancer."

I think about that comment now, and it makes me sad that I said it.

The Nationals finale was delayed a day because of weather, but Ted headed home early. When we got home Monday, we found out he was in the hospital for a bunch of tests.

There was a nurse at the hospital, and Ted was madly in love with her. For Ted, she was the fireworks. On Wednesday I went back up to see him, and she met me in the hallway.

"He's just now coming out of surgery," she said, her voice low. "They took his left testicle out."

What's a testicle? I didn't ask, but I really didn't know what she meant.

I went into his room, and his family is all sitting around the room. He's pretty groggy, just coming around.

"How you doin', Ted?" I asked.

"Jack, they took the big one out," he said.

Now I knew what a testicle was.

He was soon sent to the Indiana University Medical Center in Indianapolis for cancer treatments, but he was just loaded with it. Just ate up.

Ted had just about the nastiest, kinky hair in the world, just absolutely nasty. He told me they were going to give him chemo treatments.

"Jack, they said I might lose my hair," he said.

"Well...Ted, I don't really see that as being a problem, do you?"

He looked at me and we both laughed.

I was running Doug Howell's car at that time, and we were scheduled to race at Mansfield, Ohio, for an All Stars race. I asked Ted if he wanted to go with us, but he said they wouldn't allow him to go farther than 100 miles away. Well, Mansfield was 130 miles away, so we kind of fudged it a little bit. We got a great big cushion for him to sit on, and we took him to the races.

I won the feature that night. I owed Ted $800, and my share of our $2,000 winnings was $800. I gave the money to Ted, right there on the spot.

"Now you know what it feels like to win the feature," I told him.

He died three weeks later. I was racing in California, and I wasn't able to get home for the funeral. It seemed so strange, so unreal: I called Ted on the phone from California and we talked a while, and then the next day Jody called me and told me Ted had died.

A couple of months later we headed for Australia. Larry Laughman, who lived near me in Pleasant Hill, was scheduled to arrive in Sydney a few days after we did, then come to Adelaide to hook up with us. Instead of flying from Sydney, we hooked him up with a friend of ours who owned a trucking company, and he arranged for Loffy to ride in one of the trucks into Adelaide.

We were waiting on Loffy to get into Adelaide, and we were calling around, trying to find him. Finally, we got the news: there had been a bad accident. The local cop didn't want to quit drinking beer and help us that night, so we really couldn't get any news until the next morning. Finally they gave us the word: Larry was dead.

It was halfway between Sydney and Adelaide, and the truck driver was taking a shortcut and ran off the road, rolling the truck over. Larry died instantly of a broken neck, and the truck driver died at the scene.

We went to this little hospital, and they directed us out back. The man pulled out a slab, and there was Larry, lying there in perfect peace.

There was just a little bit of blood from his nose, but it was just so...hard, because it looked like he could just sit up and go home with us. Get up Loffy, get up, we've got to go racing...

We drove out to the scene of the crash, and looked around. It was getting dark, and the evening felt very sad, and somber. Larry had made a bunch of buttons with my picture on them to give out at the races. There were all those buttons, scattered all over the ground, where Loffy died.

I had to call back home and give the news to Larry's brother. Man, that was difficult.

Instead of going back to Adelaide, we went back through Sydney to make sure we could get Larry's body through customs, to be shipped back home for burial. Then we returned to Adelaide to get ready for that weekend's racing.

It was a few days later on Saturday afternoon, when I got this crushing feeling like somebody had hit me in the chest with a hammer. When we lost Ted a couple of months earlier, I didn't cry at all; and I didn't cry right away for Loffy. But it all hit me at once, like a giant weight that crushes you. My emotion just poured out of me. I sat at the kitchen table and sobbed and sobbed; I just couldn't stop crying.

I was going to drive Scruff's car that night, and he was very kind. "We don't have to race tonight," he said, real quiet.

"The hell we don't," I said. "I've got to do something to get my mind off this."

It was really difficult, losing two good friends within two months. Ted was 28, and Loffy was 29.

I told you earlier about how the Australian people get all wound up about the Team USA versus Australia thing, and I remembered another incident. We were racing at a little three-eighths-mile oval at Newcastle, and we got there early in the day. People were lined up so far back, they were cutting off the lines, because they were going to have too many people to fit in the grandstands. It got closer to race time, and Nick and the other guys were in the pits getting the cars ready.

They were set to take Charlie Swartz and me around the track in a parade lap, riding on this platform on the back of a truck. The people in the stands were booing and raising hell, throwing stuff at us, calling us names. This one group of guys had an American flag, and they were acting like they were wiping their ass with the flag.

Charlie and I jumped off the truck, hopped the fence, and took off into the crowd after 'em. When they saw us coming, they dropped their stuff and hauled ass. If we'd caught 'em...

Charlie Swartz. Now there was a funny, wacky guy. He's been my friend my entire life; I can still remember as a really little kid sitting in the stands at Eldora with Charlie and his family.

His dad, Audie, was a helluva racer. In fact, Audie finished second in the very first Knoxville Nationals, in 1961. They lived in Muncie, Indiana, and most summers I would spend a week or two with Charlie and his family, hanging out.

When we were kids, Charlie was our "Fonzie." He was the coolest guy, the hot dog, and we looked up to him with awe.

As we got older and both started racing, we became even closer friends. We spent a lot of time together, both in Australia and the U.S. You never knew what we were going to do to each other...it was pranks and practical jokes, nonstop. And there were times I laughed so hard at something Charlie did, I just about fell apart.

In Australia they wear these little shorts they call "stubbies," which are small shorts with an elastic band. Charlie and I were in a McDonalds (no Wendy's close by, trust me), and there must have been 60, 70 people there in line. The lobby was full. Just as I got to the counter, in front of everybody, Charlie leans over and yanks my shorts down, clear to my ankles. Nobody there wears white underwear; the popular deal is these funky, bright-colored briefs. There I am in my bright white undies, right in front of the whole world. Damn, I was embarrassed.

Most of the time I spent in Australia, I lived with John and Helen Silcock, who were truly among the nicest people I've ever met. One year Charlie and I were working on the race cars at a little garage just down the road from John and Helen's. We had arrived late and were hurrying to get the cars together. There was still a lot of detail work that needed done, and we had maybe six or eight Australian guys there helping us.

Charlie had driven for some top car owners, and he wasn't used to having to do some of the detail work himself. Every other word from him was a gripe. It was, "If it's not gonna get any better, I'm going home!" It got on my nerves, and I got sick of hearing it. I finally spoke up.

"Charlie, instead of whining and pissing and moaning, next time just go home! I'm tired of hearing about it."

"By God, don't think I won't!"

"Well, go then!"

Pretty soon he and I are screaming at each other, in this little, dark garage. Next thing we know, we look out the front door and there are all the Australian guys standing outside, staring and not saying a word. When we started to argue, they hauled ass outside, because they thought we were going to fight. Charlie and I looked at each other and laughed, because we'd never fight with each other in a million years. But those guys sure thought so, because they cleared out.

Charlie is not real tall, maybe 5'5", 5'6". I bought him some thong sandals down there with a gigantic heel, to make him taller. He appreciated that, let me tell you.

We were going down the highway one time, in two trucks. Nick and I in the first truck, and Charlie right behind us in another truck. We saw these three girls, and we stopped to pick them up. Charlie jumped out and yelled, "Whoa, now, at least one has to ride with me!" So one of the girls ran back there and jumped in with Charlie.

We headed down the road, and Charlie started screwing with me. He pulled alongside and yelled at me, "You ain't got no sense!"

I grabbed some change from my pocket, and when he pulled alongside again, I pelted the side of his truck. "Don't tell me I ain't got no sense," I yelled back. (Get it? Sense...cents? A lot of race drivers might read this book, so I have to help 'em with some of these stories.)

Charlie must not have had any change, because he pulled back alongside and threw a $1 bill at us. We pulled back out front and I threw a $2 bill at him. Then he threw a $5. All of a sudden I realized: if I throw a $10, he'll throw a $20, and I'll have to throw a $50! So I broke the rules and threw a $20, so I won.

Maybe the best story is between Charlie and Bruce Maxwell. One night at a disco they made a bet on who could dance with the ugliest girl. Charlie had this ugly skag out on the floor, and you could tell right away that he held a commanding lead in the contest, and was putting Bruce a lap down. But sitting at this table in the corner was a bunch of cross-dressers; guys who were dressed up like girls. Bruce not only unlapped himself; he beat Charlie by five laps.

The deal on the bet was that Charlie had to shave one side of his moustache off. *Just one side!* So he did, and the next night at the races he was walking around with half a moustache. It was wonderful. Finally later that night, when the races were over, Charlie said to Bruce, "Look, you've got to let me do something...I've got to have some way to shave the rest of my moustache."

The lights are out, the races are over, and just about everybody is gone. Bruce finally says, "Okay, Charlie, you can shave your moustache if you streak naked around the race track." You've got to understand, Charlie's legs aren't very long, and they're pure white. To see that glow-in-the-dark butt running around that dark race track, that was priceless. But he did it, and he got to shave the rest of his moustache.

It was really neat, having someone like John and Helen Silcock take us into their home all those years. I felt like I was raised right alongside their children. Even the few trips that I didn't stay with them, I never made a trip Down Under without visiting with John and Helen. When people booed me and threw beer cans, John and Helen understood that it was not really as hateful as it seemed, it was just an "us versus them" situation on the race track.

My Australian experiences really changed me. Before, I had actually been kind of quiet, almost shy, and very backward on a microphone. The first year there I tried to open up more, and the second year I got better at it. After that you can see the results for yourself: It's hard to shut me up once I get going.

We were in Lizmore, Australia, and one afternoon they asked each of us Americans to spend some time being interviewed on a regional radio show, promoting the upcoming races. The interviews came like 30 minutes apart; each of us was interviewed once, and they asked us to do a second round. I asked 'em, "Instead of us doing one at a time, can Charlie and I do an interview together?" They said that would be fine. We walked downtown and set it up: I acted like it was an American affiliate station, and I was the disc jockey, interviewing Charlie for all our American fans back home. It went something like this:

"Charlie, I understand you just spent a very interesting winter this year."

"Yes, I spent three months down in Australia, racing with Team USA."

"No kidding! How did you find the Australian drivers, Charlie?"

"Well, truthfully, I never did find anybody down there you could call a driver."

"Well, now surely Charlie, after three months in Australia at least one driver had to make an impression on you."

"Well, come to think of it, Max Marr did. He left an impression all down the right side of my race car."

"Charlie, what about the Australian driver, Grenville Anderson?"

"Grenville drives a truck through the week, a cement mixer, and he drives his race car the same way he drives that truck."

Before we were done we managed to badmouth every one of the Australian drivers. It was all in fun, and the fans ate it up. The radio people loved it, too. It was a great, great time. They figured one thing out: Charlie is bad, and I'm bad, but please don't put us together and turn us loose!

Later, when we had switched to sprint cars, they asked us to tape a TV commercial for Claremont Speedway. It was Tim Green, Rick Ungar, and myself. I was the spokesman, and we had the cars all lined up and ready. My line was, "Hi, I'm Jack 'the Jet' Hewitt, from Troy, Ohio, and this is Rick Ungar from Memphis, Tennessee, and over here is Tim "the Mean Machine" Green from Sacramento, California..." That sounds easy, doesn't it? It's not. We went through 10 takes, and I was having trouble getting it perfect within the allotted amount of time. A bunch of spectators had gathered, adding to my nervous tension.

Finally on the next take we had it perfect on our timing, but Ungar didn't come out from behind his car exactly like the director wanted. So we had to do it again, and I'm starting to get irritated. I told Ungar, "The next time you come out from behind your car, have your finger in your nose." We started over, and when he stepped out he had his finger jammed up his nose to the second knuckle. Our timing was perfect that time, and the director stuttered and stammered, and said we had to do it again. We hit it just perfect, and my line to finish the piece was, "and we're here to give your boys driving lessons!" I got to snickering, thinking about Ungar with his finger in his nose, and it sounded funny. It made for a good commercial, it was one of the best crowds we ever had at Claremont. It really stirred the people up. And that's what it's all about.

I had good success there in sprint cars. Their equivalent to the World of Outlaws is the World Series Sprintcars (WSS), and in 1990-91 I finished second in points to Max Dumesny. In 1991 I won the Grand Annual Sprintcar Classic at Warrnambool, Victoria, which is their version of the

Knoxville Nationals. My best finish prior to my win was third in 1983, when Danny Smith and Garry Rush beat me.

My win at Warrnambool was especially nice because Dad made the trip down that year, along with Bobby Snead.

I got a chance to drive for Bob Trostle in Australia. Bob is regarded as one of the best mechanics and car builders in the history of the sport, and I found him to be a really neat guy. He's got these little short legs, and he looked funny in those "stubbie" shorts they wear. Dorotha, his wife, was there traveling with us, and Trostle would be laughing at me because I eat ketchup on my pizza. Before it was over with, Trostle was eating ketchup on his pizza, too.

One day we were going toward Adelaide, and it was Bob and Dorotha, Tim Green and his wife, and me. I was in the back seat, and up ahead I could see two big jackasses standing on the side of a hill. I yelled, "Look up there, it's Bob!" I'm hanging out my window, yelling, "Bob! Bob! Look, it's Bob Trostle!" Dorotha didn't think it was too funny, but Bob laughed. When he laughs his eyes get all squinty, you know, and it was funny. And he liked the beer down there, that's for sure.

I wouldn't trade all those memories for anything. Tim Green, Ungar, and myself that year, and the next year Jac Haudenschild and Mike Sweeney joined me. We had so much fun.

Do I miss going to Australia every year? I sure do. My last trip was before I got hurt in 1993, and the exchange on their dollar is so crappy now, it makes it really difficult. The U.S. dollar is worth so much more than theirs, so it's hardly feasible for them to pay enough in their money for an American to come out okay. Scruff's got two two-seaters down there now, one's for Garry Rush and the other for me. But their dollar isn't worth enough to make it work, getting there and everything. Hopefully their dollar will come back, and I can get back down there.

I'm very proud of my standing in Australia, and I'm very happy the fans there have been so supportive, and so loyal. The number one American race driver ever in Australia is Bob Tattersall, no doubt. And I won't say we're second, but I believe we're in the top five for Americans.

If you ever get a chance, make the trip to Australia. It truly is a wonderful place.

Talking about Jack...

Jack is perhaps the most "people" person I've ever met. He drove my cars for many seasons in Australia, and I watched him relate to people and I was always just amazed at how well he gets on with a crowd of fans.

Our schedule always took us to Bunbury, a small town about 100 miles south of Perth. Each year there would be a group of seriously disabled people from a nearby facility, and they would come through the pits as a group. Someone obviously organized the outing, because they stayed together as they walked through the pit area.

As they came walking through, you could literally see the other racers and crews hurrying to load up and leave, or hide, because they just didn't know how to deal with these people. Not Jack. He would stand right at the back of the trailer and smile at the people and wave them over. My trailer always turned to chaos, because this group just gravitated to Jack, and they were ecstatic as he signed autographs, gave hugs, and welcomed them. They would hang around for the longest time, and the happiness just beamed from their eyes and their smiles.

I watched that, year after year, and it told me so much about Jack Hewitt.

Brian "Scruff" Donaldson
Australia

11

LATE MODELS

I never set out to become a late model driver; it just kind of happened. And I'm glad it did.

I mentioned earlier that I grew up around Charlie Swartz. My dad and Audie Swartz raced together, like forever. Charlie was a really big influence in my life, because growing up I looked up to him. When he suggested something, I would always listen.

With one exception; Charlie got married when he was 16, maybe 17, and I had no interest in that deal. However, I sure had a crush on Gale, his wife. She was beautiful.

As an adult I spent a lot of time with Charlie, especially in Australia. He was a great late model racer, just great. Mr. J.W. Hunt was sponsoring Charlie in the early 1980s, and that's actually how I met Mr. Hunt. Charlie had a really good Ray Callahan late model, a Bullitt chassis factory car with sponsorship from Mr. Hunt.

Charlie called one day and asked if I would like to drive one of their late models at Eldora's World 100. That's the biggest, most prestigious race in the world for late models, at least in my opinion. That sounded cool, because even though I was a sprint car guy, I had run stock cars in Australia, so I felt like I could do okay here in the states in a late model.

My problem was that the World 100 was the same weekend as the Hoosier Hundred for the Silver Crown series. We chartered a plane to fly us from Indy to Eldora, and hoped we'd arrive in time to qualify and race that night.

The format was different then, at least the qualifying format. You could qualify as many cars as you wanted. Obviously, you could only drive one in the race, but that meant guys could qualify several and race the one with the best starting position.

There were three one-lap rounds of qualifying. Charlie brought three cars, and he qualified each of 'em in the first two rounds. The third round was Saturday afternoon, with the race the following afternoon. Time was getting kind of close, and I still hadn't arrived from Indy in the airplane. Charlie was just getting ready to put Chick Hale, a local driver who had been racing for years and years, in my car to try and qualify. I finally got there, and there were only about 20 cars left in line to qualify. Time was running out, quickly. Chick hopped out, and I was forced to try and qualify with no warm-ups.

It was a difficult idea. I had never before been in the car, and I was supposed to be on the gas for one banzai lap. However, at least it was at Eldora, a track where I had a ton of experience in sprint cars and Silver Crown cars.

"Don't worry about it," Charlie told me. "You'll like the way it works, just gas 'er up."

I was rushed to get into the car, and my only practice was the back straightaway as I built up my speed. I hammered the car down the front straightaway, and here came the first turn.

Mr. Hunt was up in the tower. He told me later, "I saw you go into turn one, and I just turned around and scrunched my back all up, bracing myself for the hit, and thought, 'well, we won't have to worry about that car any more.' Because I knew that baby was in the wall.

"Then I heard this noise going down the backstretch, and I looked around and you were somehow still on the track. When you took it into three, any doubt I had after the first turn was gone, because I knew you were junk then. You *had* to crash it this time."

Such a wonderful vote of confidence, I must say.

We qualified twelfth, out of 127 cars. I didn't out-qualify Charlie, but we were faster than Rodney Combs and Larry Moore, two good friends who are great late model guys. Which was pretty cool. They were on my ass about that, for sure. We ended up running eighth that next day in the World 100, which I felt was pretty good for my first start.

I really liked late models. It's a very different deal than sprint cars, a completely different feeling. My problem in late models was always confidence. Now, I could get in a sprint car and be downright cocky, expecting to win; but I never had that kind of confidence in late models, certainly not in the beginning. With my schedule I didn't have the opportunity to race 'em a lot. Maybe once a year in those early years.

I'll tell you this much: Anybody who thinks those things are not race cars had better look again. They're very racy and you're up against some stout competition. Yes, sprint cars are more difficult to drive, no doubt about it. At the same time, late models are serious cars, too.

I'll tell you a funny story from my early exposure to late models. I saw Charlie Hughes win the World 100 in 1976, and later that year we went to Phenix City, Alabama, for a sprint car race. Phenix City is definitely in late model country, and the promoter there arranged a match race between Charlie Hughes and the fastest sprint car qualifier.

I was sitting in the grandstands behind these two big ol' boys from that area, and they were exactly the stereotype of a Southern farmer. Bib overalls and a cheek full of chewing tobacco. These ol' boys were saying, "You just wait till ol' Charlie gets done with them ol' skeeter cars...them Yankees gonna go back home talkin' to they'selves!"

The sprint cars came out to hot lap, and after their first lap the one ol' boy looked at the other and said, "MY GOD! Them skeeter cars...they fly!"

Roy Hicks had fast time, and he ran off and hid from Charlie.

Even in those first couple of years, you could tell the World 100 was going to be something special at Eldora. It's really something to see: all those people, all those cars; it's a once-a-year shot at accomplishing something really special.

There is a lot of prestige, and racers thrive on that kind of stuff. It's not just the money, either. There are late model races that pay more money; for example, the Eldora Dream pays $100,000 to the winner, and the World 100 is $29,000 to win. But you give most guys a choice on which race they most want to win, they'll almost always choose the World 100.

If you win that race, you've won the Knoxville Nationals for late models, the Indianapolis 500, the Daytona 500. Those four are the biggest races going, in my opinion. There are races that pay more money, but it's the tradition, the history, and the heritage. That's what makes the World 100 so special.

Man...I sure wish I had won it.

I raced mostly with Ray Callahan in the beginning, driving whatever type of car Charlie drove. At first it was a Bullitt chassis, and later on Charlie was building his own cars, called a Swartz chassis. A few years later they switched to C.J. Rayburn chassis from Whiteland, Indiana, and I've stuck with them ever since.

Over the years I raced late models at Eldora; Pennsboro, West Virginia; West Virginia Motor Speedway; the Springfield, Illinois mile; the Sedalia, Missouri mile; Chillicothe; Fremont; Florence, Kentucky; Lawrenceburg; East Alabama Motor Speedway in Phenix City; Volusia County, Jacksonville, and East Bay Raceway in Florida; just a whole bunch of different tracks.

I probably won more at Eldora than anywhere. For a while I held the track record at Fremont in both sprint cars and late models. It didn't last long, but I held 'em for a year or two.

I always had to juggle my schedule to make it all work. I was lucky, because I had the right rides that made it all fit. Later, when Mr. Hunt owned the car, Bob Hampshire took care of it. That worked really well for a lot of reasons, because Bob and I worked together really well at the race track. Plus, it helped with the scheduling, too.

In recent years I've driven for Tom and Paul Kistler. I'd always keep my schedule open for the World 100. On about five or six occasions I had to get a flight from Indy because of the Hoosier Hundred being on the same day as the World 100.

Actually, that's how I first met Bob Parker. He had a helicopter flying service, and he flew us over one year. It's funny; he didn't have his instrument rating or something like that on my first flight, because we visually followed I-70 and U.S. 127 from Indy to Eldora as our flying route.

One of the big differences between late models and sprint cars is obvious: you can bump and do things in a late model that you wouldn't dare do in a sprint car. But guys don't drive late models that way; they don't really drive with their bumpers or fenders. They can, but maybe their fender will cut their tire. So they have to be careful.

I did have a couple of incidents with Freddy Smith. The first time Freddy and I got together was a $10,000-to-win 100-lap race down at the Governor's Cup at Volusia County. I was in Ray Callahan's car, and I led for 97 laps. With three laps to go, Freddy just spun me out for $10,000. Not long after that he spun me out of a heat race at Eldora, and we almost fought over that one. That was a bad one. Then he got me last year, too. But if you ever meet Freddy Smith, he's such a nice guy I don't know how you could get into it with him.

Overall, the late model guys seemed to accept me. They didn't say, "Aw, he's just a sprint car guy." They all came around and talked which made the whole deal pretty neat. To have that respect in another form or racing, that meant a lot to me.

It wasn't all that different; just new guys in bigger cars. The first few races I had to figure out how to find bigger holes in traffic, but over time you'll learn that. To me it was just another stepping stone: midgets, sprint cars, Silver Crown cars, to a dirt late model. It's just the weight that's different.

I wouldn't have minded having a career like Charlie, Rodney Combs, or Larry Moore. It's a neat thing to say you're a killer late model driver, because that series is really growing in popularity right now. I think it's because people relate to fenders more.

There are a lot of great teams in late model racing today. If you go to the World 100 you'll see a lot more big haulers and high-dollar teams than at a World of Outlaws race. The late models have a weight rule, but they spend their money on haulers and killer motors.

I can remember a really good late model race at Eldora, the Johnny Appleseed Classic. I was driving the Kistler car, with Mr. Hunt as our sponsor. John Gill led the first 23 laps in Ray Godsey's car, and we're coming down for the white flag. Donnie Moran and I had been swapping second place for much of the race, and we're right behind John, coming off turn three and four, with Billy Moyer right behind us.

Donnie started to go low, then moved back up. But I had filled the hole when he moved, and I passed Donnie right at the flag stand. Then I dropped below John and beat him to the flag to win the race. It was awesome. When I beat those three guys, that was a big feather in my cap.

My best shot to win one of the really big races came in 1994. It was the first year for The Eldora Dream, and I was still wearing a patch on my eye from my crash there nine months earlier. They had to run the race in the daytime, and the track took rubber. We took off and hid in our heat race, so we started on the pole for the feature. I'm on the bottom, biding my time, and Scott Bloomquist spun me out, broke my wrist, and took me out of the deal.

I didn't like Scott for a lot of years, but now I talk to him like anybody else. It's just racing, I guess, and there is no sense holding a grudge.

Right now late model racing is all about chassis setup. Billy Moyer, Donnie Moran, the guys who win consistently, they know just what to do to their cars. You can't just jump into 'em and go good that quickly. Tony Stewart might jump in one and be quick right away, sometimes I can, sometimes Kenny Schrader can, but we're not going to beat somebody who is winning two or three times a week with 'em. They're just too sharp. You might make the show, but you're not a threat to win.

I think you can race a lot later in your career in late models. Sprint cars are a young man's game, for the most part; but that's not true with late models. Experience and patience count for a lot in late model racing.

If things had worked out differently, maybe I'd still have another 10 good years left in late models. I always said that if I couldn't run sprint cars any longer, I'd go run late models for another five to 10 years.

Who knows; maybe I will. Maybe I will.

12

A VERY BUSY TIME

From early in my driver career, I raced for a living. I didn't want to have a job during the week, for two reasons: one, I wanted to have the freedom to race wherever and whenever I wanted, and a job gets in the way of that; and two, who wants a job, anyway?

By the early 1990s I had become really busy. I had consistently raced 120-plus nights per year throughout the 1980s, thanks to going to Australia in the winter. It really took off in 1991, my busiest year ever.

I raced 152 feature events that year, which is a pretty full schedule. If you average it out, that's racing almost every other night, for the entire year. That's a bunch.

But I was happy as a hog in, well, you know. I would have raced every night if it had been available.

Did I get sick of it? Nope.

I wasn't just busy in 1991; I had some good success, too. I won a total of 35 races that year, including the Belleville Midget Nationals, and the Jayhawk Nationals for winged sprint cars out in Topeka, Kansas.

Before I forget, I want to talk about a couple of races I won in 1990, the Sheldon Kinser Memorial, and the Brad Doty Classic. Both those races meant an awful lot to me.

I mentioned earlier how much I liked Sheldon. They named a race after him at Bloomington, and I won it in Hamp's car. I don't get all that sentimental about a lot of things, but I do think about guys like Sheldon who aren't around any more. It was neat to win the race and think about him.

The Brad Doty Classic was a benefit that was put together after Brad was paralyzed in a crash at Eldora in 1988. Winning that race was special for a couple of reasons. One was because it attracted some of the best racers in the country; Steve Kinser won it the year earlier, and Bobby Allen won it the year after I did. So I was in good company.

But the Doty race was also special because it felt good to be a part of an event that truly benefited a friend. I don't know what the exact finances were between the race and Brad, that's not my business. But I knew he got some benefit, and that was good enough for me.

When Brad got hurt, and ended up in a wheelchair, that was a tough deal. I've known lots of brave, tough guys in my life, and I've told Brad that he's just about the bravest. I've told him, "Man, I couldn't have handled it like you have." But he just smiles and says, "Aw, you'd figure a way." But I don't know about that. It takes a lot of courage to face a situation like his.

I guess you never know what you're capable of until you're challenged. Brad was challenged, and he stepped up. I admire that.

I'm kind of amazed when I look at my stats for 1991. One of the things that stands out, that I'm most proud of, is that I won in a lot of different race cars. That means a lot; when you win a bunch in one car sometimes people might think it's the car. Well, it is the car, sure, but you've got to drive the thing. When you win in several different cars, you're proud because you're kind of proving yourself, proving that *you* can win. That means a lot to any race driver.

By the way, I only have stats because Jody kept 'em. Prior to her coming to the races with me, I didn't write anything down. Hey, do you think Don Hewitt wrote down stuff from when he raced? Shit, no. It was, "Get the money at the payoff window, and forget it."

After I left Stan Shoff's car, I began driving for Don Murphy. Actually, that was a weird period in my career; my sprint car ride switched on a regular basis between Murphy and Hamp.

Murphy was a neat guy. He was from Chesterfield, Indiana, where he owned a grocery store. Murph just loved racing, I think he had as much fun in the sport as anybody. He didn't bitch or raise hell, he just loved to race and have fun. Later on he owned a midget, and I had some success in that car, too. We became very close friends, Murphy and I.

I'm not sure how we got hooked up. He had Tray House in his car for a long time, and after they split up Murph and I got together. We went on a tear during one period, and won seven straight features. Tim Clark was our mechanic, and Tim is a transplanted "Buckeye" living right around the corner from me.

We went to Michigan and won an All Star race, then drove clear down to Richmond, Kentucky, to win a USAC race, beating Kevin Briscoe. The next night we won at Glasgow, Kentucky.

A Terre Haute win was in the mix somewhere, and I laugh when I think about that one. USAC officials would check the displacement of the winner's engine after each race, using a pump-like device called a P&G. They only checked the top three, I think. The race was a Sunday afternoon, and we planned on hauling ass as soon as it was over to try and make it to Kokomo in time for the sprint car program. As soon as we won the feature, we're hustling to load everything up. Murphy said, "Whoa, whoa, wait a minute, we can't leave yet...they've got to pump our motor."

Bullshit, we told him.

"As soon as we got here, we went ahead and had them pump our motor in advance, because we figured we'd be tight on time."

Murphy just grinned.

"Man...you guys are getting cocky, ain't ya'!"

We had several different mechanics during that period, in addition to Tim Clark. Phil Poor was with us for some races, and Lenard McCarl. We raced with USAC and the All Stars, but we also ran a lot of weekly tracks, unsanctioned races at places like Lincoln Park Speedway, Kokomo, and Bloomington.

I remember one night when we won at Lincoln Park, it was just Phil Poor and me, with no other help. We had to hump to make it happen, but we did it. That was neat.

I got a call from Gary Zarounian in 1991, asking if I'd be interested in running his midget at the Belleville Midget Nationals at the Belleville High Banks in Kansas. I had very little midget experience at that time, but Belleville was a big race, and Gary had a good car. I had never met him before, but it sure worked out okay.

It was a scheduling nightmare, because I had also committed to running Hamp's car at Liberty, Indiana, on Friday night, smack in the middle of the Belleville deal. But Zarounian bought me two plane tickets, so I flew to Belleville and qualified on Thursday; flew home on Friday and raced Hamp's car; then flew back to Belleville early Saturday for that night's race.

I ran second to Stevie Reeves at the Thursday qualifier. Stevie was really good in the Wilke midget.

That weekend was my first visit to Belleville. It was unlike any track I had ever seen before. It's kind of a D-shaped track, with a lot of cornering. I had heard how high banked and fast it was, and they weren't lying. It is actually kind of hard to pass there, because it's so fast. Even the lapped guys are fast. You've got to be pretty sharp to make it work. It reminds me a lot of Eldora, with the high banks. I could see right away that an Eldora driving style would suit Belleville, which helped me because I've got a lot of laps at Eldora.

It was a little bit treacherous on Saturday night, because the cushion pushed right out by the fence, and it was dry and slick by feature time. That was okay as far as I was concerned, because I felt like I could really get around that kind of race track.

After you've driven a sprint car, you're just brave as hell in a midget. You can go into smaller holes, and you feel like you can do anything with 'em. But you've got to be careful, because they will bust your ass.

Gary Zarounian always had top-notch stuff, and I was honored that he called me. Just to be on his list was a neat thing. I felt like I was on equal equipment at Belleville, and I went out there to win. Gary, his dad, and his uncle were all helping on the car, and they knew what to do to hook up the race car. It turned out to be a great weekend.

Steve Lewis also had good equipment then, but they weren't the unbeatable cars he has today.

The feature was 40 laps, and I was starting fourth. Stan Fox took off at the start, and led the first 25 laps. I had a good race with Johnny Heydenreich and Stevie Reeves, and eventually I worked my way into second. There was a caution on lap 25, allowing me close right up behind Stan for the restart. That was the difference; I beat him on the restart, and they never caught me.

The race paid $7,500. A nice payday.

I was just thinking about the first race I won in Don Murphy's car. It was at Terre Haute, and after the race he had his three little girls get in the picture with me. I think that moment meant a lot to Don, because they were just little things then. It was kind of a bond, that moment with his little girls in the picture.

I'm sure they're all grown up now. I hope he still has that picture. That was a good memory.

It was fun working with Phil Poor as my mechanic. I liked Phil and we got along pretty well. My first experience with Phil came when he was the mechanic on Jeff Stoops' sprint car, when he and Steve Butler won a bunch of USAC sprint car championships.

It was 1989, when Steve got hurt trying to make the Indy 500. He wasn't able to race, so they called me to fill in one night at IRP. Phil was his usual serious self, and we did okay in our heat. But I made some recommendations on changing the car, which we did. Problem was, I jacked us clear out of the ballpark. The car was terrible.

After the race, I teased Jeff Stoops.

"Jeff, I hope you learned your lesson tonight," I said.

He seemed very surprised.

"Well...what do you mean?"

"Let me tell it real plain...DON'T LISTEN TO YOUR RACE DRIVER!"

He laughed.

Actually, that's why most mechanics are kind of difficult to work with. They're just as intense at their job as the driver is at his. They can see things better than we can, and they're always wanting to change the car to make it better. At the same time you have your ideas about what the car is doing, and what it needs, so there's often a conflict.

Sometimes the mechanic just changes it, without any discussion. Even if it makes the car better, that pisses you off. So then you'll start pouting. It drives a wedge in there. But the good mechanics are going to be more intense, and a little harder to get along with, because they want to win. Period.

You see those discussions in every pit area, every night. The mechanic and the driver standing there, talking. "Let's tighten it up," says the mechanic. "NO! We need to loosen it up," says the driver. Usually the mechanic wins, because he's the one twisting the bolts.

You'll usually know right off the bat if you're going to be able to work with somebody. You'll either click, or you won't. You can still do okay if you're not on the same page, and win a few races, but you'll never be great unless the driver and mechanic develop an ability to communicate. The teams that win all the time: Mark Kinser and Karl Kinser; Steve Kinser and Scott Gerkin; Jack Hewitt and Bob Hampshire; they've figured each other out and they stay together for a long while. It takes a special something to win lots and lots of races.

I still see Phil quite a bit at the USAC races. He's been helping Dave Darland for the last couple of years, and he'll come down to our pits and we'll talk. He'll ask what tire I'm on, what setup, stuff like that. No matter what we're doing, he'll give us lots of tips on what we *ought* to be doing. Whether we need the advice or not.

A quick story on that win at the Jayhawk Nationals in '91. It was a period when I was bouncing around some in terms of running a lot of different cars, and I hooked up with Phil Durst to run his car for a few races during that period. Phil is in the car business in Lincoln and is truly one of the neatest guys in racing. The Jayhawk Nationals was in Kansas, just a couple of nights prior to the Knoxville Nationals. We qualified fairly decent, and Phil asked me what I thought it would take to win the race. I didn't pull any punches. "McCreary Tires," I said. They were loyal Goodyear guys, but Phil said, "Do you really think so?" "I know so!" The track was perfect for McCrearys: shiny, dry-slick. Just perfect.

Phil said okay, so I went to the tire truck to get some McCreary tires. But nobody was selling the brand. Somebody told me Gary Wright might have some, so I went to his trailer. Gary was a McCreary guy, and he did have some tires, but he normally ran a 3418, and I liked the slightly more narrow 3417. He did have a used 3417, and it was an awkward situation. I didn't feel right asking him to give it to me, and he didn't feel right about selling me a used tire. "I've got to have $75 for it," he finally said. No problem, we paid him and took the tire back to our pit.

We went out and won the race, and guess who finished second? That's right, Gary Wright! He just kind of grinned at me and said, "That's the last tire you'll ever buy from me!"

I remember being pretty pissed off at the track officials. When we signed in, they charged me $15 to get in for general admission, then charged me another $15 for my pit pass, which was just ungodly high for that period. That really chapped my ass.

We were leading the race with just a few laps to go and there was a red flag. We were stopped on the race track when an official came walking up to our car. "If you win, we need you to take an extra lap or two to let us get set up, and then stop on the front straightaway for the ceremonies and interview."

"Fuck you," I said.

He was just stunned. "Wha...what's wrong?"

"Hey, you guys charged me $30 for a pit pass," I said. "If you're gonna treat your racers that badly, then I'm not interested in helping you out with interviews."

He was telling me how sorry he was, and he said, "Oh, it's all right, Jack. We'll refund your pit pass if that's what's bothering you."

I looked him right in the eye.

"We've got five guys on this crew," I said.

He swallowed really hard, and walked away.

They restarted the race, and after we won I just drove back to my pits. I told Phil, "Hey, this car shouldn't move until they make it right on the pit passes."

It wasn't even a minute when the guy who ran the track came running up with the money for five passes.

We pushed the car out on the front stretch and I gave 'em the best $30 interview I've ever done in my life. Who says money can't buy happiness?

Back closer to home, my period of ride swapping between Murphy and Hamp eventually came to an end. I ended up back full-time with Hamp, and it created a difficult situation with Murphy. It was brief, but still difficult.

Hamp and I went to Granite City for a race, and Murphy was there with his car, thinking I was driving for him that night. I guess it was just a miscommunication, because I had already committed to Hamp. Boy, Murphy was pissed at me. He called me an asshole, he was so mad.

The next two nights we were in Chicago racing for Hamp, and when we were finished I rode back to Indiana with my good friends, Steve and Barb Remington. The next day I drove over to Chesterfield to Murphy's store to apologize. At first he wouldn't even see me; he was apparently still pretty mad. So I left, then came back a little later, and he still wouldn't see me. Then he called back and said, "Well, since you've come this far..." So I went back to his store one more time and we talked.

I explained that it was a miscommunication, and it was never my intention to screw him in any way. Hell, even people who are in love have spats, and that's what it was: a spat.

I guess Murphy and I thought enough of each other that we got through it all right. We hung together as friends, and not long after Don bought a midget and we went racing together. So I was back with both Hamp and Murphy, with two good race cars. That was a good situation, both from the racing side and the friendship side.

I just thought of another funny story from that period: I've got to tell you about the snowmobile trailer.

Murphy had his midget, but for a little while we didn't have a tow rig. We had been using Hamp's trailer, but one particular weekend we didn't have the trailer available, and we wanted to race the midget somewhere. I started scrounging around, and borrowed a little snowmobile trailer from Bobby Snead.

Don't laugh; it was as basic as you could get, but the car fit just fine. We strapped 'er down, tied on a couple of spare tires, and we were in business. We might have looked like the Beverly Hillbillies, but what the hell.

Donnie and Don Hewett were in town, and they went with us to Kokomo. Those guys are late model racers; they didn't know anything about working on the midget. But they helped change tires, push the car up, stuff like that. We ended up having a helluva race with P.J. Jones. Man, it was awesome. Swapping the lead, sliding each other, just racing like hell. It was fun!

P.J. got by me going into turn one, with a big slide job. I gave one back to him going into three, and there was the checkered flag, and I won. P.J. was like his brother, Page; when you beat 'em they were the first one down to congratulate you. That was neat.

We were parked between the Wilke pit and Doug Kalitta; both of 'em had great big trailers, and there's our tiny, open snowmobile trailer. As I'm pulling into my pit I'm teasing them, yelling, "Fire up the generator!" Hell, we barely had a flashlight, let alone a generator.

We also won at Michigan with the snowmobile trailer, and again at Granite City on the quarter-mile.

One of my friends was sitting in the stands at Terre Haute not long after when we pulled in with the midget, and they overheard somebody who noticed us coming in.

"Look at that trailer Hewitt's car is on!" they laughed.

Somebody else spoke up.

"Don't make fun of Hewitt and that little trailer...every time we see 'em bring it in, they've won!"

I'm proud of that little trailer. That's one neat thing I hope never changes about racing: you don't have to have a big trailer to kick their ass.

13

DUKES UP!

You've stayed with me for a long time in this book, and right about now you're probably wondering, "Hey, Hewitt, when are you going to talk about the fights?"

I guess it's time. So here we go.

I didn't fight a lot when I was a kid. In seventh grade I was the backup quarterback on our football team, and one day at practice a bigger kid took the ball from me, and was teasing me with it. I was the smallest kid out there; still, that kid really pissed me off, and I socked him in the eye. Normally I would have been in trouble, but I was so little the coach thought it was funny, and nothing more was said.

Probably the biggest misconception about me is that people think I'm fighting all the time. I don't remember when my last fight was, or who it was with, it was that long ago. Still, I'm living off my reputation. The first time some young kid walks up and whips my ass, they're all gonna have a run at me. Because then they'll know that "He's not what he used to be."

Right now people leave me alone just because of my reputation. They think I'm still the guy I was 10 years ago. Unfortunately, I'm not. But I'm not gonna tell 'em any different, because maybe they'll still leave me alone.

Intimidation is a big factor in racing. A big, big factor. Half the races are won before the race even starts. Earlier in his career, when Steve Kinser was winning all those races, when he pulled into the track people would think, "Well, we're running for second." Whenever you can beat somebody like that before they even get in the car, it's a huge advantage. That makes your job as a racer that much easier. Whether they give you an inch or not, that makes a difference. That's what Dale Earnhardt was good at: intimidation.

When other guys figured out I wouldn't hesitate to fight, I believe that made 'em think a little bit. Maybe it wouldn't change anything on the race track, but it might make 'em hesitate to come down and jump my shit about something.

Just about every one of my fights was about racing. I never picked fights, because I believe a guy who goes around looking for fights is a bully. I don't want to be a bully.

I've scuffled with a lot of different guys, and they were my friends, both before and after. I wasn't trying to hurt 'em; I was trying to make a point. I'm not smart enough to know how to talk to somebody and work it out real nice. I'll poke him in the eye and then the problem is solved. Right or wrong, that's how it is.

I have a motto as a racer: the first one's on you, the second one is on me. That means I'll tolerate getting crashed once by a mistake or a stupid move. Not twice. The second time we're going to discuss it.

Maybe other guys don't have that motto, or maybe I've not crashed anybody twice. The problem is, I think, most guys know I'll fight, so they don't come down and get after me if they think I'm wrong. And there are times I know somebody *should* have come down and ripped my ass, because I screwed up.

The only guy who's done that has been Tony Elliott. We were at Lawrenceburg one night at a non-winged USAC race, and the track was dry slick. Tony was second and I was third, and I bumped him and spun him out. I definitely didn't do it on purpose; but I was to blame because I didn't have enough control of my race car. It was my fault.

Tony came down and chewed my ass and pushed me a couple of times, and I took it, because I had it coming. I told him at the time, "Hey, I've got it coming, take your best shot." If he would have hit me, I would have taken that, too.

There are three ways you can crash somebody. One is to do it on purpose; the second way is to just be stupid; the third way is that you're just racing hard, and you bump. I never bitched about the third one; the first two, well, we had to talk about those issues.

I guess Tony could make the argument that mine was being stupid, because I didn't control my car well enough. I ended up winning the race, which probably fired Tony up even more, but I took my ass-chewing when it was over and moved on.

People have asked if I'm scrappy because my dad was scrappy. I don't think so; most of the fighting my dad did was when he was drunk. At the race track he got into a couple of scrapes, but not many. And with me not being a drinker, I had to ride mine out sober.

I never tried to hurt anybody, not really. I guess I have one exception to that, a long, long time ago, before I started racing. A local kid, Mike Mowery, went out with my girlfriend and I was pissed. Mike had been in prison for shooting a guy, so he wasn't exactly a softie. I caught him out and dragged him out of his car, and he grabbed his pistol and threw it under his car. I got to beating him so long with my fists that they started hurting, so I started hitting him with my elbows. It gave him a concussion, and bloodied him up pretty bad.

When it was over, it was over. No more hard feelings. I still see him around Troy every now and then, and we're very friendly. Mike and I have a very clear understanding: He knows not to mess with my wife, and I know that if I touch him again, he'll shoot me. Pretty good understanding.

The first real scuffle I remember in racing was with Sammy Swindell. People don't let me forget that; it seems like every year somebody mentions the couple of times Sammy and I got into it.

We were running a two-day World of Outlaws show at Butler, Michigan, in 1982. I was racing for Doug and Joanne Howell, and Sammy ran into me on the race track and I punched him after the race. People blew it all out of proportion, said I hit his wife Amy, all kinds of stuff like that. Well, there was none of that. We just both paid our fines and moved on. Actually, I won the next night out, so I felt better right away!

Sammy and I got to be good buddies after that, and then we got into it again a few years later at Lawrenceburg, and I hit him again. A lot of people were there that night, because people talked about that one for a long time.

That's a long time ago, and Sammy and I are very comfortable friends today. I don't hold a grudge, and I don't think he does, either. When I'm done fighting, it's over and done with.

I'm not saying that every guy I've fought is a close friend; that's not true. But they aren't going out of their way to hurt me, either. We might not go to dinner together, but we're still friendly.

Not too long ago Sammy told me he'd like to take his son Kevin for a ride in my two-seater one of these days. If we're ever running the two-seater at a race where Sammy is running, he can take Kevin anywhere he wants to in that car. That's just how it is. And for Sammy to ask me, well, I don't think he'd ask somebody he totally disliked. He knew he could feel comfortable asking me, because he knew I would be glad to let him and Kevin take a ride in my car.

I don't believe in holding your emotions inside. That's why I don't understand why more guys didn't come down and chew my ass out when I had it coming. Instead of yelling at me or punching me in the eye, they held their anger inside and stayed mad, letting it boil inside them. That's not healthy. After I'm done fighting, it's over; I don't even think about it any more.

Usually the drivers don't have a problem with stuff like that. It's the other people who drag it out; fans, car owners, other people. They want to keep talking about it, keeping it alive, not letting you forget it.

I don't really like having the reputation of a fighter; it's not something I'm proud of. But I believe in sticking up for what I think is right. I was doing what I had to do. I can't expect some sanctioning group or organization to put a fine on somebody for running into my race car. Then it becomes a judgment deal, and why give those officials that much authority over what we do? Racers can police their own deal if they would let us. We would stop a lot of the crashing and stuff like that, because if you get your ass whipped a couple of times you're going to start thinking about it before you crash into people every week.

When you hit somebody in the mouth, it does two things: one, it makes me feel better because I feel like I'm sticking up for what's right; and two, I'm getting you to stop running into my race car. Your fat lip goes away in a day or two, and nothing's hurt. It might piss you off a little bit because it embarrassed you, but it doesn't hurt. How can you stay mad at somebody over something like that?

When I was a kid and I got a black eye, people would ask me, "Who gave you that?" I'd say, "Gave me, hell, I *earned* that thing." They don't give black eyes away; you have to earn 'em.

I remember one other big scuffle from my high school days. Whenever you fight somebody, you're bound to wonder the next morning who won. Not that it matters, but you naturally think about it.

We were hanging out uptown one night, and a kid named Mike Fox was there, all drunked up. He hauled off and sucker-punched me, and my eye was swollen shut almost immediately. And we were friends! But he was drunk, and he had just had an argument with his girlfriend, and he took it out on me. I grabbed him and I'm trying to run his head into the bumper of a Corvette, I'm so pissed. Somebody yelled, "The cops are coming!" So I let him go, and I said, "Let's you and me go out into the country."

There were three carloads of us heading out there. We started fighting again, and I hit him and knocked him down. I'm still pissed; I can only see out of one eye, and I'm thumping his head into the pavement. The other guys are yelling, and they grabbed me. I went home when the fight was over, and I'm lying in bed and it's probably 4:30 in the morning. I jumped out of bed and went back downtown. Mike was still there. I walked up and looked at him, and we hugged each other.

"Mike, I'm sorry," I kept saying.

"Aw, hell, forget it," he said. "I was just mad at my girlfriend..."

After you've had time to cool off, you think about it differently.

Most of the time with a racing fight, it's one punch and it's over. When I fought with Terry McCarl that was different, though. I hit him once and we went our separate ways, and then he came back down to our pit and said, "This baby ain't over yet." So we had to walk down after the races and fight, and we walked back together. Hell, we got tired of wallowing in the mud. It got to raining when we were down there, and we both looked like total idiots. But we felt better about it when it was over.

You know why we fought? I can point to the fact that he ran into our race car, but that's not why we fought. We were at Baylands out in California, and we had both ran really shitty that night. We were running in the B-main, and he hit my front end once with his rear, cut me off. We both missed the show and we were both in a crummy mood.

Some of it, too, was that Terry was raised the same way I was. His dad Lenard was of the old school, a hell-raiser. He is still a hell-raiser. So we just went off and fought. Today he'll laugh about it and think it's just as funny as I do.

There was also a scuffle with Danny Smith. I was running Stan Shoff's car, and everybody knew Billy Anderson messed with nitro sometimes. But he didn't the night in question; I'm sure of that. I ran my butt off that night, probably one of my best races in Stan's car. We won the Vegas Dash and the feature that night. Danny said, "Man, Hewitt *should* have won, I couldn't even follow him because of the fumes. He had so much nitro in that car I couldn't see where I was goin'!"

Well, that really, really pissed me off. We were in Alabama, and I told him to leave my pits.

A few minutes later Danny came walking by, and he gave me a little smirk. That pissed me off, and I hit him. We wrestled on the ground a little bit, and finally Smitty said, "Okay, that's enough. I give." And that was it. I let him up and we were all done.

Don't think that made Danny and I enemies. Not by a long shot. We went way too far back to let one scuffle mess up our friendship.

I'll tell you a funny story about Danny Smith. We were racing at Winchester for a two-day show, and he was maybe 16 years old. His dad, Mike Smith, had a speed shop in Indy, and Danny was going to the races long before he started driving. Well, Nick Gwin and I decided we'd take Danny to the Triangle Bar over in Ohio, and we borrowed somebody else's ID for Danny. He got drunker than shit, and when we went back to Winchester he's standing in front of the tent, swaying in the breeze, and he yelled, "I just want to be a race driver!" And then he fell right onto his sleeping bag, out like a light. It was great.

Sometimes it's fun to screw around with people. At the Chili Bowl one year, Andy Hillenburg (Oklahoma Andy) tried to pass me and we got together and damn near crashed. I almost stalled, but somebody else hit me and pushed me straight and I got going again. The crowd really got stirred up about it, thinking Andy and I were mad. We weren't; still, I wanted to have some fun.

A few minutes after the deal, we're all being introduced on the stage for the feature race. I told Andy, "Now, Hillenburg, when we get up on this stage, you come over and knock my ass off, right in front of everybody."

Well, he wouldn't do it. I wish he would have; we would have had everybody so wound up, the next year they would have to give us $1,000 each just to show up and keep it going.

Just because you crash, doesn't mean you should fight. In 1992 the CRA guys came to the Midwest, and raced at Eldora. We had been struggling, but we were running fourth that night and finally got to third, then second. Lealand McSpadden was leading, and I ran him down real quick. All I had to do was be patient for a lap or two and I would have passed him, I believe. But I wasn't patient; I just hauled it down into the corner and gave him an Eldora slide job.

An Eldora slide job is this: Use your momentum and pass somebody on the inside, and drift up in front of him and steal his line. He has two options: back off the throttle and settle for second; or he can turn left and keep his momentum and try to pass you back.

I don't think Lealand knew this. I really don't. When I went in and committed in turn one to sliding to the cushion, he had his choice: back off or turn left and pass me back. But he kept his nose in there, and we were going to crash. Because I have no choice at that point: with all that momentum, I'm going to the cushion even if I want to change my mind.

I kept coming. Lealand kept coming. And then we hit each other. WHAM! It was a helluva crash, with both of us sailing high into the air, turning over. A really bad deal. It knocked me goofy, and it broke his collarbone, or shoulder, I think. A hard, hard crash. Lealand's car wound up hanging on the fence there in turn two.

A few minutes later I'm lying in my van, and Steve Victor and Mr. Hunt are sitting there with me. Suddenly I sat up and got out of the van.

"I've got to go apologize to Lealand," I said.

"You already did," they said.

"No, you don't understand," I said. "I've got to go apologize to him again, so that I'll remember."

I must have been awake when I apologized the first time, but nobody was home. Again.

I had a scuffle with Rich Vogler, too. The second time he crashed me was at a World of Outlaws race at Santa Fe Park Speedway in Hinsdale, Illinois. He hit me hard, and pulled away, and then hit me again. He hit me one more time down the front straightaway, trying to get me into the wall. It didn't tear up my car, but I went to his pit and just laid him down. I mean, I hit him. And he didn't get back up. I wanted to beat him up; not just hit him, but beat him up. But he wouldn't get up, and I'm not going to hit somebody while they're on the ground. I guess he knew that.

I think that deal did a lot for Rich Vogler, too. That following Thursday night we were both racing midgets at the Indianapolis Speedrome. I was running maybe twelfth or something, in Tom Piascik's car. Vogler was running behind me, and I figured he would blow past me at any minute, because he was really good at the Speedrome.

There was a red flag, and we stopped. I was parked on the front straightaway, and I got out. I told somebody standing near my car, "Go over there and tell Rich Vogler that things between us are even. Tell him to not be worried about going around my race car."

They dropped the green flag, and he drove right by me. I think he was afraid to go around me, thinking I was going to crash him. He didn't understand, that's not how it works. Not with me, anyway. Maybe nobody had explained the rules to him.

I had a fight with Steve Butler at Terre Haute, in 1984 when I was running Dick Briscoe's car. He crashed me again, and we were loading up after the races, pitted right next to each other. I said something to him, and then I hit him. He got up, and I hit him again. He kept getting up, and I kept hitting him. Finally his wife jumped in the middle, and she was pregnant at the time, so that ended it right there.

The next week we went to Granite City, and Steve and I talked. I know I hurt him again with what I said, but I was being very honest with him. I liked Steve Butler, very, very much. I still do. But I told him the truth about Steve Butler the race driver.

The problem was, Steve just crashed you. And I was trying to tell him, you've got to stop doing that shit. I believe it to this day: a lot of the time Steve and Rich Vogler weren't crashing people on purpose; I think because they wore glasses, their peripheral vision sucked. Not all their crashing was because of that; like when Butler crashed Billy Rose that day at Terre Haute (1993), that was just a stupid deal.

When Steve and I were talking at Terre Haute, I asked him, "How many good side-by-side races have you had?"

"Well, none that I can remember."

"Remember a couple of weeks ago on the mile (at Indy), and Sheldon Kinser and I were banging wheels, all through the corners?" I asked. "Do you know why we were doing that?"

"No."

"Because we *could.* Sheldon trusted me, and I trusted Sheldon. I'm not afraid to rub wheels with him. The reason you haven't had many side-by-side races is that people don't trust you, because you'll crash 'em."

Man, it was like I reached into his chest and pulled his heart out. But it was true. Sheldon and I were on the miles in the sprint cars, and we were rubbing all over each other through the corner. Never once did either one of us crash.

See, the fighting is not just about beating somebody up; it's about self-preservation. These cars can bite your ass, man. The sooner you get a guy to stop putting you at risk, the better. You can go down and be real sweet and maybe he won't listen; you bust his lip and you'll get his attention, right now. That's all I was ever looking for.

I did lose my cool at Eldora one night and punched the flagman.

It was the World 100; I think it was 1986 or so. I was in Charlie Swartz's team car, and Charlie was trying to dive under me on restarts. Team car or not, I'm trying to protect my position. Tiny Purcell was the flagman, and he knew me better than any of the other late model guys because I ran the track so much. Well, Tiny decided to make an example out of me, and he black-flagged me for jumping.

I was *not* jumping the start. Period. I pulled up and tried to talk with him, and he didn't even have the authority to black-flag me; he was supposed to consult with the people in the tower before he made that call. But by then it was too late, because he couldn't correct it. With the World 100 you don't get a second chance, and I was out of the race for that year.

Man, I was hot. I swung at him on the front straightaway from inside the car, but I just kind of swiped my arm at him. But no matter what, my night was over.

It was several hours later, and I'm all cooled off. I'm standing in the payoff line, near the officials' tower. Tiny came walking out of the judges' stand, with a deputy on each side. I was calm and cool; but he gave me one of those smirky looks, like saying, "Now what are you gonna do?" That really pissed me off. So I hauled off and hit him. I didn't hit him all that hard, as far as that goes, but he turned around real quick to run back into the tower. Just as he got there Terry Baltes' wife, Dee, threw the door open to let him in, and poor Tiny ran right square into the door. I guarantee the door hit him a whole lot harder than I did. The door really did a number on him.

The two deputies grabbed me and threw me up against the wall. I didn't resist them, because I knew they had a job to do. I told 'em, "I know you've got to do your job, because that's your law. What I just did, that's Hewitt's Law. I can't expect you guys to take care of everything that goes on, and this race paid $20,000 to win, and this is what I do for a living. That man just cost me a shot at this race, with a bad call. Maybe to you guys it wasn't that big a deal, but it was to me."

I spent the next half-hour bullshitting with the sheriff while Earl Baltes decided what to do with me. Finally Earl said, "Jack, if you apologize there will be no charges." I fired up again, and said, "Fuck him! I'm not apologizing no matter what! I'll go to jail first!" Well, Earl just threw up his hands and said, "It was silly of me to ask," and walked away. The final penalty was that we got barred from Eldora for the rest of the year, but I was allowed to race in the sanctioned events there, which included the 4-Crown.

An important note: Today I'm very much buddies with Tiny Purcell, and all is okay. He quit flagging after a year or two, but I still see him now and then at the races, or he'll call me. Just another chapter, I guess.

Actually, I did go to jail one night, sort of. That was when I hit Joey Saldana.

That whole episode was not a good thing. I always liked Joe Saldana, very much, and when I started racing with Joe, his son Joey was a little kid. But one night in 1995, at Chillicothe for an All Stars race, Joey and I were racing down the backstretch. I was leading, and Joey was second, when he came all the way from the top right down across the middle of the straightaway and got my right rear with his left front. Call it being young, call it being dumb, call it whatever, but to me it was very deliberate. I flipped just about all the way down the straightaway. It didn't really hurt me, but it truly did scare me. I was very shaken up by it. And very, very pissed, I might add, because I felt like it was deliberate on Joey's part.

I was so mad, I walked over to his car, and he's still sitting in the car. I've never liked to see anybody get hit while they're still in the car, but that's what I did to Joey. He was sitting in the car, and I hit him in the mouth. I was just so mad. I'm ashamed of that today, very much. But what happens to me when I'm in a fight and everybody is grabbing me and pushing me, it just gets me more wound up. So I actually got more angry when everybody was trying to break it up.

At that time the All Stars had a standard fine of $300 for fighting; we had raised the bar some time before that from $100. (After this deal it went to $1,000.) Jimmy Darley, the All Stars official, was grabbing me, and I'm yelling, "I haven't got my $300 worth yet!" So I hit Joey again.

The first one was enough to make us even; but Joey had to pay for everybody else getting me madder.

After I hit him the second time I walked to the front of his car and tried to tear the wing off because I didn't want him to win the race. I've never done anything like that before, or since. That's probably the most foolish I've ever looked at a race track, truly just the dumbest thing I could do.

They charged me with assault, and took me to the local jail. I didn't actually go into a cell; I just took care of everything at the front desk. I don't know if Joey brought charges or if it was the track, but the legal thing pissed me off for a while, too. That's the only time I've ever been inside a jail. When the court date came, Joey didn't show up, so they dismissed the case.

Later on that year I walked into Joey's trailer and started talking to him. I got tears in my eyes when he told me I had always been one of his favorites. I apologized for hitting him.

I could have called him on the phone and told him that, but when I do my apologizing, I want to look somebody in the eye. It's much harder, but dammit, it means more.

Joey and I are okay now. We still talk, and the whole ugly deal is behind us.

I think that might have been my last scuffle. No, wait; there was a deal at North Vernon with Brad Marvel. You've got to understand something, I think the world of Bill Marvel, Brad's dad, and I really like Brad, too. I don't know what happened, but he did something that really pissed me off. Brad's a scrappy little dude, too, and when I hit him, we were scuffling around and somebody else reached in and hit me right in the eye. Got me a good one, too! I think it was Brad's son Justin, or Robbie Rice. They both deny it, and we laugh about it today. After the fight was over I was back in my pits, and just a few minutes passed before I was back down in Brad's pit, all emotional, apologizing to him.

Brad and I were buddies before, and we're still buddies. And the same with Justin and Robbie. I don't care if one of 'em is the guy who hit me that night. Now, at the time I would have killed 'em, but now we just laugh about it, because whoever hit me hauled ass right away. But no big deal, we just took it and went on. Sometimes you take 'em, and sometimes you give 'em.

If you haven't already figured it out, I live for the emotions of the moment. The good, bad, or whatever. I'm not one to wait; I want to get it over with. I want my pat on the back, my ass-chewin', my ass-kickin', I want it now, I don't want to wait.

When I was a kid growing up, my dad only spanked me one time, when I fell into the river. All the other times my brother John and I needed an ass-whippin', my mom took care of it. We were usually good for one a year, from age eight till junior high. Every time it was coming, I was first in line. I want to get mine over with.

Whatever is bad, I want it to be done, right now. That's why I didn't wait until the next day, or the next week, to settle up with somebody. I just can't wait that long. I want to go take my poke and be done with it.

So there you have it: that's the story on my fights. The good, the bad, and the ugly. After reading all this you can decide if I'm a bad guy or not; as far as I'm concerned, it doesn't matter, because I'm okay with myself. I don't have a hard time sleeping at night, because all the guys I've scuffled with are still my buddies.

Me? A bad-ass? Naw. Just peaceful ol' Jack Hewitt. I'm really just a puppy dog.

Hey, do me a favor, okay? All these young kids I race against, they might still think I'm a bad-ass. I'd appreciate it if you didn't tell 'em any different.

Talking about Jack...

It's hard to describe Jack Hewitt in just a few words. To me, he's just Dad.

I've just begun to understand him, and his career, over the past couple of years. I've always been around him, but I just didn't realize everything he has done as a racer. I mean, the guy has just had an awesome career as a race driver.

When you're with him in the pits, it's obvious that he's very generous with information and advice. He tries hard to give people good advice, he would never lie to you. If he's starting on the pole, if you ask him what setup he's using, he'll tell you, even if you're trying to beat him. He's just very open.

Dad can talk your leg off, but sometimes he sticks his foot in his mouth and says too much, or says the wrong thing. But he's a killer racer.

He is by far one of the best sprint car drivers ever. He can talk the talk, because he's walked the walk.

He's just...he's just Dad. That's the guy I know. Dad.

Cody Hewitt
Troy, Ohio

14

OCTOBER 3, 1993

I had always considered myself pretty lucky in my career, because even though I had raced a bunch, I hadn't been hurt much. Whatever good luck I'd had, though, all went away on a sunny October day in 1993. It was a terrible bit of fate, falling from the sky. Literally.

Up to that point I'd had some crashes, but few injuries. A quick inventory was a broken shoulder blade at Millstream in 1985, and a broken ankle at Lernerville around 1990. I'm sure I rattled my head a couple of times with concussions, but the broken bones were the injuries that actually required treatment.

It's funny, you can break a bone and not feel a lot of pain, but you can also hurt like hell and not have any broken bones. One night at Wayne County Speedway in Ohio, a guy spun out and I hit him dead sideways. WHAM! What a hit that was. My car jumped into the air, rolled over sideways, and came down straight on its top. I had a wing on, but I still hit hard. It felt like I had broken every bone in my body. Nothing was broken, but damn, it sure felt like it.

Another time at Lima I flipped out of the ballpark, and the driveshaft jammed into my leg. It wasn't bleeding at first, but when I started walking the blood just gushed out of my leg. My buddy, Bounce, he's driving me to the Lima hospital and he can't find it, driving around all over the place, and we get lost. Finally he took us clear to Troy, because at least there we knew where the hospital was!

My broken shoulder blade wasn't a big deal, because we could just cut my seat out a little bit and I could still race. But my broken ankle was by far the worse of the two injuries. The ankle was broken at Lernerville when a big clod of dirt came through the side panel and knocked my leg under the torque tube.

The guy in the ambulance at Lernerville was having me move my ankle and kept saying, "It's not broken, it's not broken..." I was encouraged by that, but he was wrong. I had actually broken the "ear" clear off the bone. I whispered to Donnie Hewett, who was with me that night, "Man, get me to a hospital...get me out of this ambulance and get me to a hospital." He and Brent Kaeding took me to a local hospital for X-rays. The doctors there looked at the film and said it was definitely broken.

"It's too swollen for us to set tonight, so we'll set it tomorrow," they said.

"Tomorrow I'll be in Ohio," I said. "They can set it there."

"Well, if you're not admitted here, we can't give you anything for the pain."

"I didn't ask for anything."

We put it up on a pillow and headed for home. I went to the doctor the next day, and brought the X-rays with me. He said, "You are so lucky...the way it broke, it went right back into position. If you don't do anything else to it, I don't have to put a plate in there, and we can leave it the way it is."

"Well, I race tomorrow," I told him.

"Didn't you hear me? I said if you don't do anything, I won't have to put a plate in there!"

"Didn't you hear *me*? I said I was racing tomorrow."

He just shook his head and set it, put it in a cast and went on.

I remember a funny story from when they took the cast off my foot.

I went into the doctor's office, and the nurse put me on a table and began cutting the cast off. There was another patient in there, on the other table, a lady. The nurse cut my cast off, and just wiped my foot off with a cloth, real quick. Then she moved over and began working on the other patient.

Well, if you haven't washed your foot in about a month, it gets to stinkin'. Maybe they were used to that, but I wasn't. It was very embarrassing. When the nurse was working on the other patient, I hopped off the table and jammed my foot into a sink in the middle of the room. I'm scrubbin' that baby.

The doctor walked in and saw me, and told the nurse, "Oh, don't pay any attention to him. That's my patient who's into pain."

The big crash came on October 3, 1993.

It was the 4-Crown at Eldora; an event I kind of figured was my own personal program. I had won a lot of 4-Crown events through the years, and that day I had a car for all four divisions. They ran midgets, sprint cars, modifieds, and Silver Crown features that afternoon.

Truthfully, I don't remember much from that day. All I know is that when the lights went out, I had just won a $10,000 midget race, and I didn't have far to go to win another $10,000. We almost had it in sight, but it didn't work out.

I was in Mike Streicher's car for the midget race, and we beat Page Jones on the last lap. I was excited. I hopped right into Bob Hampshire's sprint car, which was numbered 26 (instead of our usual 63) because we were helping the guys at 6R Racing earn points toward the championship.

I was leading the feature with just a few laps to go. I was going down the front stretch, and I remember seeing a car flipping ahead of me. I turned left to miss him, and the lights went out.

The car was Mike Mann's and as I tried to go past him, his car landed right on top of mine. Then I started flipping.

Jody was sitting in the stands and saw the crash. Nobody panicked, because it didn't look like I had flipped that hard. She didn't think it looked that bad. She was watching the scene, chatting with people sitting around her, and she finally said, "Is Jack out of the car yet?" "I don't think so," they answered. "No, wait, yeah, he's out...well, maybe not." She got up and walked over to the office. Our friends Georgette and Bill were in there.

"Jack is out of the car, right?" she asked.

They just looked at each other.

"We've got to tell her," Georgette said to Bill.

"Tell me what?" Jody asked.

"They've called for Care-Flight."

My next memory was about five days later. I was very groggy, lying in bed in the hospital. I had been using a breathing tube since the crash, and when they tried to remove the tube began to awaken because I was having trouble breathing.

I was in Miami Valley Hospital in Dayton. The problem was that they kept me on morphine, out in the twilight zone. I don't know if it was the head injury or the drugs, but I was crazy. After seven days Jody lobbied to get me transferred to Methodist Hospital in Indianapolis, one of the finest hospitals in the world.

I was so zoned out, I couldn't tell them what was hurting. I had a broken neck; but since I couldn't tell 'em it was hurting, they didn't know my neck was broken. They knew my arm was broken and they also knew my eye was screwed up, but they didn't know much more than that. The impact had killed the sixth nerve in my right eye. You have a muscle to pull your eye in toward the center, and the sixth nerve pulls your eye to the outside, to keep your vision straight. But with the sixth nerve dead, my eye was turned in so hard I could almost look inside my nose.

We were in the ICU/Trauma unit. They got pissed off when Jody insisted they transfer me to Methodist. The lead doctor told Jody, "I don't know if your husband is ever going to be right again."

Course, what did they have to gauge by, anyway, when they talk about "right"?

What little hours I'd be awake, four or five days after the crash, they'd take the breathing tube out. I was trying to tell Jody that I couldn't breathe. She's calling for a nurse, and they're ignoring her. She finally stomped out there and yelled, "Get in here, now!" They came in and put the ventilator back on me. That's when she made up her mind that we had to go to Methodist.

Jody said, "I want him out of here, NOW!" So we went to Indy, to see Dr. Terry Trammell. The immediate dividend was that we went right from morphine to Tylenol 3. What a difference. Jody had tried to explain to them, "You've got to understand, this is not an average person. He is an athlete, and he's able to bear more pain. It's not doing him any good to keep him all doped up."

Dr. Trammell came in and began to look things over, and it took him a couple of days to find the broken neck. They did CAT scans and an MRI.

The breathing tube had caused some trauma that affected my ability to swallow. You could look at me and know things weren't good, because my color was just pallid.

When Dr. Trammell finished his assessment of my injuries, here was the list: a broken neck, broken sternum, broken right arm, and damage to the sixth nerve of my right eye. I had some paralysis and I couldn't swallow.

When we tried to reconstruct the accident, we came to the conclusion that Mike's roll cage flipped into mine, and that's what got me. A bar or something hit my helmet and knocked me out and broke my arm. When I rolled over, that's what snapped my neck and broke my sternum.

The two biggest problems, as far as I was concerned, was the eye damage and the fact that I couldn't swallow. You want a helpless feeling? Try losing your ability to swallow for a while. You can't eat, you can't drink, you're a helpless baby. It's awful. I began to make some progress with the swallowing, but when they set my neck fracture, it paralyzed my throat again for a while. It took at least two to three weeks before they figured out that my throat had some paralysis.

Jody told me later how difficult those first hours were. My dad is as tough as can be, and at the local hospital-Coldwater Hospital not far from Eldora-he was standing over in the corner, weak in the knees, almost ready to faint. That's not like my dad. When the helicopter arrived to take me to Dayton, he walked outside as they wheeled me away. He couldn't ride with me in the helicopter, and for a moment he had to say goodbye. He had tears in his eyes. It was a bad deal.

I was in Methodist for a total of five weeks. The second week there, Mike Mann called. He was feeling really bad, and said he was going to quit racing. I told him, "You can do whatever you want, but I'm not going to quit." There I was, cheering *him* up. I'm laying in there with an orthopedic halo, a patch on my eye, and a broken arm. I know he was feeling bad, but what good would it do him to quit? I told him, "You know Mike, the times I've crashed a race car...once it leaves the ground, I really don't have any control after that point."

There was never any question in my mind I would drive again. It wasn't if; it was when. There was no doubt. Dr. Trammell was a square shooter all along, except there at the end. He didn't tell us why, but he had sent our neck X-rays to the Miami Project (they do research related to spinal injuries) in Florida.

The doctor down there called him, and said, "Is this guy dead?"

"No, he's not dead, why would I send the X-rays down there if he were dead? Not only is he not dead, he's not paralyzed, and he's not in any pain."

"Well, we don't know why not, because with an injury like his, they are usually dead."

We didn't know it at the time, but that ring that attaches the head to your spinal cord, the injury that killed Kenny Irwin Jr. and a few other guys, my ring was already off center. That's the only thing he wasn't completely honest with us about. He told me that if somebody would have come up behind me and patted me on the back, my skull would have acted like a guillotine and severed the spinal cord.

Scary stuff.

My time in Methodist was a learning experience, seeing what they can do with the human body. It still amazes me when I think about it.

One bad experience came pretty early on, when they wheeled me down to X-ray. They had already messed with me a couple of times, so I was pretty tender. They put me on this X-ray device, but I wouldn't fit exactly right. They left me alone in the room for about 45 minutes while they went to figure out what to do.

When you're hurting, 45 minutes is an eternity. I couldn't swallow, and my mouth was full of saliva. I had contracted pneumonia by this time, and I'm coughing up all kinds of stuff. I was almost in tears. They finally came in and helped me spit and clear my throat, but I told Jody, "Don't ever leave me by myself again. That's it." After that, it didn't happen any more. She stayed with me right up to the worst stuff.

Most of the staff there were great, but there are always exceptions. One gal dropped me onto a bed, like I wasn't hurt at all. Another nurse, a young Hispanic lady, she would come by to draw blood. Let me tell you, if I had a choice between this gal drawing blood and just picking a guy off the street at random to do it, I'd choose the guy on the street, hands down. Every time, she'd take three or four tries. After about three weeks, it got pretty old. Every place was sore. She came in one day and missed, and Jody said, "Look, just go get somebody else." "No, I'll try one more time." "No, I said get somebody else." And she wouldn't let that nurse come in any more.

Later on, after I was all healed up, we stopped back in. They all thought that was great. They said, "Nobody ever comes back to show us how they came out!"

The halo was a drag. It's a metal device screwed onto your skull and fastened to your shoulders, to prevent your head and neck from moving while your fractures heal. It's a bitch. Period.

Charlie Swartz came by to visit. Charlie had buried his mother, Marcella, on the day I got hurt. Charlie stayed all day when he visited me, and when he was getting ready to go home he heard them say they were getting ready to put the halo on.

"I've got to check that thing out!" he said, so he stayed a little while longer. Don Murphy was also there, and we were cutting up, having a big old time. I had swallowed for the first time that day, so I was on a roll. Whole food! Then they took me down and put the halo on, and when I got back to my room I was in all kinds of pain. Charlie didn't like that deal, not at all. He hauled ass and went home. I wish I could have joined him.

They began my therapy while I was still in the hospital. I started walking very short distances in the hallway.

One day Dad and Mom were visiting and helped me out of bed to take a walk. Dad is on one side, and Jody is on the other, pulling the wheeled stand with my IV setup. Dad and I are both wearing eye patches, and Mom took one look at this motley group and said, "Uh, I think I'll just stay in here." She was embarrassed! It was funny.

I left the hospital on a Saturday morning. I still couldn't swallow, and I had a sling around my neck for my broken arm, and of course I'm wearing the halo. That next day, Jody moved the sling from my neck and hooked it up to a couple of posts on the halo. It must have taken pressure off my neck or something, because the next day I could swallow.

Food! Real food! I called Mom and Dad and said, "Get to Bob Evans, and get me some biscuits and gravy!"

The problem was, with the swallowing difficulty they had inserted a feeding tube directly through my stomach a couple of days before I was released.

Actually, that was a neat deal. They ran a light down my throat, all the way into my stomach. Then they turned out all the lights in the room, and where they could see the light in my stomach, that's where they made the incision for the feeding tube. Cool.

When I started swallowing a couple of days later, Jody called them to ask about getting that damned tube out of my stomach. But the lady said the tube had to stay in for at least one month, to allow my stomach to adjust.

Gee, it hurt when they took it out. It was maybe a month later, and the doctor had me up on a table and he just pulled the thing out. It felt like somebody had hit me in the stomach with a sledgehammer. The doctor said, "You all right?" I said, "Yeah..." He left the room, and I told Jody, "Get me to the elevator before I start to cry." I was in that much pain.

I also required eye surgery. Dr. MacGregor of the Children's Hospital in Columbus did the surgery. I was referred to her by my friend Roger McClain. She had performed eye surgery on him some months earlier. Roger's surgery had gone very well, but the helpers forgot to put this moistening salve in his eye, and it peeled after the surgery. He said it was very, very painful. So that was on my mind as I was going into surgery.

They gave me an anesthetic-sodium Pentothal, I think-and just as I'm going under I hear them say, "He's in here for a hysterectomy, right?"

Real funny.

The entire time I'm under, I'm still sort of awake. I kept telling the doctor, "Don't forget to put that salve in my eye!" Dr. MacGregor finally said, "Would you just shut up and go to sleep??!!"

My eye had been turned in so severely it stretched the muscle. When it's that extreme, she said, it will never heal on its own. So they decided to perform a procedure prior to my surgery where they paralyze your eye and that somehow helps it heal. I'm fully awake for that one; they gave me a couple of eye drops, and I know what they're going to do: Stick a needle in my eye. That paralyzed it for about three months, and it protected the muscle from further damage.

Right as they're getting ready to do that procedure, I said to the doctor, "Does this mean I won't be seeing double any more?"

"No, if you look off to the left or right you'll probably still have some double vision."

"That's good, because I like going to be with two women every night."

Jody said real quick, "Yes, but you always choose the wrong one!"

While they had the needle in my eye, I had to move it back and forth. Man, you can see that needle coming which is bad enough, but to try and move your eye... It was pretty gross, and scary.

I wore that damned halo for three months. It was a miserable son of a gun, let me tell you. It came off in December.

Not long after, Mr. Hunt passed away. That was a really dark period, with my accident and then losing one of my very best friends. We went to the funeral in Florida, and that's where I got to know Dr. John Miller a lot better. Doc is a chiropractor who also does a lot of work with alternative therapies, things like acupuncture. Doc said, "When you come back down in February, come see me, I'd like to see if I can stimulate that nerve to your eye."

Pretty soon Doc is working on me, and he had about 16 needles sticking in me, all around my ear, my eye, and my toes.

The first day I was in his office, after he had taken a bunch of X-rays, he grabbed my head and turned it, just like a chiropractor does. My neck popped, big time, the worst pop I'd ever had. He also continued to work on my eye.

After two weeks in Florida, we went back to Methodist for a follow-up examination. Dr. Trammell took another X-ray of my neck, and he seemed puzzled. He said, "Would you mind taking another MRI?" I said no, but I didn't know what to think, what was up. Dr. Trammell's secretary called later and said, "You tell Jack he's got a guardian angel riding with him." The ring on my neck was centered like it was supposed to be.

I called Doc Miller and said, "Did you know that ring was off-center?"

"Well, yeah," he said. "That's why I fixed it." It wasn't a big deal to him.

I began to exercise at the first opportunity, to try and regain my strength. I took the therapy they provided and tried to maximize it. If they told me to climb one flight of stairs, I did two. We'd always do more than they said, trying to get stronger.

We had lots of visitors while we were at Methodist, and in the weeks following. Hamp called me up one day, crying. He was just so torn up that I had been hurt in his car; it really worked on him. Well, I teased him a little bit, and told everybody, "That big bawl-baby called me." He was mad that I told everybody and said, "You sumbitch...I'll let you die next time! I won't feel bad for you at all!" Man, he was hot. I thought it was funny, but he didn't think so.

Another good friend from Indiana, Jimmy Rayl, came by one day. Jimmy was a great basketball player for Indiana University. He brought me a neat flannel shirt, and he was trying to make me feel better. He's sitting there, talking to me, and he said, "Can I do anything for you?" Well, I grabbed his hand and put it on my crotch. "Bless this for me, would you Jim?" He pulled his hand back real quick and he hauled ass.

I didn't want everybody coming in to feel sorry for me, so I was giving everybody a hard time. Jokingly, of course.

Jim Keeker was my teammate with 6R Racing, and he sent a get-well card with a picture of a booger on it. Later, when I had this feeding tube in my nose, and I'm telling you, that's like a greenhouse for boogers. One day they were cleaning my nose and they pulled out a booger, I'm not lying to you, that thing was as big as a 50-cent piece. It was a dandy, the booger of all boogers. They got it out and I said, "Don't throw that away!" We wrapped it up in a Kleenex, and when Jim came by to visit I handed him the Kleenex, and said real serious-like, "Jim, I saved this for you. I grew it just for you, buddy. It's something special." He opened that thing up, and he didn't know what to think.

It was a fine moment.

I just remembered one day in the hospital early on, when they were trying to get an evaluation of my head injury. The nurses and doctors asked me all kinds of questions, and one was, "Who is the president of the United States?"

"Hillary Clinton," I said.

They looked at me kind of funny, and I said, "Hell, everybody knows that...we all know who is telling Bill what to do."

The kind of shook their heads, and they quit asking me so many questions.

I wish I could tell you there is a magic time when you're healed up from such a crash. There isn't a single threshold, a point where you know you're all the way back. It's more like a long, drawn-out deal, and you learn to take it a day at a time, and try to be patient.

In February 1994 I flew to Phoenix to watch the Copper Classic race, and I was really yearning to race again. All those emotions were still there: the desire, the excitement, everything. The crash hadn't dimmed any of them.

But physically I was nowhere near ready. When I was healed up enough to try, though, that's what I was going to do.

There was never, ever any doubt.

Talking about Jack...

Jack Hewitt is a very passionate man. If he feels like you did him wrong on the race track, you're going to hear about it. If he feels that the flagman screwed up, that's the first person he'll be looking for when he gets out of the car. As a believer, he's passionate about God, just as he was passionate about being an atheist most of his life.

Another thing with Jack is that there is no veneer. What you see is what you get. He doesn't have to wear fancy jewelry, or fancy clothes, to impress anybody. Jack is very comfortable being Jack.

He is very intelligent, and has a great awareness of life and how it's going. When you tell him a story, he is very quick to grasp what you say, and he'll remember it for a long, long time.

Coupled with all of this is his tenacity. In treating people, we often grab them and hold them, restricting their movement, as we ask them to move another part of their body. When you tell Jack to move in that situation, hang on, because his first move is going to be wide open. That's probably how he wins his fights, he doesn't need to warm up on the first punch.

He's also a very compassionate person. Although he's probably the toughest guy I know, he's also probably the most softhearted person I know.

I was riding with him from his house to Eldora, followed by several loaded vehicles trailing us to the race track. There was a turtle crossing the road, and Jack could have simply moved the steering wheel a little bit and missed him. Instead, Jack slams on the brakes, stopping the whole convoy, and gets out and moves the turtle off the road. As he does this, I hear him say to the turtle, "You big dummy, don't you know you're going to get ran over out here?"

Guys like Jack Hewitt are genuine heroes to a lot of people, because they have the courage and the conviction to do and say what the rest of us wish we would do or say, but we don't have the guts.

Dr. John (Doc) Miller
Tampa, Florida

15

FAITH

Do you believe things happen for a reason? I do.
When you go through an ordeal like my 1993 crash, it's hard to find many positives. It was painful, expensive, and it robbed me of many months of my career.

On the flip side, getting hurt put in motion a series of events that brought great changes in my life, and my outlook toward the future.

You might say it changed me forever. Literally.

I mentioned earlier that when I went to Florida for Mr. J.W. Hunt's funeral in January 1994, I was re-introduced to Dr. John Miller. I first met Doc many years earlier, when my friend Jack Nowling was promoting races at the Tampa Fairgrounds. Doc was well connected to the racing scene in Florida.

Doc was good friends with Jan Opperman and Rich Leavell; shoot, he's friends with everybody.

We were at the cemetery, and when Mr. Hunt's services ended, Doc came up and started talking to Brent Kaeding and me. Everyone was leaving, but we just sat there and talked. While we sat there, Cody sat nearby and watched as they took the tent down, rolled up the grass carpet, loaded all the chairs, took half the flowers away, and put the dirt over Mr. Hunt. What an experience for a 10-year-old kid.

Doc first talked about my eye issue, and asked how it was going. Toward the end of the conversation, Doc asked, "Do you believe in Jesus?"

"Well, I don't want you to think I'm bragging about this," I answered, "because I don't think anybody could brag about being an atheist. I want to believe in God, but I need to see a miracle."

"Oh, you're not an atheist," he said right away. "You're agnostic."

When he told me that, it was a gigantic step. I had never been exposed to any kind of Christian teaching, and I was so ignorant I honestly didn't know anything. To understand the difference between an atheist and agnostic was really a breakthrough for me. I guess it opened the door because I realized I was never *against* believing; I just didn't believe anything.

I came back to Florida a few weeks later, and Doc worked on me every day. He worked on my eye, my neck, and my arm. In January I couldn't raise my arm enough to get my wallet out of my pants, but after working with Doc my arm really made progress, and was soon nearly normal. The only thing we didn't really make progress on was the eye, and of course I had the surgery later to help that.

I had raced against Rich Leavell, and Rich and his wife, Queenie, were very close with Doc. They were also very close with Jan Opperman, who had witnessed to them about Jesus many years ago.

I was never a Jan Opperman fan, because I had him figured as a dope-smoking hippie. And I thought he used his charity project, the Boy's Ranch in Montana, to get money by using Jesus' name. After talking with Doc and Rich about Jan, I realized Jan was so sincere, so loving, and so giving. I had always respected him as a race driver; who couldn't, since he was one of the greatest of all time. But after learning more about him, I felt like I had cheated myself because I had misjudged him so badly.

Here's the bottom line: Jan Opperman got Doc back to the church, so you have to give Jan Opperman credit for getting me to Jesus, through Doc.

When I began to listen and learn from Doc, it all made sense. He had answers to my questions; he didn't just say, "Because the Bible says so." I always thought we came from monkeys; he can show you that there are two different theories there, and he showed me other ways of looking at issues like that.

There are so many questions most of us can't answer. Why are little kids crippled when they've done nothing wrong? Things like that. Doc can point to scripture in the Bible to help explain some of that. He could answer all the questions I had for years, and he helped me understand.

Once he got me interested, I never let up with the questions. We'd go to lunch and I'd ask him questions constantly. Because once I had opened my heart, then I couldn't get enough. "Tell me more," that was my feeling.

Somewhere along the way, my heart opened up and my mind accepted and I believed in Jesus. I believed! After all those years of not having any idea, I finally understood what Jesus was about, and that He had a connection with me personally.

It wasn't just me; Jody and Cody were listening, too. And accepting. Jody was already a believer, but she had never been baptized. In April, Doc came to Ohio, and Rich Leavell came over from his home in Indiana, and we all went uptown to the Lincoln Center in downtown Troy. Jody, Cody and I were all baptized by Doc there at the pool.

It was a wonderful moment. I felt like the entire world had changed. Actually, it *had* changed. I was always operating under the belief that this life on earth is all there is to it. When I accepted Jesus, that opened the gates of Heaven for me. Now, I could live forever in Heaven. Think about that for a second: going from believing in nothing to receiving a blessing to go to Heaven when I die.

Suddenly, the trees went from just being green to being the most beautiful shade of color in the world. Not just green; a beautiful shade of green. I sometimes ask people if they believe, and I ask them what changed for them when they began to believe. My good friend Tommy Worth from Tulsa said, "The skies got more blue." And I knew right then that he was sincere, because you can't describe such a feeling, when you accept Jesus into your heart, not just your mind.

After I was baptized, I still asked Doc lots of questions. The main question I had was this: No matter what, you can't get to Heaven if you don't believe Jesus is the Son of God?

"Doc, I never considered myself a bad person," I said. "Other than fighting a little bit, I never smoked, I don't drink, and I never intentionally hurt anyone. But you're telling me that I can't get to Heaven unless I believe in Jesus?"

"That's right," he said.

"You mean to tell me that if Hitler had accepted Jesus and asked for forgiveness right before he died, he would go to Heaven?"

"Yes, that's right."

But Doc also said, "I'll tell you this right now, Jack: There are a lot of bad people in Heaven, and a lot of good people who aren't in Heaven."

"Well, that sucks," I said.

"But there are such things as rewards in Heaven," Doc said.

"Wait a minute, Doc, that isn't going to work, either...I mean, how bad can the wrong side of the tracks be in Heaven?"

Doc just threw up his hands and said, "You're right, all the streets are paved with gold, aren't they?"

My life had changed, and I was anxious to tell people about it. I tried not to be obnoxious, but I do try to witness to people. I don't consider myself a braggart, but I will brag to people about being friends with Jesus. I don't try to get people saved, that's not my job. I'm not the guy who will baptize you and all, that's for guys like Doc. My job is to spread the word and help other people get to the right people to answer their questions. People who will witness and lead and baptize.

Everybody has a calling; Doc's calling is preaching, Rich Leavell's is to be soft-spoken and calm as he witnesses, and that helps lead people. Me, I feel more like Johnny Appleseed: people look at me and see this hell-raiser who did all this bad stuff, and he wasn't going to Heaven, but now he's made a complete turnaround. I can still cuss and things like that, but I'm still going to Heaven. Other than taking God's name in vain-which I don't do-all the other words are just expressions that people made up, and that's not a big deal.

Most of my profanity is just a bad habit. Should I lose it? Sure I should. But I'm a flawed person, just like the next guy, and change like that comes hard for me. I've been around profanity pretty much every day of my life. My heart changed when I accepted Jesus, but I couldn't change my environment. You get around a race track, and cuss words flow like water. That's just the way it is. Is that good? Nope. But it is what it is. You ain't gonna change that; certainly not overnight.

I guess the main message I want to spread is this: The door to Heaven is open for anybody. If you'll believe that Jesus died for your sins, and you ask forgiveness for your sins, then you can go to Heaven.

I truly can't think of a better deal than that.

Even after I accepted Jesus, I still had a few scuffles and fights. You're allowed to ask for forgiveness, but the key is this: When Jesus died on the cross, it was for our sins. Not *His* sins; *our* sins. It's all been paid for. We just have to look to Him and ask for forgiveness, sincerely. He didn't put expectations or limits on our sins; they're *all* forgiven. But if you have your heart right, you'll know when you've done wrong, and when you'll want to ask Jesus for forgiveness.

As far as the scuffles go, there is an angel in Heaven named Michael, and all he does is kick ass! That's what I'm thinking; I don't want to be hanging around the streets of gold when I'm an angel in Heaven; send me back to earth for the battles. That would satisfy me.

Sometimes people say to me, "Well, Jack, what do you know about this, anyway?" I tell 'em, "Because Doc said." I trust him and I believe what he said.

I struggle as a reader; I just don't like to read. I know I need to read the Bible for myself, and I'm working toward that.

You want to hear something funny? When I got hurt earlier this year, an old friend and former racer, Joie Ray, gave me a Bible. That was the only Bible I've owned in my life. I'm 51 years old, and I just got my first Bible. So bear with me, because it's going to take me some time to get caught up.

When I go to church, and listen to preaching, for some reason I get very little out of it. I don't know why; I just don't feel like the words are for me. But when I talk one-on-one with someone about Jesus, and they're teaching me, I absorb that really well.

This is my personal message to you: If you haven't ever connected with Jesus, please don't give up. He is there for you; trust me. Hey, if He is making the offer of Heaven for an old hell-raiser like me, He obviously isn't too particular, is He?

Keep searching. Get interested. Find the right person who will help you learn about Jesus.

I know there are people out there who truly don't believe; they really are atheists. A friend of mine and I were talking the other day, and he told me a story that Rev. Billy Graham wrote in his newspaper column some years back. A lady wrote in and challenged Rev. Graham, saying that since he can't offer absolute proof of God, then God doesn't exist. Rev. Graham's answer made sense to my friend and it makes sense to me, too. He answered the lady something like this, and forgive me that I don't have his exact words: "Look around at this world, and all the amazing living creatures. The trees, the flowers, the animals, human beings, the sky, everything. It is all so very complex and intricate, isn't it? Which theory makes more sense: It all happened totally by accident, all by itself; or some greater being created it and made it exactly right?"

I'm a practical guy. But I believe Rev. Graham is right. All of this around us, it didn't just happen. At least I don't think so.

Two years ago, Doc anointed me with oil to help protect me. After I got hurt earlier this year, we got to talking about that. Doc said, "You know, when you have a race car, maybe you're fast. Then all of a sudden you start slowing down, and pretty soon you're back to square one. So you put it on the setup blocks and start over. I think we need to start over with you."

So he and Rich Leavell anointed me again, and it was the neatest thing. We did this out by the pool at Doc's one evening, and as we were walking back toward the house my feet were just floating off the ground, I felt so good.

But I was just having some fun with Doc and Rich. I stopped walking, and said, "Hey, wait a minute, guys...I just want to make sure of one thing: when you put me back on the setup blocks, you did use the winged blocks, and not the non-winged version, right?" And we all laughed.

You know how I always say I like both winged and non-winged racing? Well, that's only for racing. When it comes to heavenly beings, I definitely prefer the winged variety.

My life has changed since I accepted Jesus. I hope you know Him, too.

16

COMING BACK

I mentioned earlier that when I got hurt so badly at Eldora, the idea of quitting racing never crossed my mind. I was certain I'd race again; I just wasn't sure when.

I've got to tell you, that crash took an awful lot out of me. It was a long winter, trying to rebuild my body, retrain my muscles and nerves, and figure out where I stood in terms of physical ability.

Bob Hampshire was a great friend, and stood by me through it all. That winter we treated just like any other winter; making deals and plans for a full season of racing in 1994. Even if there was a question of whether I'd be able to race, I think Bob would have waited and kept a seat open until we were sure. As long as I had the desire, he would have helped me, I believe. He was much more than a car owner; we were good friends.

After I was released from the hospital, I still had to wear the halo for a long time. I had a patch on my eye, the halo, and my arm in a sling, so I was a mess. I slowly started healing up, though, and got rid of the sling, and with Doc Miller's help regained the use of my arm.

When I had the halo on, I couldn't sleep very well. After I got home, Jody missed a lot of sleep right along with me, because I'd wake her up with my tossing and turning. One night she went to bed and I'm sitting there, and I got the keys to the van. I got myself outside, got in the van, and drove around the block. I just wanted to try it. I knew I could see the lights coming, and it wasn't like I had to turn my head to see. Jody was awake when I got home, and I got my ass chewed for that one. Big time.

I got into a race car at Eldora for the opener in April. I had not yet undergone the eye surgery, and I still wore the patch. It wasn't until after the surgery that I could start taking the patch off.

The Eldora race had sprint cars and modifieds. I won the modified feature in John Orr's car, but I didn't do that great in the sprint car, and missed the show. It was a good outing, though, because you really don't know where you are in terms of ability until you get back in the car. It was a matter of adjusting your driving to accommodate the changes in your physical ability.

The biggest adjustment, by far, was learning to drive with one eye. I didn't think it would be a big deal, but it was. I watched my dad race and win with one eye, so I figured it was no problem. After all, Dad won everything at Lima a couple of weeks after he lost his eye. I figured if my dad was that tough, I had to be almost that tough, too. At least give it my best shot.

After a while I started using a piece of gray racer's tape instead of the patch. A lot of people laughed at that, but there was a legitimate reason for using the tape. By putting the tape in front of my eye, I could leave the sides open, and still have some peripheral vision. That's a big issue in a race car, peripheral vision.

It took a while to get myself back to 100 percent. I didn't feel completely comfortable until I got the patch off, which was later in the season. I finally won a USAC sprint car feature in July at Lake Odessa, Michigan, then won again two weeks later at Eldora. However, they found water in our fuel at Eldora, and we were disqualified. The rule at the time was that any foreign substance in the fuel brought a disqualification; but you often get water in your fuel from the inside of the tank or the fuel jugs sweating. They've since amended the rule so that water doesn't bring a disqualification.

The crash had really affected my confidence. I found that I didn't try to get the car into the same holes as before. Maybe your brain remembers the pain from crashing, so it holds you back a tiny bit when you race. After a crash of that magnitude, I'm not sure you ever go completely back to the way it was before. I don't know if anybody does; I know I didn't. I had gone all those years with really minor injuries, and it never slowed me down. I could race through all that stuff.

But this crash knocked the shit out of me. There's no denying it. I tell people I'm a lot like a Honda car; it didn't take a very big crash to tear up a lot of stuff.

We stuck with it, and by the end of the season I had it going pretty good again. I don't mean to say I was back to normal, because that wasn't the case. I was competitive, but I had to work pretty hard to be competitive. Gradually it came back to the point where I was comfortable that I had a shot to win on a regular basis.

One of the key steps came at the 4-Crown in late September. It was one year since my crash, and I won the Silver Crown feature that day. That was a big win, for obvious reasons.

All things considered, I didn't have a bad 1994 season. I won a total of seven races, and under the circumstances I was happy with that.

When I won the 1994 Silver Crown race at the Eldora 4-Crown, I was driving the Team 6R Racing car. Like Hamp, the boys at 6R stuck by me through my recovery.

My relationship with 6R Racing went back to 1990. 6R is a bunch of successful businessmen from the Indianapolis area who love racing, and wanted to get involved. I ran second in my first start for them, and after that I became their dirt driver. Jim Keeker drove their car on pavement.

They're a neat bunch of guys. They don't care if you win or lose, the outcome is the same: They're gonna have a beer. As long as you don't get hurt, they'll have fun, win or lose. There is absolutely no pressure there, and it's just a great time to be with all of 'em.

By 1995 I felt like I was pretty much back to normal. I won 16 races that year, which was pretty decent. I was still with Hamp in the sprint car and Silver Crown car, which was sponsored by the 6R guys. In fact, Hamp and I won five USAC sprint car races in a span of six weeks early in the summer.

Here's a footnote to history: When Tony Stewart won the USAC Silver Crown title in 1995, it came down to the very last race at Sacramento. There were three of us in the hunt for the championship: Stewart, Dave Darland, and myself. Darland blew up early in the race, so I had a good shot at the title. But Billy Boat ran into me, and I slid out of the groove and hit the fence and my night was over. Damn. That turd Stewart knew what had happened to Dave and me, so he charged up through the field and finished second to Donnie Beechler, giving him the title by two points over Darland. I was third, just nine points back.

That had been a good season for me in Silver Crown racing. I won one of the most memorable races of my career in June, on the pavement at Richmond International Raceway in Virginia.

It was the series' first race there, so everybody was pumped up. I'm not a pavement guy, I'll be the first to admit, but I still try just as hard on pavement as I do on dirt.

We hot-lapped the car, but we had motor trouble. We were running a Ford V6 engine, but the coil was apparently bad. At that time I absolutely despised Glen Niebel, but it was Niebel who loaned us a replacement coil so we could race. Honestly, I felt so strongly that I would have rather not raced than asked Niebel for the part. But the 6R guys liked him; he built the engines for their other cars.

We qualified so poorly we had to start on the rear of the consolation race. Jeff Bloom was leading, and I passed him toward the end and won. We had to start 25th in the feature, which sure was a long way back.

Right from the start, that car just started going right up through the field. The race was 134 laps, and I followed Jim Keeker for a while before I made a banzai pass to take the lead on lap 118. We had a late yellow, and Randy Tolsma pulled alongside me. Randy should have been a lap down, but he snuck through a wrinkle in the rules to stay on the lead lap. He had pitted for fresh tires, and going into turn one on the last lap, he got under me. We went into the next corner, though, and I dropped down inside and he had to go to the flat part of the race track. We won it, on national TV.

After the race they interviewed, me, and I told 'em, "They say Virginia is for lovers, but I don't know...you'll have to ask my wife about that in the morning."

The neat thing about that Richmond race was that we were using a Ford V6. We had been talking a lot with Lee Hampton and Lee Morse of Ford, and the next day following the Richmond race was the Winston Cup race at Michigan. Robert Yates walked up to Lee Morse and said, "Well, I see your boy kicked butt last night." All the Cup guys watched the race on TV. It was cool.

Hamp and I met with the Ford guys in Detroit, along with Carl Best, a local Ford dealer who liked racing. They didn't throw a lot of resources at the project, but we wound up with a pretty good little V6 for the pavement. The engine was a little heavier than the Chevy, and the crankshaft was located a little higher in the block. But our biggest obstacle was the aftermarket situation. For every two companies building parts for the Ford, there are 10 building pieces for the Chevy. There just aren't enough people experimenting and developing pieces for the Ford. You're kind of the lone ranger with that engine.

Was the program a success, overall? I think so. We won some races with that engine, and I know the relationship with Ford saved Hamp some money. But it was a big learning curve, with an awful lot of time invested. The engine changed the handling of the car a little bit, and the power range was different. They were pretty reliable, though; we didn't have problems with them blowing up. Only a few at the beginning.

I ran a 454-cubic inch small-block Ford at the World 100 one time, and that thing was a rocket...before it blew up.

Here was my history with Glen Niebel, by the way. It began when I was in 6R's car at Milwaukee, and we were using one of Niebel's engines. He had his own race car, but he also built engines for other teams and was famous for making the Chevy V6 work in sprint car racing. Our engine at Milwaukee was blowing oil real bad, and I told Niebel, "Look, just put some long hoses on the valve covers, and maybe it will breathe better." But he didn't want to do any of that. We finished third, and we should have had second. Everything was just covered with oil.

Some time later, Bob Parker called and asked me to drive his sprint car at IRP. Bob used Niebel's engines, too. I'm standing around that evening at IRP, waiting, waiting, waiting, and no race car. I finally got my uniform on, and hot laps are almost over. Bernie Hallisky, who worked for Niebel, came up to me and said in a low voice, "Jack, I hate to tell you this, but your car isn't coming. Niebel won't tell you, but he blew up his engine on the dyno, so he took yours to run in his car tonight."

Mike Bliss won the feature that night in Neibel's car. After that I didn't care if he heard me or not, I told anybody who asked that Glen Niebel was an asshole.

Niebel died a few years ago from cancer, and I realize it isn't right to speak ill of somebody who has passed away, because he isn't here to defend himself. With all due respect, though, I just didn't like the way he treated people.

I've always been an emotional guy, and after my accident found myself getting more emotional, more quickly than ever before. When I hit my head, it must have affected my nerves. Ten years later, I'm still like that. The urge to cry kicks in very easily. And I don't get just a little bit choked up; I cry and cry and cry. I don't know what causes it, but I can't control it like I could before.

Also, it affects my voice when I get mad. Used to, when I got mad and told somebody I was gonna kick their ass, I had the fire in my eyes and the sound in my throat, and you knew I was sincere. But I discovered pretty quickly during my recovery that when I was mad, my voice got all high and squeaky.

When you're telling somebody you're gonna kick their ass and you sound like Pee Wee Herman, well, you lose the effect.

I found that out with Billy Shipman.

We were at Macon, Illinois, in 1996 for a USAC midget event, on the pace lap getting ready to start a race. I was in Don Murphy's Ford-powered midget, and we were kind of chugging around, and the motor died. I was right in the middle of the back straightaway. I saw the yellow light come on, and I thought, "Okay, he sees me." But then the green light came back on.

Billy Shipman was the flagman, and I think he panicked. Rather than doing nothing, he panicked and turned the green light back on. I'm sitting there, dead in the water, and here comes the full field of cars. They're flying past me, and that isn't a good feeling, not at all. As each car went past, I got more angry. Everybody got past except a number 10 car, and I don't remember who that was. Man, he drilled me in the ass, really hard. It didn't hurt me, but it pissed me off, because it was all so unnecessary. And it scared, me, too. He never turned the yellow on until after I got hit.

I climbed out of the car and walked straight over to the stand in the infield, and I wanted to kill Billy. Bill Carey, another USAC official, tried to stop me, and said, "Now, Jack, don't go over there and do something stupid." I just ignored Bill, and got to the stand and looked up at Billy.

"Get down off there," I told him. I'm telling you, if he would have climbed down there, I would've killed him. If the steps up to the stand were in place, I would have gone *up there* to kill him. I would have had his neck.

I'm madder than shit, but I'm yelling and my voice is all high and squeaky. I'm not scaring anybody, I'm sure.

Part of what made me so mad is that Billy just turned his back on me, and told me to go back to the pits. Boy, that sent me into orbit.

"You little queery fat bastard, I'm gonna twist your head off," I told him.

"If you call him another name, that's $50," Bill Carey said.

I didn't even take my eyes off Billy Shipman.

"You little faggot son of a bitch, I'm gonna kill your fat ass!"

"That's $100."

When I got up to $350, I guess Bill Carey figured his approach wasn't working, because he quit quoting me prices.

I finally had enough, and I walked away.

To this day I'm kind of sore at Billy Shipman. I don't have anything against him personally, and in fairness to him he was just learning at that time, but I'm glad he's not flagging for USAC any longer. He just panicked that night, and made a big mistake. And I paid the price, along with poor ol' Murph, whose race car was all bent up. And the car that hit me, too.

D.O. Laycock caught the whole episode on video, and it's probably his best-selling tape. If nobody else capitalized on it, he did. It's there for eternity.

I raced with Hamp through the 1997 season, when we split up again. Every relationship has some ups and downs, but Bob and I had very few downs. We rarely argued or disagreed. We could talk about almost anything on the race car and work it out so that we were both happy.

My last ride in Hampshire's sprint car was a win, at Terre Haute in October 1997 (I also won the midget race that night, in Murphy's car.) It's good to know that our sprint car relationship ended on a winning note.

I'm not really sure how it came about, us splitting up. I wasn't the same Jack Hewitt I used to be; I didn't dominate races like I had before. Bob was probably thinking I was getting old. At the same time, I was thinking his race cars weren't running like they used to, they were too heavy, etc. So we just went our separate ways. Obviously, I would never do anything to hurt Hamp, and I know he feels the same way toward me, so it was just two friends having a friendly parting of the ways.

Still, it's very hard to actually quit. I called him on the phone to tell him I was quitting, and I don't usually do that. Good or bad, I do my deals face-to-face. I was so upset, so emotional, I actually had to take a shot of whisky before I called him. I was bawling. That's how much it meant to me, leaving Bob. I just told him, "It's not working out, and I need to go get another ride."

Quitting a good friend like Bob Hampshire is the hardest part of this business. I don't like it. I don't like it at all.

17

THE BUSINESS

Racing is a business. There is so much money changing hands, so many companies building parts, sanctioning bodies, stuff like that, there's no other way to look at it: It's a business.

That's always been hard for me to accept, because when I began my career it was purely for the joy of racing. No matter what happened since that time, the wins, the losses, the crashes, whatever, I always had a lot of passion and joy in my heart for racing.

The sport has changed a lot from the time I started almost 30 years ago. The biggest change is financial; racing is obviously way, way more expensive today than when I started. I tried to adjust to the change, knowing I had to help hustle product deals and sponsors, because it's so expensive just about every car owner today needs some help.

It must be hard to be a car owner today. Everything costs so much, and most of those guys race for pride. But it escalates to the point that unless you've got a ton of resources, you've got to have help. That's hard for a lot of guys to accept, because that hurts their pride. Don Murphy, for example, rarely comes to the races since he quit fielding a car. Murph had his own business, but hell, everybody has a budget limit. He got to where he just wasn't comfortable spending the kind of money it takes today, so he quit. I think he imagines that people look at him differently because he quit. But nothing lasts forever.

Not everybody can own a car. I can't own a car; I don't have that kind of money. And Murph ought to look at it like this: The years he was involved, he did it! He ought to be walking around telling everybody how proud he is. His cars won some pretty cool features, races other guys never won. And for him to think he should be embarrassed, that just isn't so.

As the cars have become much more expensive, we're seeing more and more guys driving for 30 percent or less, plus they had to bring deals or money to get the ride. I always drove for 40 percent. Some car owners would pay 50 percent if you won, and other car owners only paid 30 percent if you finished out of the top 10.

Many car owners today say they couldn't race if they paid 40 percent. It's a mess, really. Once they find a driver willing do drive for 30 percent, it's all over. I can't imagine them going back to paying 40 percent.

Right now, the guys making money in sprint car racing are the mechanics, I think. Guys who really know their stuff, like Jack French, they're paid pretty well. Some of 'em are making good money off the fathers of some of the rich kids who have come into the sport in recent years.

I've never worried about money. If I've got it, I'm fine. I'll either keep it forever or spend it right away. I can blow money just like anybody else. Then again, I can go fishing and not need any money. I can be broke but as long as I can charge my boat battery, I can go out to the gravel pit and fish for free, all night long.

Jody takes care of our financial details, and that suits me. We've had some good years where we put money back to last us for a while, and then we might have a lean year and not have any money put back. Oh, well. I don't worry about it, because something always seems to come through and we make it all right. Some things just fall onto our plate, stuff we weren't anticipating.

When we're winning, we eat steak; when we're not winning, we eat baloney. But I like baloney, so that's okay, too.

When I look at doing different appearances and programs, I usually don't think about the money part of it. For example, earlier this year I was invited to speak to a fathers-sons group at a nearby church. I figured it was going to be young men and their little boys; it was actually 65-year-old dads and their 40-year-old sons. I didn't ask for any money for speaking, but when I was finished they gave me a check for $200. That's the kind of money that seems to fall out of nowhere that has always helped my family get by.

Sometimes I do get a little bit uncomfortable in those situations. There is a really neat deal each winter up in Celina, Ohio, put on by the Chamber of Commerce. They pack the place with fans, and they'll bring in speakers like Bobby Allison, Ned Jarrett, Benny Parsons, guys like that. Every year they would send me three tickets for my family, and they'd get me up on stage to speak for about 15 minutes. Now, I realize their primary speaker is a famous Winston Cup guy, and they were paid

$5,000 to show up. But in the 15 minutes I was talking, I always got just as big a reaction as the Winston Cup guy. And I really liked the program, but it got to where it made me feel uncomfortable, because of the financial arrangements. So I quit going for a couple of years.

Then I got a call from Steve Schmidt, who works really hard to organize the program. He said, "I'll pay you $500 to speak if you'll make a commitment to be here." That sounded fine, so I agreed. He also booked Sterling Marlin, and it turned out that Sterling didn't show up because his plane was fogged in or something like that (truthfully, I think Sterling just wanted to stay home and watch the Tennessee Volunteers game on television). Well, I wound up doing my 15 minutes, plus Sterling's hour. I didn't ask for more money, although Steve called later and said, "Man, you really got us out of the ringer." Which was good, I was glad to do it.

They eventually got Sterling to come back on another date, so I guess it worked out. But it's just that I knew when I was standing up there talking to those race fans, it meant a lot to me and it meant a lot to them, because I was so sincere. To big-time stars, there is no way they have the same emotion. And, damn, if you're paying somebody $5,000 to speak, they ought to get absolutely fired up for that kind of money.

I guess that just shows how things get complicated when money gets involved. Even if you're not a money person-and I'm definitely not-money gets to be an issue in this sport, in many different ways.

I talked earlier about my loyalty to the people at McCreary tires. I also have a long relationship with Carrera shocks. I've used both products on my race cars for many years.

I began to understand racing deals in the mid-1980s. The deals I'm talking about are when a driver and/or car owner makes arrangements with a supplier to use their parts. The financial arrangements go anywhere from a small discount to the supplier paying you to run the part. You'll see deals with just about everything: shocks, tires, engines, wheels, you name it.

I was on a deal in the early 1980s with Pro Shocks, and I got my shocks free. In 1985 when Hamp and I won all those features, later that winter we switched to Carrera shocks, for the same deal of free shocks.

George Gillespie of Pro Shocks approached me that following spring and asked me why we switched. I said, "George, the main thing is this: go back through the issues of *Speed Sport News* and look at the ads you ran to congratulate your winners. Look to see if you congratulated us in your ads."

I saw him a few days later, and he said, "Yeah, I checked it out, we had your name down seven times!"

"Absolutely, that's what I'm saying," I said. "We won 29 features last year. The reason we switched is not so much that Carrera wants us; it's just that you don't really want us; you just don't want anybody else to have us."

There is a big difference there.

The last couple of years, I began to wonder if my loyalty to people like McCreary and Carrera had hurt me. One of the problems with deals is that if the company falls behind in its development, you're in trouble, because you're stuck with equipment that might not be capable of winning.

That's the problem with racing being so expensive. Too many car owners have to choose products they would rather not run, because they can't afford to pay for the parts they prefer. There is something wrong when that is happening.

A year or so ago, I began to feel like I couldn't afford to experiment with parts and stuff, because every race I blow off with the wrong tire or wrong shock or wrong whatever, is a race I've wasted. You begin to realize this doesn't go on forever; you need to capitalize on every opportunity to win while you're still able.

I have begun thinking a little differently about my deals. Sure, I'm a loyal guy, but I'm probably not going to be quite as firm as I used to be.

By far and away, the best part of this business is the fans.

I know, I know; nowadays all the drivers gush in their interviews, "Gosh, our fans are the greatest..." Then they'll hide in their motorhome after the races.

For me, the best part of my career has been meeting and greeting people. Even when I've had a crappy night, the fans cheer me up afterward. If I did well, the fans and their reaction made it even more special.

Let me give you an example. In May 1992 we were at the Indiana State Fairgrounds for the Hulman Hundred. We had a tire going bald at the halfway mark, so we stopped and changed. We came all the way from the tail to finish third, behind Lealand McSpadden and Jeff Swindell. If there had been one more yellow, I would have got 'em both. Everybody else was running the bottom, and I'm clear out in the loose shit. Banzai! After the race there was a ton of people coming by my pit to congratulate me, and I couldn't have felt better if I'd won the race. All those people, shaking my hand, patting my back, it's just an awesome experience.

I remember this one guy walked up, he was a major in the Indiana National Guard, stationed at the air base at Terre Haute. "You're nothing but a fighter pilot on four wheels," he grinned. I'll never forget that.

See, I could have done the same thing on the race track, without the fans, but what's the point? If nobody was there to see those moves, it wouldn't be satisfying at all.

I guess that's why I've always been so devoted to the fans. Lots of guys give lip service; I always made sure the fans were my top priority. I'll stay as late as I need at the race track. If there are still people there who want an autograph, I'm staying to make sure they get one.

If we leave early, which happens maybe one or two times during the season, it's because we have somewhere else we've got to be. Most of the time, I don't schedule things that closely, because I want to make sure to leave enough time to meet with people after the races.

When you've crashed, or broke, it's still good. All those people who take the time to come see you after the races, that helps you forget about the bad stuff. Maybe they'll bring up an old race where you did good, and help you smile. Anybody in racing has to realize that you're going to have a lot more bad nights than good nights; that's reality. So you have to learn how to make the best of it, even when it's been a crummy night. The fans can help you do that.

If I were in charge (isn't that a scary thought?), I would require the racers to unload all their stuff in the infield at every race track. The fans could see the racers working on their cars, walking around, and that adds to the show. Plus, after the races, the guys couldn't hide in their trailers right away, and a fan might even help roll a tire up into the trailer. That brings the fans much closer to the racers.

When I was a kid going to Eldora, you'd walk down into the infield after the races and there would be dozens of people gathered around the 20 or 25 open trailers. I remember walking up to the Gapco sprint car, Rufus Gray's car, and watching Mario Andretti wiping the grease off his shoes, sitting on the fender of the trailer. Awesome!

Your hero might be sitting there drinking a beer, and you might sit and talk to him for a minute. The next week, you're going to feel like you're a part of that team, that you have a special closeness with them. He's going to be your guy because he sat and talked to you. There is a bond there, and we shouldn't underestimate how important that emotion is in this sport. Maybe next time you'll bring a friend, and let him go into the infield with you and meet the guy.

Today it's harder to get to know the racers. I think the enclosed trailers have been a big part of that. I realize they're wonderful to work out of, but they haven't done the sport any good. That ability to get close to the drivers is something short-track racing has all over Winston Cup or the IRL. But even in short-track racing, they're starting to alienate the fans. One of these days, they probably will. That will hurt our deal a lot, because people won't hang around because they can't see 'em down in the pits after the races.

Four years ago I got a call from the local Joint Vocational School that serves some of the area high schools around Troy. They asked if I would bring a race car over to display at their annual open-house program. That's when they bring in all the area sophomores who are interested in the school, and give a speech on all the different areas of the school available to them. Body shop, machine shop, woodworking, whatever. While we were there, Frank Anthony, the teacher who invited me, began telling me that the body shop section was about to close because of lack of interest from the kids. He just barely got enough kids that year to do one more year of classes.

Later that year he called back, and said, "You wouldn't happen to need any race cars painted, would you?" I said, "Are you kiddin' me? Absolutely!" "Well, then, we'll paint one for you," he said. So I took a car over and let the students paint it. The kids were so fired up and excited, I eventually took two other race cars there for painting. It really went over well, the kids really got into it.

They must have told all their friends, because the following year they had to hire another teacher, because the class had doubled in size. I'm not saying it was the race cars that made the difference; that's not what I mean. What I'm saying is that if people help the kids get excited about what they're doing, that makes a difference.

We always put the school's sticker on each car they paint, and that pumps the kids up even more. They get so excited! Every year since, I've made sure to take a race car up there for painting, and they get right on it. Mr. Anthony has them do it over if it isn't exactly right, so the quality is very good.

It's one thing to tell everyone that a bunch of high-school kids painted your race car, but I try to give 'em more than that. I'll bring pictures of the car on the race track, and sign them for the kids. The kids see the car on TV or on the race track, and they can say it with pride: "We painted that car." When they come to the race track and visit us after the races, Jody gives every kid from the class a free T-shirt.

I tell everybody I know: If you have a vocational school near you, you need to take your race car up there and see if you can have them paint it, because it helps the school out a bunch. The newspaper comes out, and they usually get a story in, which is really good for the school and for the kids.

Car-Paint Racing is out of Dayton and Columbus, and they have four or five stores selling auto body supplies. They found out about my deal with the vocational school, and offered to provide the paint and supplies at no charge. See? Things like this just grow and grow, and it's neat.

The kids usually don't get to see the car after it's lettered, but this past year I brought the car back by the school and the kids were very excited. I had planned on taking the car up there to show just for a little bit, but they asked if I would allow them to display the car, and they kept it for a whole week! Now they've asked me to take the car up in the spring, and park it in front of the school. Those kids are so proud of it.

It's neat to be around kids, and work with them. However, it can be heartbreaking, too. When we had the Silver Crown race at Sacramento, they had a deal out there called the Day With The Racers. It was a bunch of young cancer patients, and they would meet a bunch of us racers at a nearby go-kart track and spend the day together. Each kid "adopted" a racer, and you spent the day with that kid. They were our co-pilots in the go-karts, and we had pizza afterward, and everyone had a great time.

But it's really tough, knowing the kids are so sick. It just tears you up. A lot of times I would come back the next year, and ask about the child I was with the previous year, but the child had died from cancer. That's really, really hard. You feel sad, doing that program, but you feel good, too.

I like making people feel good, helping them know there are people out there who care about 'em. Whether it's a fan or a sick kid, I want them to know there are people who care.

Sometimes when you're close with the fans, you get some odd requests.

One night at Eldora, I was asked to help with a very unusual thing. Roger Clevenger, a former driver and longtime race fan from

Knightstown, Indiana, had died from cancer. Roger had asked that some of his ashes be spread at Eldora.

Someone from his family asked if I would help spread Roger's ashes around the track. I agreed, and after I strapped in to warm the car up and iron the track out, they handed me the little plastic bag containing Roger's ashes. Problem was, when I got going on the track, I caught the bag on something and tore it open. I'm fumbling around trying to get the hole closed, and Roger's ashes were here, there, and everywhere. Some did get on the track, yes; but a lot of him was all over me.

So Roger got the bonus deal; he got to race with me all night long. I'm sure he would have been very happy about that.

I like people. I've never felt like a star...even when we were at Indy, I was still just ol' Jack. That's why I like the fans so much, because I'm a people person. It's not something I have to do, sticking around signing autographs; it's something I *want* to do. I enjoy it.

One time my buddy Bill Parton came with me to the races. Afterward, a cute young girl stopped by the pits and I kissed her on the cheek. After she walked away, Bill said, "Man! I want to be a race car driver!" Not a minute later a great big lady came by, and I kissed her on the cheek, too. She walked away and Bill said, "Well, maybe I *don't* want to be a race driver!" I said, "Hey, you can't sort 'em...you've got to kiss 'em all. You treat 'em all the same."

From age two to 92, I kiss 'em all. Besides, when you can get a 60-year-old gal giggling like a second grader, that's a lot of fun.

We were coming back from I-69 Speedway in Gas City, Indiana one night, and a guy's car broke down right there before you get on the interstate near the track. We stopped to help, and I asked him where he was going. He said the next exit, that's where he gets off. That's the way we go, too, so I offered to tow him down there with my tow strap. I towed him to a station, and he called his wife to come and get him. A couple of years later, he stopped by our pits and re-introduced himself. Now, I guarantee you, the guy remembered that little act of kindness, and he will for a long time. Who knows, maybe that got him to do something nice for somebody else.

That theory of treating other people right doesn't just hold for racing; that's how I want to live my life. Being nice to others, being a good person, that's what I'm shooting for. I'm certain it pays dividends we don't even realize.

Jackie Lee Hewitt, age 2

*Christmas, 1962. I'm on
the right.*

*With my little brother, John,
sitting in Dad's race car.
December, 1963*

I'm on the left with Charlie
Swartz in the middle and
little brother John on the
right. We're in the stands
at Eldora.

My tenth-grade picture from Troy High School.

This bunch was quite an outfit! I'm in our demo derby car with my army buddies alongside. L to R is Benny Robertson, Eddie Musgrove, Rick Willoughby, Sammy Mills, and Jerry Kneemiller.

I was a very eager young racer in this photo.

Don Hewitt, my all-time hero.

Dad on the right, with his car owner, Harley Haynes.
(Dusty Roads photo)

Proud papa Don Hewitt with John and I.
(Jerry Clum photo)

Man, that hair is downright scary! I'm at Limaland in 1977.
(Dusty Roads photo)

Ouch! An early sprint car crash at the Indy Fairgrounds mile.

I raced a lot of nights in the Nickles Bros. car.
Don and "Hurald" are special friends.
(Steve Remington photo)

LaVern Nance helped me get a one-night ride in this Kansas supermodified. Isn't that a cool-looking car?

Tijuana, Mexico in 1978. I'm on the left with Charlie Swartz on the pony and Nick Gwin alongside.

*I'm in the Tognotti No. 18 at Skagit Speedway, racing with
Rick Ferkel in his famous No. 0.*
Elaine Blackstock photo)

*Sharing a happy moment with Rick Ferkel and friends,
at New Bremen in July 1980.*
(Dusty Roads photo)

After my Australian scuffle with Ben Ludlow and Tony Giancola, this cartoon appeared in the local paper the following day.

More Aussie action: Team Australia beat Team USA on this night, and I had to pose for this PR shot with Tim Montcreif. We sure had fun Down Under.

Eldora Speedway, April 1982: My first USAC sprint car win, with Johnny Vance and mechanic Jim McQueen. That's Duke Cook peering over Jim's shoulder.
(Tracy Talley photo)

Sharing the podium with two great racers: Kenny Schrader (l) and Steve Kinser (r).

You know it's an old picture if I'm wearing a Hoosier Tire shirt! This is at the 1982 Eldora Nationals.

With Earl Baltes (c) and Dad at the Eldora banquet, 1986.

This was Gussie: a very special race car.

On the way to a win in Dick Briscoe's car at Kokomo in 1984.
(Ken Coles photo)

In Bob Hampshire's sprint car at Eldora in 1987.
(Ken Coles photo)

*I have some
very wacky
friends.*

Giving the needle to a very young Jeff Gordon.

A mid-1980's photo with two good friends: Mr. J.W. Hunt (c) and Jac Haudenschild.

He was as much a great friend as he was a great car owner and mechanic.
Bob Hampshire and I had some terrific years together..

Sharing a win with Mr. Hunt at Eldora, 1988.
(John Mahoney photo)

In Stan Shoff's sprint car.
(Steve Remington photo)

*Talking with
Doug Wolfgang
at the 1991
Kings Royal at
Eldora.*
(Phil Kunz photo)

I wish I could have talked Stan Shoff into running more non-winged races.
I'm two-wheeling his car at Kokomo in '89.
(John Mahoney photo)

I loved racing late models.
(Max Dolder photo)

Sign language: This guy is telling me, "Go get-em, Jack!" I'm telling him he's number one.
(Allen Horcher photo)

Winning the Putnamville Clash at Lincoln Park Speedway in 1991. I'm pictured with Phil Poor (l) and car owner Don Murphy (c).
(Randy Jones photo)

*Pictured here with
Mr. J.W. Hunt
and Eldora
promoter Earl
Baltes.*
(Cyndi Craft photo)

*Charlie Swartz
has been a life-
long friend.*
(Cyndi Craft photo)

Winning at Belleville in the Zarounian midget. What a great experience!

I'm driving the M&L No. 4 at the 1991 Hoosier Hundred, racing with Jimmy Sills in the No. 1.

(Bob Mount photo)

It's Eldora, April 1994, and this is an important moment. I've won in my first race back from serious injuries six months earlier. For the moment, all the pain and difficulty is forgotten!
(Chris Pedersen photo)

Wearing my eye patch as I recover from my 1993 crash.
(Randy Jones photo)

Father and son: with Dad at Terre Haute in 1996.
(John Mahoney photo)

Father and son, part 2: With Cody in 1997.

*A happy scene in 1995 after winning the USAC Silver Crown
event on the pavement at Richmond, Virginia.*
(David Giles photo)

*Pictured with the great
Australian racer,
Garry Rush.*
(Cyndi Craft photo)

Dream come true: at speed at Indy in 1998.
(IMS Photo by Jim Haines)

My expression says it all.
I don't think I stopped
smiling during the entire
month!
(IMS Photo by Walt Kuhn)

With Cody and Jody at the Indianapolis 500 Parade.
(Rolland Rickard photo)

After finishing 12th, Jody was right there to give me a hug.
What an emotional moment!

Jack and Jody.

*Sharing victory lane with Bob Hampshire and USAC official
Norm Shields at Lawrenceburg in 1995.*
(John Mahoney photo)

I've just won the Silver Crown portion of the '98 4-Crown Nationals, sweeping the entire event. Truly a fairy tale night.
(John Mahoney photo)

Sharing the 4-Crown stage with Cody and Jody, and Berneice and Earl Baltes.
(John Mahoney photo)

With the Team 6-R Racing guys at Terre Haute in 1999.
(John Mahoney photo)

With a bunch of the 6-R guys on a trip to Roman's Oasis,
a great club in the Phoenix area.

Running my two-seater at the Chili Bowl. I hope I can give you a ride one of these days!
(Randy Jones photo)

99 percent of the time, I'm a pretty happy guy.
(Cyndi Craft photo)

With my buddy, Tony Stewart.
(Jim Haines photo)

With my friend and sponsor, Randy Steenbergen. I'm letting Randy help me with the fish I caught!

*Winning with Dennis Kaser and crew at North Vernon, Indiana in 2001.
Dennis is the guy at Jody's left.*

*Sharing a laugh with two of my favorite people: Page (l)
and Parnelli Jones (c).*
(Greg Tyler photo)

One of my proudest moments, being inducted into the National
Sprint Car Hall of Fame.

INTERLUDE
September 2, 2002
10:45 a.m.
Troy, Ohio

I'm home now, back at my home just outside of Troy. Yee-haw and Hallelujah! I'm still pretty beat up but at least I'm home.

My spirits are improving by the day. I can stand up by myself, and I'm beginning to take very short walks. My range is growing; I'm able to walk maybe a quarter-mile using a walking stick.

My arm is still messed up. The feeling is there, and I can move my fingers, but I don't have the ability to use my arm much. My leg is much better.

In a few days I'm going to Florida so my friend Doc Miller can help me with some therapy. When I got hurt in 1993 Doc was a huge help, and I'm hoping he can help me again.

I'll admit something: I've begun to accept that my racing career has changed. I haven't given up on racing again: in fact, that's a great motivation for me to get better. I'm going to drive again someday, even if it's only to close out my career on my terms.

But I know it will never be the same. I've got to be smarter about things. I can't keep jumping into sprint cars on the bullrings with these brave kids. I've accepted that. But I'm not going to rule out some Silver Crown racing, and some late model racing.

I had a big surprise the other day. A writer from the *Dayton Daily News* came over for an interview, and we were sitting at the table talking. He asked me if I felt any differently about racing, and I said, "Absolutely not."

Jody was sitting nearby, and he asked her the same question. She just looked straight ahead, and kind of clenched her jaw, and said, "No comment."

That surprised me. Our entire life together has always been around racing, and I never dreamed she would feel that way. I guess we never talked about it. She has a right to feel differently; I've put her through a lot.

It isn't just that I've been through this twice; so has Jody. She would never say, "Jack, don't drive again." She might like to say that, but she won't.

I still think about racing all the time. I have a great desire to race again. Will I be able to? I don't know. And that bugs me.

18

MY BEST FRIEND

When I look back across my life and think about the people who shaped me and influenced me, I have to think about my dad. The first 16 years of my life, he was just my dad, like most other kids have a dad. But when I turned 16 I entered his world, and we became best friends. We had such a great relationship for the next 30 years it's difficult to think about Pop without getting emotional.

When I was young, he wasn't the father figure a lot of kids had. He was my dad, he drove race cars, and he didn't do everything as a dad they way the books today tell you it should be done. But when we grew into an adult relationship, I saw him not for his faults, but for the things I loved about him: his toughness, his funny stories, his outrageous attitudes toward life, things like that.

Trust me, Don Hewitt was a one-of-a-kind person. I've traveled far and wide and met lots and lots of people, but I never met a guy quite like my dad.

I can't even begin to estimate the hours we spent together. I guarantee I did more with my dad than almost anybody has with their father. So many long trips...we went to Australia together, and I can't even count the many trips to California.

When Dad quit racing, he continued his driving through me. If I did well, he did well, too.

I liked hanging out with him. Not just because he was my dad; but because he was fun to be around. He kept us laughing, all the time. The thing about older people, they can always tell stories; they've just got some great stories. Between Dad and Mr. J.W. Hunt, I was around some pretty good storytellers.

How did he get involved with racing? It was a pretty unlikely thing, but I'll bet a lot of guys start out that way. Dad and his brothers were going to Shady Bowl Raceway near DeGraff, Ohio, when Dad was 15. It was a roaring roadster race, and those cars were just death traps. A guy had been killed in an earlier crash and they didn't have enough cars for the feature. Dad spoke up and said, "I'll drive it!" So he climbed into a race car that a man had just been killed in, and drove in the race. That was the start of his career.

There were six boys in my dad's family: Darrell, Dick, Don, Delmer, Danny, and Dallas. All of 'em but Dallas and Darrell eventually raced.

My grandpa hated that Dad was racing. It scared him. One day Dad talked Grandpa into coming to Shady Bowl to watch him race. Grandpa stood behind the concession stand, peeking around the corner at the track, because he just couldn't bear to watch. He eventually did warm up to it, and in fact Grandpa also drove in some races.

Frank Dickey was the owner of New Bremen Speedway, and he used to say that his favorite race of all time was the Hewitt Duck Race. It was Grandpa and all his sons, in one special race. They had to do several laps around the track, pull up to the pond in the infield, dive into the pond, and capture a duck that had been turned loose. The guy who caught the duck was then to jump back in his car and do one more lap, and that was the winner. Uncle Delmer caught the duck, but he gave it to Grandpa, who took the lap and won the race. Believe it or not, I still have old-timers come up to me and tell me about that race, and they always laugh. I was just a baby at that time.

Dad raced during a tough era. He raced against some really good racers, guys like Chick Hale, Audie Swartz, Bob Pratt, Dick Pratt, Rollie Beale, Doc Dawson, and lots more. That's a competitive bunch of drivers, right there.

I got to race against my dad for seven or eight years before he retired. Racing beat my dad up some; he lost his eye at Eldora in 1971, and a couple of years later got a couple of fingers burned off when he crashed, again at Eldora. The crash knocked him out, and when the car stopped he was all stretched out, and his hand was laying on the exhaust header.

He basically quit in 1980, but I remember at least one time he raced after that. We were at Fremont, and the night's program called for a make-up feature from an earlier rainout, followed by a full racing program. I was driving for Bob Hampshire at the time, but the Nickles Bros. asked if I would run their car in the first feature. Brad Doty had qualified the car on the original night, but he couldn't make it back for the rain date. So they asked me to fill in.

I finished third or fourth in the first feature, then hopped out to run Hamp's car for the full program that followed. I told Harold and Don Nickles, "Why don't you put Dad in the car?" Well, they're always worried about their driver getting hurt, and they really didn't want to see Dad get hurt any more. But they thought about it and finally said, yes, Dad could run the car.

We both transferred to the feature through our heat race, and it was going to be Dad's first feature event in several years. Problem was, Dad overheard Don Nickles say right before the feature, "Hell, I only put five gallons of fuel in, he won't last long anyways."

That's the wrong thing for Don Hewitt to hear.

"Your ass!" he yelled. "You fill this sumbitch up! I'm gonna run this feature!" Man, he was hot, just ripping their ass.

They filled up the tank, and Dad ran the entire feature. When it was over he pulled in and stuck his arm out to Don Nickles, and yelled, "Feel this arm!" Don did, and Dad said, "Does that feel like I'm tired??!!" He was pissed.

I won the feature, and later that night somebody asked Dad how he did. "Jack's the only one who lapped me," he said, all puffed up.

Here's a funny story: Earlier that night, when I talked to Dad about running the car, I told him, "The only way you're allowed to drive this car is that you've got to run all the safety equipment I run: rock screen, arm restraints, gloves, everything." I had learned a lot from his safety mistakes, and I'm extremely picky about making my race car as safe as possible.

When he came in after hot laps, he told us, "Hell, there ain't no wonder you kids are brave! Look at this...you handcuff me (arm restraints), then you blindfold me (full-face helmet), then you put me in a cage (rock screen). There ain't no wonder you're so brave!"

Did I tell you about the time we stole the ambulance at Eldora?

Well, wait a minute...it wasn't *we* stole the ambulance; Don Hewitt stole the ambulance. For the record, that's how it went down.

Dad was well-known for partying and getting drunk after the races. We rode to the races that night with Glen Caldwell, and as the party was going on he told Dad, "Hey, I got to go home." Dad was still having fun, so he told him, "Hell, go on home. We'll get a ride."

Pretty soon we looked around, and we were in trouble. The party was winding down, Dad is drunk, and there's nobody at Eldora but a few campers, and they're all going to bed. It looks like we're stuck there for the night.

We start looking around for a place to sleep. Steve Victor and I spotted this old civil defense car they used for an ambulance, a 1956 Cadillac. Steve and I hustled to the car, and the back door was unlocked. We climbed in, with me laying on the stretcher and Steve sitting in a little seat back there. I've got me a bed, so I'm grinning.

In a minute or two here came Dad and Nick Gwin. Nick jumped in the passenger seat up front, and Dad hopped in on the driver's side. That's where we're all going to sleep that night.

But there was a major, major problem: The damned keys were in the ignition! Dad fired that baby up and we headed for home. I was so embarrassed, I covered myself up with the sheet so nobody would see me, because Dad found the switch for the red lights and turned 'em on. Thank goodness they couldn't find the siren. They were looking, believe me.

So we're driving across the Ohio countryside toward Troy, with a drunk hauling underage kids in a stolen ambulance that probably hadn't had legal license plates in 10 years. Just another day with Don Hewitt.

How we made it home without being arrested, I have no idea.

The next morning Earl Baltes' brother-in-law said, "Hey, Earl, where is the ambulance?"

Earl was appalled.

"That damned Don," he said. "I'll bet he took it!"

"He can't take the ambulance!"

"Whattaya mean, he can't??!! The sumbitch is gone, ain't it??!!"

The next day, Dad said to me, "Hey, you want to ride with me to Eldora to take this ambulance back?"

"NO WAY!" I said. "And wipe my backprints off that stretcher, too. I don't want anything to do with this."

He took it back, and Earl just shook his head. Dad and Earl were tight, that's for sure.

I've got to tell you a related story about the ambulance. Uncle Dick, Dad's brother, was even more outrageous than Dad was. He was a little, uh, shifty sometimes.

He pulled into our driveway that day and saw the ambulance.

"Where'd you get that?" he asked Dad.

"I stole it from Eldora last night," Dad said.

Uncle Dick looked at the ambulance, and back at Dad, and said, "Don, I've stole some serious shit in my life...but I've never stole an ambulance."

Traveling with Dad was a treat. Actually, he helped me a lot on those long trips, because he was a big help with the driving.

I hated traveling down the road by myself. I hated to drive, especially if I was alone in the car. If a bunch of us were traveling together, I'd drive my share, but I still didn't care much for it. Dad was just the opposite; he could drive forever. That's why we traveled so well together; we really got going good together.

We'd pile in the car, or van, and head out West. When we'd leave I might pop in a Conway Twitty 8-track, and we'd get to Wyoming and I'd say, "Dad...ol' Conway is getting hoarse. He can't go no more." It would just keep playing around and around on the 8-track. I guarantee you, though, by the time we got to Wyoming, Dad still didn't know the words to any of the songs. He could listen to anything, as long as it was noise, but then he really didn't pay any attention to it.

There were lots of times when I had a hotel room, but he didn't stay with me in the room. I liked to sleep till 11 a.m., and he wanted to get up at 6 or 6:30. So he'd go out and sleep in the van. There we were, with a motel room complete with a shower, and a lot of times he'd get up in the morning and drive around till he found a creek somewhere, where he'd wash his face, brush his teeth, and clean up for the morning. That's just how he was. He liked doing that kind of stuff.

I remember riding down the highway with Dad, and they had just come out with Fuzzbuster radar detectors. We're flying down the road, and the thing starts beeping. Dad doesn't slow down; he's still going 75, 80 miles per hour. Up ahead we see a cop sitting in the medium.

"Dad," I said, "These Fuzzbusters are to detect radar...they don't make the car invisible. You've got to slow down."

My dad and I were very close, but he still didn't express a lot of emotion to me. Or anyone else, for that matter. He'd never tell me I did a good job, things like that. He would be proud of me and would tell other people things, but he didn't say them to me.

In later years when I'd do well you could tell he was proud, because he would just be grinning at me. I've got some neat pictures from when we won the Warrnambool Classic in Australia, and Dad was there with me. He's got this sash across his chest, holding a big bottle of champagne, just drunker than shit. I knew he was proud, but he just wasn't one of those guys who would tell you when you did well. He'd just tell you when you did bad.

He and Mom would sure raise hell with each other. Here's a classic story. One night Mom and Dad are lying in bed, arguing, with the lights out. Each was smoking a cigarette, and Dad was lying on his back with an ashtray on his chest. Dad finally puts his cigarette out in the ashtray, and sets it aside. My mom doesn't see him move the ashtray. She's bitching at him, and she reaches over and puts her cigarette out on his bare chest.

He leaped out of the bed, with blankets tangled all around him, wide-eyed. He's yelling, "Woman, you're nuts! You're friggin' crazy!"

That's one of the nights he slept in our room.

When I was a teenager, Larry Laughman had a Ford Torino, and in the winter four or five of us would get together and go to Fort Wayne, Indiana, to the indoor midget races at the Coliseum. When we left the building, we'd all break out in a dead run to the car, because the last one to the car had to drive home. My dad was probably 40-plus at the time, but he was right there with us, stretching out those long legs, because he didn't want to drive, either. That's a really good memory, picturing him grinning and running with all those young guys.

Dad was good friends with Jeff Crawford, who owned the Kozy Kitchen, right down from where we lived. Jeff had a big Harley, and Dad liked to ride the motorcycle around. We had a big German shepherd dog, and when Dad fired up the motorcycle the dog would come running, and would jump on the back and ride down the road with Dad. True story.

One evening Dad was drunk, and Mom heard the Harley fire up. She heard him start to take off, and all of a sudden there is the sound of a big crash. She ran outside, and there is the motorcycle on its side, with Dad's leg pinned underneath. "Help get this damned thing off me!" he's yelling and cussing.

Mom ran over and helped him lift it enough to get his leg out, and he stood up and started to brush himself off. Mom asked him what happened.

"Aw," he said, "that damned dog leaned the wrong way!"

Dad loved to tease me about being dumb, or clumsy, just to ride my ass. That's when I was an adult, and I'd get right back at him. We were going to a cafeteria one day, and I stumbled a little bit on the sidewalk.

"You're so damned clumsy!" he yelled, just giving me hell and laughing. We went inside and got some food and sat down, and he's still laughing and ripping my ass. He has a small plate of cottage cheese, and while he's reaming me he's shaking the pepper shaker over the cottage cheese.

"Dad," I interrupted, "I don't ever want you to rip me again about being dumb."

He looked at me, kind of indignant, and said, "Why the hell not?"

I reached over and brushed the pepper off the cellophane on the cottage cheese.

My brother borrowed my car one night and was riding around with six boys near the little town of Lena, not far from Piqua. About 3 a.m., there was a knock on the back door of our trailer. Dad answered the door, and there was a highway patrolman standing there.

"Are you Donald Wayne Hewitt?" the trooper asked.

"Yes."

"Do you have a son named John William Hewitt?"

"Yes."

"Mr. Hewitt, I'm sorry to have to tell you that your son hit a train tonight with his car."

"Christ," he said. "How much is a train? I ain't never had to buy one of those before."

My dad was working in the garage on Junie Heffner's race car when our trailer caught fire from a nearby lightning hit. Mom rushed out into the garage, yelling, "Don, come quick! The house is on fire!" Dad didn't even look up; he just kept working on the race car. Mom is hysterical. "Don! I said the house is on fire!"

He finally looked up at her. "Lady, I ain't no fucking fireman...what do you want me to do about it?"

Later on Dad worked for Polling's junkyard, working for his friend Bill Didier. One day Dad was in the wrecker, picking up cars. Dad went over to pick up and old car near the gravel pit where we fish. He got it lifted, but the emergency brake was locked up. He couldn't get it to release, so he just started dragging it down the road toward the junkyard.

Pretty soon the rear tires blew out from the friction, and he kept going. The wheels were dragging on the pavement, sparking like crazy. It started three or four small fires in the ditch along the way.

He got the car to the junkyard, just like he had been told. Then the phone rang: It was the fire chief, chewing Bill Didier's ass about all those fires throughout the countryside.

We took Dad fishing on our Canadian trip several times. A bunch of us were standing around one day, and Dad walked up all excited and said, "I found a big pile of bear shit!"

A lady nearby said, "Well, how fresh was it?"

"About 45 minutes," Dad told her.

She gave him a real puzzled look, and said, "How do you know that?"

"Because I stuck my finger in it!"

The lady was just aghast, she just about shit. And Dad looked at her, totally serious. Knowing Dad, I wouldn't doubt that he did, either.

Those are all funny stories, and I promise you every one of them is true. But now I have to tell you about the end of the line for Don Hewitt.

In May 1997, Dad was working at Polling's junkyard. One of the jobs on those old salvage cars is taking the gas tank off before it can be crushed. Well, Dad is an impatient guy, so when he'd see those other kids dicking around trying to unbolt an old gas tank, he'd run over there with a torch and cut the straps, zip, zip, and the tank is out. That's terribly dangerous, obviously, and Bill Didier fired Dad twice for doing that. Bill was basically trying to protect Dad from himself.

Dad was really excited during that May, because John Orr promised to let Dad drive his modified at Eldora. That was the most excited I had seen Dad in a long, long time, because he was ready to race. John Orr was feeling pretty tickled about it, too. Eldora had been rained out a few days earlier, but Dad was still hopeful he'd get to run the modified soon.

On a sunny summer day, Dad was supposed to be running the wrecker at Polling's, but it was a slow day. Dad was never the kind of guy who could just stand around much. So while he's waiting on another wrecker call, he walked into the shop, and sure enough a couple of younger guys were having trouble getting a fuel tank off a car that was up on the lift. You guessed it.

He ran in there with a torch, and told the younger guys to stand back. He reached up with the torch...well, the top of the tank had rusted through, and the torch ignited the gasoline fumes, and the entire tank exploded. Here Dad is standing right underneath, and when it blew it just splashed burning gasoline all over him. He had a hat on, so it didn't burn his face real bad-it burned his nose a little and part of his ears off-but then it was kind of a "V" down his chest, and the rest of his body was burned. Bad burned.

He ran from the shop, and they said the flames were going 15 feet in the air. He knew where the water was, and he put himself out. They called an ambulance to come get him. He was conscious and talking, and insisted that he walk to the ambulance. He was a tough old fart.

I had run an errand with Tim Clark, and when I got home the phone rang. It was Billy Didier (Bill's son), and he said, "Jack, you'd better get down to the hospital, your dad got burned pretty bad."

I kind of dismissed it, and said, "Yeah? How bad is he?"

"Jack, your dad is burned pretty bad."

"We'll go down and see him, then. Just don't worry about it; he'll be all right."

At first we went to the wrong hospital, but eventually we tracked him down. What made it very hard was that by the time I got there, they already had him on morphine, and he couldn't talk. Looking back, that was a huge issue, because we never had a final conversation, a chance to say goodbye.

There was very little they could do for him. He was terribly burned, both on the inside and the outside. They tried to keep him comfortable, but he was just so badly burned, they couldn't do much for him.

He lay there for two weeks. And I felt like the world was coming to an end.

The first few days I refused to believe he would die. He just *couldn't* die. Not Dad. He would beat this thing, because he is so strong and so tough. But as the days slipped by I began to realize he wasn't going to recover, and this was going to be the end.

I had to go to Butler, Michigan, for a NAMARS midget race, to run Don Murphy's car. We were almost to Fort Wayne and I told Jody, "It's been two weeks since Dad got burned, and when we get back, I've got to take him off the morphine, let him come back, and tell me what I need to do. He's the toughest guy I know, but I want him to tell me what he wants."

When we got back from Michigan, the hospital cut back his morphine to see if he would be able to communicate. But his kidneys were shutting down from his injuries, and his body couldn't cleanse itself from the morphine. So he never did come around, and I never got to talk with him like I had hoped.

I was there at his side, along with Mom, and I didn't know if he could hear me. I said, "Dad, it's bad...don't stay here for us, you do what's easier for you. I'll take care of Mom." Man, he opened up that eye, and gave me a look that would kill. I was getting an ass chewin' with his glare. Like, "Who in the hell do you think you're talkin' to?" Jody saw it as something different; she saw it as Dad saying it was okay, that he knew it was coming, and he was grateful that I said what I did.

His body began to shut down, one vital organ after another. They said they could put him on life support, and they probably could have, and he might have been able to live for a while longer. If they would have had the right healing process going, and there was hope, maybe that would have been the thing to do. But he was burned so badly...there was almost no hope. My mom and my brother and I talked it over, and we held a vote on what to do. We voted two to one not to put him on life support. And I believe that's what he would have wanted.

They told us it was only a matter of time, and we all stood there with him and waited. I was holding his hand, and I could see on the monitor his heartbeat going down, down, down, and I started being a cheerleader. "C'mon, Dad, c'mon Dad, please, Dad, you can make it..."

And then he just slipped away.

He was 67 years old when he died, at the end of one helluva life. I'm so grateful for all the years I got to spend with him, and I'm grateful we were able to have such a close relationship.

I just felt lost for a long time, because I felt like a part of my life had been cut away, and I kept missing him at every turn. When I'd take a trip, I'd think of Dad. When I'd hear a funny story, I'd think of Dad. When I would look at old racing pictures, I'd think of Dad. When I signed in at the pit shack, I'd think of Dad.

I suppose it's like that for everyone who loses a parent. It's just that I had lost *more* than a parent. I had lost my best friend. The best damn friend a man could ever have.

My mother had always suffered from blood sugar, just like her parents. It got progressively worse as she aged, mainly because she didn't watch her diet like she needed to. She would always take her medication, but she would eat whatever she wanted. She was a stubborn lady.

In 2001 she started to have circulation problems, and her feet began to turn black. She became very high-strung, very nervous, and began to slur her words a little bit. Her kidneys began to fail, and she was on dialysis three times a week. They finally put her in the hospital because her feet were dying, and they were concerned about gangrene.

Jody and I met with her doctor, and he explained what he wanted to do.

"We need to amputate one foot, and at a later date we'll take the other foot," he said.

"Will she ever leave the hospital?" I asked.

"She'll survive the surgery, but we can't guarantee she'll ever leave the hospital."

"What options does she have?"

"If you take her off dialysis, her body will become infected and she will die within two weeks."

"Well, that's probably what we'll do, take her off dialysis."

After Dad died, we took Mom up and had them draw up a living will. We had already talked about this scenario. She had watched her dad lose his leg to sugar, and she didn't want that. She had already told us, "Don't let them amputate anything."

So I went to see Mom. I asked her, "Mom, do you plan on dancing in heaven?"

"Yep."

"All right, then, we're going to take you off dialysis."

And then I sat there and cried with her.

She had entered the hospital on a Friday, and they kept her there until Tuesday morning, when we took her home. She died two days later, at 5 a.m. Jody and I were there with her, along with my brother John and his daughter, Tonya.

They say time heals all, but not that. There is no way. Jody's dad passed away about 10 years ago, so we had dealt with that before I lost both my parents. Ten years later, I know Jody's pain is still there from losing her dad. So both my parents are gone, and her dad, so Jody and I have shared our grief.

I miss them as much today as the day they passed away.

It still seems empty, them being gone. Losing them brought Jody and I closer together, along with Jody's mother, Millie. She's more a part of my life now than ever. I've always gotten along great with Millie. Lots of people make jokes about their mother-in-law, but I never did. She's only 87, so she'll be around another 20 years or so. At least I hope so.

Sometimes Dad would joke around with this old poem he knew:
"The sky was blue,
The track was fast.
I started first,
And finished last.
Send me another $100 to get home on."

Mom and Dad were both cremated, and we spread some of their ashes at Eldora. I still have the remainder of their ashes at home; I haven't taken them out to Grandma and Grandpa's place yet to spread them. I just can't bring myself to finish. I'd rather have them at the house with me.

Ride on, Don and Jake, ride on. I miss you both, every single day.

19

INDY

From the time I first pulled a helmet down over my head, I always thought about getting to the Indianapolis 500. If you're a race driver in America, that place almost always holds a special meaning for you. That great big track, all those people, the balloons, the blue May sky, the sound, the history, the jets flying over, man, there isn't anyplace like Indy.

Early on, I held out hope that being a successful sprint car driver would get me there. But CART screwed things completely up in the 1980s, changing Indy car racing into a series for road racers. Dirt track sprint car drivers? You might as well have been from another planet, because those guys laughed at us like we were second-class racers.

Piss on 'em.

CART may have had the upper hand in the 1980s and early 1990s, but Tony George, head of the Indianapolis Motor Speedway, took the lead when he formed the Indy Racing League in 1995. There have been some people critical of Tony George, but I'll tell you this: he gave us a chance. I think he's got a lot of guts to grab things by the horns and make changes.

Tony George got me to Indy, along with Bob Parker, my longtime friend and sponsor. I'm very grateful to those two guys for having faith in me, because it helped my dream come true.

In 1997, Steve Kinser ran the Indy 500 for Sinden Racing. I was very happy for Steve, and felt like he deserved the shot. Hey, who's been a better race driver over the past 25 years than Steve Kinser? The guy is a helluva racer, and he's exactly the kind of guy who *should* be at Indy.

Seeing Steve run Indy kind of gave me hope; got me fired up a little bit. Every year I spent at least one day at Indy during the month of May, sniffing around and seeing if there might be some way to get a shot. Everybody wanted money, or they had never heard of me, or both. So I never really had any good leads. But when Steve got there, my interest picked up a bunch.

In the early years of my career, I'm sure my long hair and beard turned people off when I walked the garage area at Indy. I was having a great time racing, doing what I loved, but didn't realize that to go to the next level I needed to cut my hair, shave, make myself more presentable. Not that it mattered; there were lots of clean-cut short-track racers who deserved a shot, and they didn't get a look, either. Still, I've wondered sometimes if I had changed my image a little bit it would have helped.

In early 1998 I got a phone call asking if I'd like to come to Las Vegas to take my Indy Racing rookie test. I don't remember who called; I don't know if it was somebody from the IRL, or somebody from PDM Racing. Bottom line, as far as I was concerned, was that Tony George was behind it. I'm not sure if I'm supposed to say it like that, but it's true. He was responsible for helping me, I'm sure.

I went out to Vegas, where several guys were scheduled to take their rookie tests. Dave Blaney was in the car when the engine blew up, and that ended the weekend. But a few days later they called again and asked if I'd come to Phoenix for another try.

John Paul, Jr. was there; he had been PDM's driver. He told me a lot about the car; I asked a lot of questions, because I really wanted to know. That was the first time I had a chance to get to know Paul Diatlovich and Chuck Buckman, the owners of PDM Racing. I liked those guys.

We finally got in the car, and I got through my test quicker than normal. In a way you cheat yourself a little bit when that happens, because you get fewer laps in the car.

Paul pointed down toward turn three and four there at Phoenix, and told me the Indy Car guys would flat-foot it through there. But I wasn't allowed to, not yet. So the guys were teasing me about that. The car was working so well, there was no doubt in my mind that I could have gone through there flat. After my turn in the car was over, I stuck around and watched a couple of other guys do their test. When we were finished for the day, I just started grabbing tires and stuff, and helped the crew start loading up. The other drivers saw this, and they started helping, too. The PDM guys were surprised; they said it was the first time they had drivers helping them load up.

Not long after, I was back home in the Midwest. I was driving Bill Biddle's sprint car at that time, and I needed to go to his shop in Terre Haute to work on the car. I got finished up and was heading back to Indy in my van when I got tired, and stopped for the night at a rest area on I-70. I got up early the next morning and called Bob Parker. "Get over here!" he said. "You've got to get to the Speedway and get your rookie test done!"

I hauled ass for Indy. Apparently, they had been looking for me the night before to get me set up for Rookie Orientation Program, but nobody called me. They sent me over to the Sinden Racing garage; they were going to provide the car for my ROP. It was raining, though, so it looked like there wasn't much urgency after all, because the day was likely to be rained out.

Jeff Sinden and Joe Kennedy of Sinden Racing were in their shop, and they fitted me up in the car. They took one look at me and both said, "We'll use Steve's seat," and they bolted in the seat Kinser had used the year before.

It stopped raining at the Speedway late that day, and they opened the track at about 5:15. They asked me, "Would you like to take a couple of laps today?"

"Damn right I'd like to take a couple of laps today!"

I got in the car, and I felt pretty comfortable. They asked if I'd like to try to get through one of the phases of my rookie test, and I agreed.

On my very first time to go around the track there at Indy, I began to cry. I couldn't stop thinking about Dad, and how empty if felt that he wasn't here to share this with me. Obviously, I was elated to be here, but one of the key parts was missing; having Pop standing down there in the pit box, right there with me. He had never made it to Indy, and I know what it would have meant to him to come there with me. I literally cried and cried as I was slowly circling the track.

I ran a few laps at speed, and they waved me in. "You've gone through your first phase," they told me. "The 185 to 190 phase."

"All-right!"

"You all right? You want to try another phase?

"Yeah, but I feel pretty slow."

I went back out and passed another phase, and by then it was 6 o'clock, quitting time. Brian Barnhart, or whoever was in charge, said, "Do you want to take your third phase?"

"Absolutely."

The next one was 195 to 200, and we did our 10 laps and got through it. I was amazed that it had all gone so smoothly, I didn't think that was possible. By then it was time to quit, with one phase left on my test.

But I still didn't have a ride. Bob Parker got to talking about helping me, and he talked to PDM and they got together. Bob had some money from his company, Parker Machinery, that would help me, and it worked out. It was like a dream come true.

Our next outing was Opening Day, Sunday, May 10. It was nice and sunny, but my day turned dark in a hurry.

I still had my fourth phase of my rookie test to get through, and I was working up to speed in the PDM car, getting the feel of things. At about 2:30, I was coming out of turn four and I let the car push up too much into the gray stuff, and I couldn't get the car back down. I hit the wall with the right side of the car, did a half-spin, then hit the inside wall with the rear, and slid back across the track into the outside wall, where the car stopped.

I had never crashed at that speed before, and it was a pretty good smack. I was still going maybe 100 miles per hour backward, I had no steering or brakes, and I just reached up and started flipping the off switches, waiting to hit again. When the car stopped there was some fire on the right side of the car, and some guys from Pagan Racing's crew ran to me with pails of water and a water hose to put the fire out. I didn't have a scratch, but the car was really hurt. I unbuckled and climbed out, one miserable son of a bitch.

I know it aggravated the PDM guys, but what could I say? I tried to tell them what the car was doing. That's why it's so difficult for a beginner in any kind of racing: you might well be right about what your ass is feeling, but you don't have any credibility so nobody listens, because they're just sure you're full of crap.

Because of the damage, they told me we wouldn't be back out until Wednesday. As good as things had been going it seemed like it all went away, just like that.

I suppose I could have gone back to Troy and waited for them to get the car repaired, but that was the furthest thing from my mind. I decided early on to make the most out of my Indy experience, no matter what happened. I wanted to stick around for every day, every function, that I possibly could. Like a kid at the carnival, I wanted to ride every ride on the midway and see every sight before it was over.

At 8 o'clock the next morning, I was at the PDM shop. I spent the next three days there, while they worked on the car, just to lend moral support. They were amazed, but I think they appreciated it. I just wanted them to know how important this deal was to me.

The crew got the car finished in time to return to the track on Wednesday, but we lost an engine that morning and ran out of time to get back out. We came back Thursday morning and got through our final phase, which cleared the way for us to try to qualify that weekend.

But our crash had been a big setback. Since we missed three days of practice, we were really behind the eight ball in terms of finding enough speed to make the race. We had just two days (really, a day and a half) to find some speed. We had done a 206.3 on Wednesday, but we believed it would take at least 10 mph more than that to make the race.

Was there pressure? Sure there was. But not pressure from Jack Hewitt. The pressure I felt was in my mind, from Don Hewitt, Rick Ferkel, Bobby Allen, Brent Kaeding, Chuck Amati, Johnny Beaber, all those guys from that era who should have had a shot but didn't get one. I had them all in the car with me, and they didn't want me to screw it all up, because if I screwed myself out of the show, they were out, too. Damn, I wanted to make it, because it was all about so much more than Jack Hewitt. I mean that.

It was challenging, because I had never been in anything like that car. But if you're a race driver and you get into a different car, you learn. Besides, the PDM guys knew what they were doing. If you're a race driver and the speed doesn't bother you, and you know where the throttle is, you can figure it out.

The biggest thing was the sitting position. I'm not used to lying back like that, unless I've got a TV remote in my hand. That was different, but I got used to it.

The speed was just a blur. You're kind of amazed when you're going through the corner, wondering, "How does this thing stay stuck like that?" It overrides your brain, because your brain is telling your foot, "Hold it on the floor because this car is going to stick." Then you look down at the dash and see you're going 225, and there is nothing down at the end of the straightaway but that little ol' wall, just waiting on you. Your instincts are trying to tell you, "Look, you're not this stupid. Let off." But you override that and make it work.

We were struggling to find speed, but we had a breakthrough Thursday afternoon. Johnny Rutherford leaned into the car and told me, "Listen, run it just like you're at Winchester...back off down the straight, and flat-foot it through the corner." (I wonder if anybody ever told Johnny I was never worth a crap at Winchester?) It wasn't 10 laps later, and I was flat all the way around the race track. That was a giant leap forward. Once we got there, it was a matter of trimming the car out and finding more speed. We ran a 213.7 on Thursday, and improved to a 214.5 on Friday, one day before qualifying began.

Qualifying at Indy! There is pressure there, let me tell you. We drew second position, which meant we'd be the second car out Saturday morning. But Scott Goodyear scratched his backup car, so we were the first one to try and qualify. We ran a 214.9, a 215.0, and a 215.1, when Paul waved us off. Talk about your heart dropping...you're coming around for the white flag and they're waving you off.

We tweaked some things, and Paul approached me.

"Do you think you can flat-foot it for four laps?" he asked.

"Will it turn?"

"Yeah."

"Then I can flat-foot it for four laps."

We got back in line a few minutes before 5 o'clock that afternoon, and at about 5:30 we tried again. This time, we were faster: we ran four laps of 216.8, 216.5, 216.138, and 216.2, giving us a four-lap average of 216.450 mph. It looked like we were in the show. Paul, who hadn't said much on the radio during either qualifying attempt, was whooping and hollering.

I was blinking back the tears, thinking about Dad and all those other racers who were riding with me. We had made it to the Indy 500.

Our timing was perfect; we found speed at exactly the right time, and we'd start the race in 22nd spot, on the inside of row eight.

Right after my qualifying run they interviewed me, and I slipped when I said something like, "Aw, shit, thanks Mom!" Tony George and George Snider were sitting right there watching me, and they looked at each other when I said that. It was such an exhilarating moment, I guess I just forgot to watch my words.

Later on Tony said in an interview, "We like having Jack here, but we never know what he's going to say!"

I hated to tell Tony this, but *I* don't know what I'm going to say. It's hell living with this mouth, let me tell you.

Indy was all about emotions. From taking my rookie test out in Phoenix, to doing the ROP deal at Indy, to hot lapping, to practice, to crashing, to qualifying, to starting the race, it was emotional all the way. It's so much pressure off your mind when you're qualified I can't even describe it. Then again, nothing was set in stone, because we could be bumped on Sunday afternoon during the second day of qualifying.

We were sitting ducks to be bumped, because we had no backup. We had used up our one shot. I spent Sunday in street clothes, hanging out in the suites with my friend Russ Dellen, one of the guys involved in 6R Racing. We were a good ways from the bubble, but we were still sweating bullets. A couple of times I had to walk out on the balcony so I could be by myself, because I was crying. It was just that emotional, even though everyone was telling me, "Yeah, you've got it made, you've got it made..." But all I could do was wait. I can't imagine what it would be like to be 33rd, right on the bubble. Unbearable.

The bumping got to within four cars of us, and then it was over. We were safely in the show. I breathed a big sigh of relief at 6 o'clock when qualifying ended.

I had a little encounter with Arie Luyendyk that week. There were a lot of rookies in the field that year, and Arie made the statement to some writers, "The only thing we have to worry about are the rookie drivers," or something like that. Right away, a sportswriter came to our garage and told me, "Arie made a statement about you..." I was kind of irritated about the whole thing, and I just kind of tossed back, "Aw, who cares what that little faggot says?"

No big deal. I wanted Arie to know I didn't care for what he said, but of course he can say anything he wants. That's what's beautiful about this country; so can I.

The reporter kind of blew it out of proportion, and a few weeks later at Louden, New Hampshire, Arie approached me.

"Did you call me a faggot?" he asked.

"Yep."

"Why did you say that?"

"Because you badmouthed me."

"No, I didn't."

"Sure you did. You said something about the only thing you've got to worry about are the rookies, didn't you?"

"Yeah, but I didn't mention your name."

"What's the difference?" I said. "I'm a rookie, and you badmouthed me."

It was maybe a year later, and I was sitting and signing autographs at a charity event in Indianapolis. Arie walked up behind me, leaned over real close, and said, "You faggot..."

I turned around and grinned at him and said, "You're not still mad about that, are you?"

Then he laughed and we started talking, and we were fine. I don't think he liked it, but we got over it. Besides, he's got bigger and better things to do than worry about what Jack Hewitt says to a newspaper reporter.

A year or so ago, I gave a talk at a big charity function up in Celina, Ohio. The place was packed with rowdy, partisan Ohio race fans, and we were having a good time. A guy yelled from the crowd, "You should have punched Arie!"

I acted real serious, and I said, "Sir, now wait just a minute. A guy with the stature of Arie Luyendyk, you don't punch a guy like that...you bitch-slap 'em."

Boy, that got 'em going.

In the week following qualifications, they had a function called the Mayor's Luncheon. The room is full of important politicians and stuff, and they sat me at a table with a bunch of fancy people. I got there a few minutes late, after lunch had been served. They brought me a plate of food, and of course I'm the pickiest eater in the world. It was all stuff I don't like: iced tea, salad, roast beef, baked potato. They had green beans, which I like, but these health-nut people cook them differently and they're stiff and hard, like right out of the garden.

Everyone at the table was kind of looking at me, and I looked around and said, "Gee, is this what you rich people really eat? It's no wonder you're all so skinny." By the time the luncheon was over, my table was hootin' and hollerin', having a big ol' time.

Because I had arrived late, they didn't have my name in the proper order on their list, and they introduced me last, instead of in my proper starting spot. Most of the guys had said, "I'm here to do this," or "I'm here to do that..." I got up there and I'm almost jumping up and down, I'm so excited. "I'm at the Indianapolis 500!" I said. The audience saw how enthusiastic I was, and you could see them just feeding off of it, and they got excited, too.

I think it meant a lot to Tony George to see the excitement on my face, to see how much we got from the experience.

During the month of May I stayed at Mike Spaulding's house, he's one of the guys from 6R Racing who lives in Indy. He owns Café Santa Fe, an excellent Mexican restaurant on the north side, on 82nd Street at Clearwater Crossing.

On race day I had to get up pretty early. I swung by Bob Parker's place, then got a police escort to the track. Now, in the past I've had cops *behind me* with the red lights on, but never in front of me. It was a cool deal, going 70 mph through downtown Indy. You're treated like royalty, like you're somebody special. When you've made the field for the Indianapolis 500, you can swell your chest out a little bit.

It's like everyone was a player in my dream. The cops, the crew, the fans, everybody had a role on my special day.

When you walk out on the grid just prior to getting buckled into the car, you can't help but notice all those people. You *have* to see 'em. My uncle Dallas came in from Maryland, and he and my cousins were sitting in turn two. I told Gary Lee in a radio interview before the race, "As soon as this feature is over, I'm hurrying to Eldora to run the sprint car." Gary laughed and said, "Well, I don't think I've ever heard the Indianapolis 500 referred to as 'a feature' before!"

My biggest concern on race day was pit stops. We hadn't been able to practice them much, and I was having trouble keeping the engine going pulling out of my pit. I didn't have any confidence; I wouldn't rev it up high enough, because I didn't want to hurt the engine. I really struggled with that. But it turned out okay, because I didn't kill the engine once, all day.

We got the race started, and I tried to be careful. J.J. Yeley and Eddie Cheever came really close to crashing, right in front of me. I got on the brakes to miss 'em, and flat-spotted my tires, requiring a quick pit stop for new tires. That hurt us a little bit, because we were immediately at the back. It wasn't long before Tony Stewart came by and lapped me.

During parts of the race I felt pretty racy, and I passed some cars. As the race wore on I gained some confidence, and the car was working great. The big issue was that with my lack of confidence, I didn't want to make a mistake at 225 and hurt somebody.

We were 15th at the halfway point, and I was very focused on being smooth and steady. I really wanted to finish this thing. The track is pretty narrow, but it wasn't a problem passing guys or getting lapped. I knew when guys were coming up behind me, and I'd make sure to give 'em lots of room. Actually, using mirrors was a big thing for me. That was the first time in 25 years of racing that I was in a car with mirrors.

Prior to this race, the Little 500 sprint car race (500 laps) at Indiana's Anderson Speedway was the only really long race I'd been in. That part was an adjustment, too. It wasn't a physical thing, but mental. Sure, you lose a little weight during the course of the race, and you're slipping around in the seat a little bit toward the end because you're a tiny bit smaller, but it's much harder mentally than physically. You're concentrating on so many things...pit stops, hitting your marks every lap, things like that.

We were running 11th with just 20 laps to go, and I spun on a restart coming out of turn one. I was on cold tires, and I just drove down there and spun. I'm not good enough there to have any fancy excuses, so I have to be honest and just say I lost it. A lack of experience and cold tires, and I lost it.

When I spun I kept the engine going, but I had three flat tires. The tub was dragging a little bit, but I could drive it back to the pits. It's neat to listen to the radio broadcast I have on tape, because the announcers were talking about how they felt bad for me because I had spun out of the race, when all of a sudden one says, "He's driving back to the pits! Guess who is coming down pit lane, right now..." It was cool.

When I finished the race, we were running 12th. As soon as I crossed the finish line, I thought of Dad, and I started to cry. I'm crying right now, as I tell this story. I was happy and sad, all at the same time. I was happy to finish, but sad that the dream was coming to an end. And it wasn't just Dad I was there for, it was all the guys from my age group who were riding with me.

When I crashed that first day, I felt bad that I had let them all down. And the guys who stepped up to help me: Tony George, Bob Parker, and a couple of my short-track car owners and sponsors: Bill Biddle of Hannig Construction, and Jim Mills of Turbines, Inc. I really wanted to represent them all very well because they believed in me.

When I got out of the car, and all the fans were swarming around, I just forgot all about running at Eldora that night. Bill Biddle had a car there for me, but we just called over there and explained we couldn't make it. I didn't want to leave one minute too soon, because then the dream was over. I wanted to stay until the last person was gone, enjoying every possible moment.

The fans had been just awesome, all month. There were a lot of short-track fans there, and I'd like to think it was because I was in the race. A lot of people told me they had quit coming, but "since you came back we had to come back, too." That made me feel really good. It seemed like everywhere I turned, there were people wanting autographs, and I made sure to take every possible moment to accommodate them. We always had a long line of people at our garage, which just added to the great atmosphere.

The entire experience was wonderful, truly wonderful. Actually, if you'd look at our month, it was almost like a script right out of Hollywood. From not being there, to getting there late, then we crashed, then we made the show, then on race morning we walked out on the grid and saw that our car was lined up straddling the famous yard of bricks at the finish line. Then the spinout at the end, and finishing the race.

The only thing missing was a little sex and violence, and it would have been a great movie.

I ran Louden with PDM later in the year, but that was the end of my Indy Racing career. I didn't have the financial backing to put a full-time deal together.

Was I sad my Indy 500 deal was for only one race? Sure, but I have to be realistic. I got a chance to make the show, and that's far more than most other short-track guys get. So I've got to be happy with how it worked out. Besides, it would be wrong for me to bitch about anything...after such a wonderful experience and people were so generous with their help. As far as I'm concerned, I owe all of 'em, big time.

If I'm sad about anything, it's that the Indy Racing deal is becoming too much about big money, and not enough about racing. The American drivers are dwindling, once again. That's very sad, because I know there are a bunch of sprint car drivers who could run well at Indy.

I've ran both cars, and I can tell you with absolute sincerity that driving a sprint car takes a lot more ability than driving an Indy car. I mean it.

Want to try an experiment? How about this deal: put Tracy Hines in Roger Penske's car, give him some laps to get the feel of the car, build his confidence, and he could race with anybody in the country. Now, if you're talking road racing that's a different deal, but if you're talking ovals, damn right he could get it done. Him and a whole bunch of short-track guys.

If they put together an event with a million-dollar purse, and ran 50 laps at Indy in an Indy car and 50 laps at Eldora in a sprint car, and scored overall points, I guarantee the first five spots would be sprint car guys. They would learn Indy cars way, way faster than the Indy car guys would learn sprint cars. No doubt in my mind. None! Hey, my butt has been in both cars, and I believe I can speak with some authority here.

You name the best five Indy guys, and I'll pick maybe Tracy Hines, Brian Tyler, Dave Steele, Jason McCord, and J.J. Yeley, and put 'em against Luyendyk, Cheever, Jeff Ward, Gil DeFerran, and Helio Castroneves. I would be amazed if one Indy guy got in the top five in points.

I'm telling you, sprint cars are tough to drive. Very tough. It's way harder to learn and adjust. Even if you did it at IRP, Winchester, or Anderson, they'd be looking goofy for a while. It isn't just being on a dirt track, it's everything: sitting upright in the car, very little aero to help you, and having to drive the car with your ass.

Aw, man, there I go again, ranting about sprint cars. I can't help it. They're just the most bad-ass cars in the world. Believe me.

Getting to Indy was one of the most wonderful, important accomplishments in my career. No matter what happens from here on out, nobody can ever take that experience away from me. I'm forever indebted to all the people who made it happen: Tony George, Bob Parker, the guys at PDM, all our sponsors, and my friends who were there to share it with me. I'll never forget it.

Talking about Jack...

Only Jack Hewitt knows how it really felt in those last few minutes before six o'clock on the evening of May 16, 1998, Bump Day at the Indianapolis Motor Speedway. He was, after all, on the verge of realizing a lifelong dream by qualifying for the Indy 500. That dream had been passed along from one hard-ass racer to another, through the genes, because Don Hewitt once had an Indy dream, too. "Dad always wanted to get here," Jack said that day. It was a goal the son never abandoned, not even when the 500 was so dominated by foreign road-racers that the Speedway might as well have been on another planet.

Only Jack Hewitt knows how it really felt that day when six o'clock finally did come, and the Indy stewards signaled the end of qualifying with a single report from a starter's pistol, fired skyward, toward the heavens. Jack Hewitt looked skyward, too, thanking God and surely also thanking his only hero, who had died eleven months earlier. "All I could think of was Pop. I was like, 'Man, where's Dad?'"

Only Jack Hewitt knows how it really felt on the morning of that year's 500, once the belts were pulled tight and the visor went down and Jim Nabors boomed into "Back Home Again in Indiana," and there was nothing left to do but run the race.

And only Jack Hewitt knows how it really felt to run that whole 500, and to finish a more-than-respectable 12th, and then to have the space in front of his PDM team's garage fill up with so many short-track friends and fans that it looked like the pit area at Terre Haute. Three hours later, Hewitt was still there, mingling. "I think we'll just stay here awhile," he grinned, "and enjoy the moment.

Yup, only Hewitt knows how those moment really felt. But here is something I'm not sure he'll ever know: just what those moments felt like for the rest of us. And how on earth could you explain it to him? How do you tell a down-home hero like Jack how our spirits rose and fell with his that month? How we exalted over his first practice laps? How our hearts sank when he thumped the wall in practice? How we choked up when he made the show? How proud we were as we looked at his yellow car on that starting grid?

Hewitt was all over Indianapolis that month. He visited a half-dozen radio shows, made every possible autograph session, ran the Hoosier Hundred at the State Fairgrounds and raced a midget at the 16th Street Speedway. He explained it with an analogy: "You take a kid to the carnival, and he wants to ride every ride."

But I'll forever wonder: Will Jack Hewitt ever know how many of us he took along on that ride?

Bones Bourcier
Indianapolis
Editor at Large
Speedway Illustrated Magazine

20

FAIRY TALE NIGHT

Of all the tracks I've raced on throughout my career, I've got to say that Eldora is the most special. I've felt that way for a long time, even before I had an unbelievable night on September 26, 1998.

Eldora is just 35 miles from my home, so naturally I always wanted to show off in front of my friends. It's the first track I have a memory of; my dad took the first laps ever at Eldora Speedway when I was a small child. In many ways, that's where I grew up: Eldora.

To this day, I get all pumped up when I do well there. In later years it has been tough sometimes, to go there and run tenth, because that's the place early in my career where I was always very competitive. But after my wreck there in '93, and with the kids I race against getting more and more brave, it's been a lot more difficult to win there.

Throughout this book I've talked often about the 4-Crown Nationals at Eldora. That's one of the most special events all year, because it's such a neat concept: four different divisions and four feature events, all on the same weekend. It's one of my favorite weekends of the entire year.

It's pretty special for a driver to *make* all four features at the 4-Crown. It hasn't happened very often; just a few guys have done it. There are always tons of cars in every division, and it's very competitive. You can find yourself missing the show very easily.

1998 was one of the years I had a ride for every division. Qualifying and heats are on Friday night, and when we got there Saturday night I was already transferred to the feature event in all four divisions. That's a good feeling, because you don't have to worry about working your way out of the B-main; you can concentrate on race setup and have your mind in race mode right off the bat.

Okay, I'll level with you. I never dared to realistically dream about winning all four features on the same night. Every good race driver-and I mean *every* good race driver-believes he can win any race he's in. But four in one night...that's so extreme, so far-fetched, you kind of laugh when you think about it. Sure, I wanted to win all four. Wouldn't anybody? That's the whole point to *running* all four; to try and win.

One year I won two features, plus had a second-place finish. That's the best anybody had ever done. Several guys had won two, but I was still the best so far with the two firsts and one second.

Eldora was my home track; I felt like I was supposed to be better than anybody else there. Kind of like defending my home turf.

Let me tell you what happened to me at the 1997 4-Crown.

I was driving Bob Hampshire's car in the sprint car feature. Kevin Doty was leading, and I was running third. On lap 13, I was just coming out of turn two, challenging for second, when my safety belts came undone. At Eldora, of all places. I'm going down the front straightaway, starting to drop down to get off the race track. But something just took over in my mind, and I decided to stay out and race, with no seat belts.

I ran down Doty and won the race. It was very strange; it was like something was pushing me back in the seat, holding me in place. I never once felt loose in the car, or scared. It wasn't until after the race that I began to think about what I had just done.

What I did was completely stupid. No excuses. Running almost 20 laps at Eldora with no belts was the dumbest thing I've done in my career.

When the sprint car feature was over I had to get right into the modified to run the next feature. That was good, because it kept me from thinking about what had just happened. If I hadn't had to race again right away, I probably would have started crying, because I would have begun to realize just how incredibly dangerous that was. It was like a high-wire walk on a windy day with no net; if you survive, you're delirious.

I joked with people a few days later, and said, "When you think about it, I was gonna win, either way. I was either gonna win the feature or go see Dad."

Let me tell you about a night when I bent the rules at Findlay.

It was probably 1988 or so, and I was already qualified for the feature. A friend of mine, Billy Deaton, was starting in the back of the B-main and really wanted to get the car into the feature. He approached me and asked if I would drive the car in the B-main and try to finish fourth or better.

I said sure, I'd help him out. The problem was, it wasn't legal. However, I figured what they didn't know wouldn't hurt 'em. We went into his little motor home, and I put on his uniform and helmet. I walked directly from the motor home to his race car, and climbed in. Nobody could tell it was me, because I kept the helmet visor down, and he stayed in the motor home.

They pushed me down to the staging area, and just then Earl Baltes decided to water the track. So there I sat, nervous as hell that somebody would realize I was driving this car. Duke Cook walked over and was leaning into the car, thinking he was talking to Billy, telling him all the things he needed to do in order to get a transfer spot. I kept leaning down like I was looking at the driveline, and I never put my visor up. It seemed like I sat there forever.

Finally we started the race, and I got to fourth place pretty quickly. Everybody was running the bottom, or screwing around in the middle, and I was on the high side. Pretty soon I was third, then second, and figured I had better ride right there. Rick Ferkel was leading...and I just couldn't hold back. I won the race, and drove back to Billy's pit. I jumped out of the car and ran in his motor home. We switched uniforms real quick. Before we went outside, I told Billy that I saw something in his cooler.

"Look! Down here! Did you see that?" I said, pointing down into his cooler.

"Where? I don't see anything..." When he leaned in close, I grabbed him and ducked his face in the cooler. He came up spittin', saying, "What in the hell are you doing?"

"There you go," I said. "It looks like you just worked up a good sweat!"

Actually, my dad pulled that stuff before. When they ran the 500-lap sprint car races at Eldora in the 1960s, guys would pay him $25 to qualify their car. He was already in the race, but you know ol' Don. He said, "Shit, yeah, I will." He would put their car right up on the wall, throwing sparks with their back bumper all the way around the track. As soon as he would qualify one car, another offer came in, and he was right back out.

After a bunch of qualifying rounds, Earl Baltes came hurrying down to see him.

"Don," Earl said, "you can't be qualifying any more cars. That's it."

Although I was already qualified for all four features in 1998, I didn't feel all that optimistic on race night. Yeah, I was qualified, but I didn't qualify all that well, and felt like my midget deal was my weakest link. Not because Bob Parker didn't provide me with a good car; that's not what I mean. It's just I was starting in the sixth row, and I'm not a great midget racer anyway, going against guys who race midgets all the time. With the Steve Lewis cars and the Willoughby cars, I wasn't sure we could do it.

As soon as we pushed off in the midget feature, I was ecstatic to see what the track was doing. It was a really dry, slick black, with a good hump across the track from bottom to top. That's just a perfect surface for me, just perfect. Had the track been wet and heavy that night, I guarantee I wouldn't have had a great night. But it played perfectly to my strength, and we just took off and moved right up through the field. I passed Tracy Hines and Dave Darland to win the 25-lap race.

I'll tell you a secret I discovered that night at the 4-Crown. I can go to almost any race and see something; a year previous I watched Donnie Moran win the World 100 by running a completely different line than I had ever seen before. He drove into three and dived down to the middle, then drove to the wall. Normally at Eldora it's best to be right up on the wall, but with that slick track I decided to see if Donnie's line would work in an open-wheel car. Well, trust me: It worked. The midget was fast in that line, and I used that same line in all four features. I kept thinking some of the other guys would notice and try it themselves, but amazingly enough nobody did, all night long.

I was driving Bill Biddle's BWB sprint car, starting 10th in the feature. The car was really working, and I charged right up through the field. I saw Tony Elliott running the bottom, so I moved down there to try it, but it wasn't as good as the line I had been running, so I moved back up. Dave Darland was really coming on the top; if Dave had passed me he would have been very tough to beat because he was goin' pretty good. But once I got up there and got my rhythm going I could pull away from 'em pretty easy.

After we won that one, I was pretty confident about the modified feature. My modified program was pretty good at Eldora, and I had won a lot of races there. Almost to the point that I was starting to get cocky, because I banged off the wall on the first lap. I was in John Orr's car, and we started fourth and won pretty handily.

Believe it or not, at that point I felt like all the pressure was off me. Why? Because I had won three features, which was more than anybody else had ever done. Already I had one-upped Tony Stewart, Rich Vogler, Larry Rice, Steve Kinser, and Kenny Schrader. It put me into a zone where I had nothing more to prove. I was farther than anybody else had ever gone before; anything else was just gravy.

The great news, though, was that I was starting on the front row of the Silver Crown race. It was the 6R car, and Darrell Guiducci would be on the radio coaching me.

From the first moment of the Silver Crown race, I knew the car was perfect. Just perfect. I stayed calm, and Darrell kept telling me, "Darland's just a car-length off you," trying to get me to race as hard as I could. Dave wasn't really there the entire time; we were able to pull to a little lead several times. On the last lap I came up on Jerry Coons in the Potter car, and Darrell told me, "You've got it made, just follow Coons. Don't try to lap him."

When he told me that, I was going to lap him or else (Darrell told me afterward, shaking his head, "Right when I said that I *knew* you weren't going to listen to me.") I just gassed it up and passed Coons, and took the checkered flag.

I pulled to a stop on the front straightaway, and you couldn't have knocked the grin off my face with a two-by-four. There was a mob of people just going crazy, and when I came up out of the car, the crowd just roared so hard it shook the trees all over Darke County. It was an incredible scene, forever etched in my memory.

If I live to be a hundred years old, I'll never forget that moment.

The whole thing was unbelievable. Today, four years later, it's so unlikely, people who weren't there might say, "Aw, bullshit, nobody can win four races the same night."

One of the neat things was that for a surprising number of people, that was the first race they had ever attended. Maybe they came away with the idea that this happens all the time. You'd be surprised the number of people who say that to me.

A long time ago the Mataka Bros. in New Jersey won three midget races in one day with Mario Andretti. But all these years later, it would be hard for people to remember which three races he won. Winning the 4-Crown was different because it's an event, something a great number of people know about.

It took so much luck, so much good fortune to do it, I don't want to discount that. It is unlikely, obviously, because when you look at the caliber of guys racing the 4-Crown all these years, and nobody had been able to win all four, that tells you something right there. Plus, I think the man upstairs had a lot to do with it, too.

I am so proud of that night. I'm proud of the job I did, sure; but I'm very proud of the car owners and mechanics of those four cars, because they gave me everything I needed to win. They were as big a part of that as I was. I got the glory, but they were right there with me.

When did it sink in, knowing I won all four? I don't know if it's ever fully sunk in. It will probably take a few years before I fully appreciate the meaning of what happened, and just how special it was. Probably after I quit, and I'm sitting around one night reflecting and reminiscing, I'll start to cry when I think of that night.

I can tell you this: At the moment I didn't really grasp it. Sure, I was pumped up, and excited to win the Silver Crown feature, but in the heat of everything, with all the people and noise, it was just so hard to believe.

Now I go to the 4-Crown and I just grin, and think, "How in the world did I do that?"

That night after the photos and ceremonies were all finished, I pulled a chair out by where all four cars were parked on the front straightaway, and signed autographs for probably two hours. It was a magical ending to fairy tale night.

Snow White and Cinderella got nothin' on me.

Talking about Jack...

I kind of grew up around Jack Hewitt, but Don Hewitt was my hero first. Jack was just a kid in those early days, but a funny thing happened along the way: As I spent more and more time with Jack, he became my hero and my buddy.

It was neat traveling with the Hewitts, because every day there was something fun and interesting going on. A lot of people would never believe the childhood Jack came from, but he made a decision to step up and make something of himself. At the same time, he's very loyal to people from every stage of his life.

As a racer, I think Jack was in the wrong era. He's made of the same stuff as Hurtubise and Foyt: hard-charging, blood-n-guts racers. If he had come along earlier, he could have had a lot of years at Indy. If he'd come along later, he'd be a great Winston Cup racer.

He's obviously changed a little bit in the last few years. He's mellowed some. He's a hardheaded son of a bitch who will only see things his way, right or wrong. But he'll also fend for the underdog; if he sees anybody being picked on, he's right there to help them.

When you're a buddy of his, you're a buddy for life. I'm not around him every day like I used to be, but even when we've been apart for six months, when we see each other within five minutes we're just as close as ever.

Probably one of the hardest things is to convince people that all the wild, crazy stories about him are true. He's led such a fun, exciting, interesting life, most people might not believe it could really happen like that. But that's Hewitt: always over the edge.

Donald "Bounce" Ryder
Knoxville, Tennessee
formerly of Pleasant Hill, Ohio

21

FISHING

When I like something, I tend to like it a whole lot.

I don't play golf, or softball, or basketball, and I don't watch football on TV. Most of my life the only thing I've cared about is racing, and obviously I've just gone whole hog over that.

But a few years ago I discovered something I like almost as much as racing: fishing. I can't explain it, but man, I love to fish.

I'm pretty good at it, too. I'm way better than my fishing buddies; I tell 'em that all the time.

Grandpa Hewitt was a fisherman, so that's probably where I got it.

When my dad lost his eye in May 1971, he took the $5,000 insurance check and bought a 21-foot Chris-Craft aluminum boat. I have a vivid memory of that boat: It is September 1971, and I'm home on leave from the army. It's 6:30 in the morning, raining, and we're on Rattlesnake Island, up near Put-in-Bay on Lake Erie. Rod Stewart is singing "*Maggie May*" on the radio, and Dad is bringing a bass in. Thirty-one years have passed since that moment, but I remember it like it was yesterday.

Of course, it didn't end peacefully; Dad and our buddy Frog (Mike Laughman) ended up getting drunk and jumping in the lake, and I had to fish both of 'em back out.

The funny thing about my attraction to fishing: I don't care much to eat fish.

I never thought I would like fishing, because to me it looked like you're just sitting there watching a bobber. I warmed up to it gradually, and ended up owning a small boat we used to fish for walleye around home. Still, I didn't like to just sit aimlessly in the boat; I liked to chase the fish a little bit, stay active.

I've always loved the water; ever since those days as a boy on the Great Miami River. I've been certified to scuba dive, and I love snorkeling.

Some years ago my Troy buddies would get together every Tuesday night to fish at Bobby Snead's gravel pit. We'd fish for carp, catfish, whatever, with a big campfire and lots of bullshitting. The other guys would drink beer and we had a great time. Instead of hanging out at a bar, we hung out at the gravel pit.

One night we kept moving because we weren't catching anything. Each time we moved, we started a new fire. After a while it looked like an Indian village, because a bunch of campfires lit up the night sky. We probably did the Tuesday-night deal for a good three or four years in the early 1980s.

Then one year Bobby's brother invited him to join a group of guys on a week-long fishing trip in Canada. Bobby wasn't keen on the idea, and I'd have to agree, because spending an entire week with his brother-Whip-would be pretty taxing. Plus, the other guys who went with Whip, that just wasn't Bobby's crowd. But Bobby finally gave in and went with 'em, and when he came back, why, you would have thought that he had ridden with Columbus to discover the New World.

Canada, Canada, Canada, that's all he talked about for six months. Bobby was just a Tuesday-night fisherman like the rest of our group, yet he was all fired up about fishing in Canada. While he was up there he saw a bush pilot across the road from where they were fishing, and asked the guy, "What would it cost to fly me around to look at this place from the air?" It wasn't a lot, so he said, "Let's go!" He had a ball, and he just raved about how beautiful it was.

He was telling Rick Mohler and me that we just *had* to make the trip next year, and I was thinking, "Give me a break...I'm not going to Canada to fish."

He kept on. "Jack, I'm telling you, it's great..."

Well, we went to Canada the next year. It was me, Bounce (Donald Ryder), and Mohler. We rented a boat and bought some cheap rain suits, and caught some fish. But it was a little 16-foot boat where you sit in the middle, with no trolling motor; just too small to be comfortable. Our rain suits didn't hold up, and we got soaked, but we still had fun.

It was a good enough time that we said we'd try again next year. Well, we've gone back almost every year since, and now it's such a tradition for our group, if one of the guys died I think we'd have him stuffed and take him with us, because nobody wants to miss.

The second year we knew more about how to prepare. We bought a flat-bottom boat with a V-8 motor, stripped the boat and put a platform on top, doubled the plywood, installed carpet, and made it pretty nice. We called it the Queen Mary Party Barge.

People would laugh at us when we pulled in with that boat, but then they'd see us fishing. We could outrun 'em on the lake, and we could go anywhere because of the flat bottom. We had a ball.

Part of the fun of writing a book is that you can tell tales on all your friends. Here's one on Bounce.

Bounce is a big ol' boy, and he's not really an outdoorsman. One of the things I learned when I was a kid is that sometimes you've got to crap out in the woods. So you find a log, hang your butt over the side, and get it done. Well, we're in Canada, miles from town, and Bounce has a nature call. But he's a city boy, and he's never been in this situation before. I explained the procedure, but he didn't execute the plan very well.

A little while later we're in the boat, and Bounce stands up. I can see a big dark spot soaking through his britches, located in a place where you can pretty much speculate what happened.

"Uh, Bounce, did you have a little trouble taking a dump?" I asked him.

"What do you mean?" he said.

"You shit your pants," I said.

(Hey, how else you gonna say it?)

Bounce is a real respectable guy, and he's all worried about people knowing what happened. So make sure you don't tell anybody.

I like to fish for smallmouth bass. They're like a largemouth on steroids. They're not as big, but they definitely put up more of a fight.

They say a bass has a brain the size of a pea, yet they still outsmart me pretty consistently. I'm afraid to find out how big my brain is, because I can't catch that fish with the pea-size brain.

I like to set goals and work toward them, things like running Indy and winning all four races at the 4-Crown. I've done those things, so now my goal is to catch a 10-pound bass. I'm at a disadvantage because I don't use live bait, and that's what most trophy smallmouth are caught on. So

I have to outsmart 'em, and so far I haven't outsmarted anything larger than a six-pounder.

I use spinner bait, because I have no patience for worms or anything like that. Besides, I feel bad watching that worm draw up and die when I put the hook in him. I'm going to throw the fish back anyway, so why should I kill a worm just to throw a fish back?

In the past I didn't care if I caught anything or not, it was just fun. I'm a little more serious now, because I like catching bass. I'll fish the rivers around home, and the lakes and gravel pits, but I haven't found anything that compares to Canada in terms of catching fish. The closest thing I've found is Don Smith's place over in Terre Haute. You don't go fishing there; you go catching.

In Canada we stay about five or six miles from town, and it's just a beautiful wilderness. There are bald eagles there, and you'll see them swoop down on the water and snatch a fish. One time we saw an eagle carrying a snake. Bob Hampshire and some guys once watched a bear swim from one island to the other. Deer, moose; the place is just teeming with wildlife. My cousin once saw a huge woodpecker. There are rock formations all around, and the place is just filled with an awesome beauty.

One day everybody was taking a nap, and Bounce and I went out by the nearby island and probably caught 50 smallmouth bass in that area within a couple of hours. It was probably our greatest day fishing, ever.

One really nice thing about those trips to Canada is that I've been able to build a close friendship with my cousin, Billy Emerick. Billy was raised in a tough, racially mixed neighborhood, with some difficult circumstances. His mother left the family when Billy was in seventh grade, and his dad went to prison for shooting a guy. Billy and his family, they had nothing, and he was forced to live with friends all the way through high school. Yet he made something out of his life. After he graduated from high school he got a student loan and put himself through college. Today he's a schoolteacher. I admire Billy, very much. I think the world of him.

We're always laughing at each other. He is smart as a whip, but has very little common sense. None. Yet he is always correcting my grammar, teasing me about how little I know about many things.

One time we were on the Queen Mary Party Barge, and the shaft connecting the motor to the propeller was bent. It was wobbling badly, so I pulled in to the bank. I walked around on shore till I found two trees that were close together. I carried the shaft up to the trees, wedged the shaft in between, and leveraged it until it was straight.

Billy was amazed. "Well, I've never seen anything like that in my life!" he marveled. Something so simple, and he couldn't believe it.

For many years after our school days Billy and I had no contact with each other. Bounce was teaching school in Troy; he was a band teacher. He ran into Billy and said, "You ever go out and see Jack?"

Billy said, "No, I don't mess with any of my family."

"You ought to go see him. He'd like to see you."

"Nah," Billy said, "he's into all that macho fightin' and drinkin'..."

Bounce told him, "Billy, you don't know Jack very well. He's not like that."

Eventually Billy and I got reconnected, and we began spending more time together. We're different in our strengths, but we get along really well. Billy makes the trip to Canada with us, and we also go to Maryland each year during spring break to visit my uncle Dallas.

You know all those great stories about racers abusing rental cars? It happens with boats, too, but it wasn't intentional.

Rick Mohler and I rented a boat, and we're out in the lake. We decided to move, so we fired up the engine and took off. We're going along, and-BAM!-we hit a rock. Then another, and another. We pulled the motor up, and the prop was bent all to hell.

One of the blades was gone, so we knocked another blade off to try and balance it. We take off again, and-BAM!-we kept hitting-BAM!-rocks. Finally we found our spot and stopped.

"Drop the anchor!" somebody yells.

After a pause, we hear, "It's already down!"

The anchor was a big hunk of concrete, and the rope was just exactly the right length from the bow to-you guessed it-the prop. We weren't hitting rocks; we were hitting our own anchor.

We didn't say much, and quietly returned the boat. The next year Rick went to rent another boat, and gave him his name at the desk. A mechanic nearby raised his eyebrows, and said, "What was the name?"

"Mohler," he replied.

The mechanic went to the back, and came walking out with our chewed-up prop from the year before.

"This look familiar?" he asked.

They made us pay for last year's prop before they'd rent us another boat. Unreasonable suckers, weren't they?

We've caught some monster fish in Canada. One of the kids in our group caught a muskie that was 52 inches long, and Hamp caught a 44-inch muskie. My cousin Billy also caught a muskie that was 40 inches long. They've also got some gigantic northern pikes there, great big slimy fish.

Lots of guys like catching those big ones, but not me. I prefer my smallmouths.

I don't just fish in Canada, of course. I spend some time each winter in Florida, and I'll fish a lot down there. I remember another good story I can tell, this one on my friend Tim Clark.

We were down at Jack Nowling's place, and Jody came down for a few days. Don and Donnie Hewett were also there with their boat. I had to run Jody to the airport, and I made plans to meet the guys on the lake when I got back. When I got back to 'em, I pulled alongside and Tim Clark was stepping from one boat to the next. As he was stepping, his legs were spread from one to the other, and he got this funny look on his face.

"Uh-oh," he said.

"What's the matter?"

"I just shit my pants."

Well, of course I was understanding and sympathetic, and I wouldn't want anyone to think I teased him during a difficult time. Hell, yes, I teased him! Like he ain't never been teased before!

A few weeks later we were going to Phoenix, and somehow the guys at 6R Racing heard about Clarkie's accident (I can't imagine how they heard, can you?). When Tim got off the plane, Darrell Guiducci and the guys had a box of Pampers waiting on him. The 6R guys have no mercy when it comes to things like that.

Let that be a lesson to you: If you're ever fishing and you have an accident like that, don't tell Jack Hewitt about it.

I've really enjoyed spending time with Donnie and Don Hewett in Florida. We met many years ago, and they spell their name differently, but those guys are like family to me. Actually, maybe they *are* family to me; they've traced their heritage back to three brothers: One spelled his name "Hewett," another "Hewitt," and the third one "Huett." Amazing.

Donnie and his dad have a great relationship, much like the relationship I had with my dad. Donnie is my age, and even with the age difference Don and I are great friends as well.

One morning we were headed for Camp Blanding, south of Jacksonville. We were towing the boat, and we're a little ways from home when all of a sudden Don says, "Oh, shoot, I forgot my boots." He had his raincoat, but forgot his boots.

We drove on another three or four miles, and I said, "Hell, that's nothing, Don...I forgot the keys to the boat."

We were well over halfway there, too far to turn back, so we kept going. We could use the electric trolling motor, so we were still okay.

The electric motor was doing fine out there, and we were fishing and having fun, when it started to sprinkle. Then the rains came, and we were almost all the way across the lake. Then the wind picked up...and my little trolling motor wasn't strong enough to push the boat against the wind. We were finally beached, about 20 feet from shore.

We decided Donnie would walk around the lake to the truck, and call somebody to bring us the keys. I put Donnie on my shoulders and carried him to the bank, and then I went back and got Don. I felt responsible because I forgot the keys, so I wanted to at least try to help those guys stay dry.

Don and I walked around on shore for a while, scouting the area. Luckily the rain had stopped, but the wind was howling, kicking up whitecaps on the lake. It was getting dark, so we found some shelter from the wind, and got some logs together for a fire. I went back out to the boat for a jar of oil to help get the fire going, and also for some food and drinks for supper. Pretty soon it's well past nine o'clock.

"Looks like Donnie might not come back and get us tonight," I said.

"By God, he'd *better* come back and get his dad," said Don. "I don't care what he does for you, but he'd better come back and get his dad!"

A while later we're still sitting there, and we've given up on Donnie.

"Don," I said, grinning, "you know, I read in an outdoor magazine that to keep warm and survive, you should take off all your clothes and lay against each other to conserve your body heat."

Don looked at me, real serious, and said, "I think we'd have to be here a couple of days before we go there."

Donnie eventually brought his dad's boat and the keys to my boat that night, and we finally got back home. Another day, another adventure.

These days I have a Team Sailfish boat. When I saw that boat I fell in love with it. It's pretty much maintenance free, and that fits me just fine.

One of the benefits of my situation is that when your job is two or three days of racing each week, that leaves four or five days for fishing. I still go a lot, every time I feel like it. I'll go to Bobby Snead's gravel pit, or the Great Miami River, or the Stillwater River. I'm located between two rivers that are seven miles apart, so it's never hard to find someplace to fish.

Fishing is very relaxing. You think about your lures and things, but you also think about chassis setup, things like that. Tires, last week's race, it all runs through my mind. That's if I'm by myself; if I'm fishing with somebody, I'm trying to out-fish him. I'll help you and show you what I'm using, but I still want to catch more fish than you do.

Sometimes the other guys don't want to fish with me because I'm hard-core about it. One evening Billy Emerick and I went to Bobby's gravel pit, and around midnight he was ready to go home. So I took him to shore and dropped him off, then I went back out on the lake. He came back the next morning, and I'm still out there in my boat, fishing away. I dozed off a couple of times, but I fished pretty much all night.

As much as I love to fish, I'm not quite to the point where I enjoy fishing more than racing. Maybe someday I'll feel that way, I don't know. I'm a lucky guy, because the two things I enjoy the most, I've been able to do a lot of both.

Say, you don't know where I could catch a 10-pound bass, do you?

Talking about Jack...

I started off with Jack Hewitt as one of his sponsors, but I quickly noticed that we had moved past that relationship: we were friends. It's never been about money with Jack; it's about a bunch of guys having fun at the races and trying to achieve their goals. Don Murphy told me a long time ago, "You've got to go to a race with Jack, because it's the most fun you could ever have." He's right. Sure, there's pressure at the race track, and you want to win, but somehow you have a great time, even if you missed the race. Jack is very competitive and he doesn't like to lose, but he's never down in the mouth.

Jack is a very driven individual who plays this tough guy routine, but who is actually very soft-hearted. He's a very accomplished racer, and he's well-liked by friends and foes alike.

He's a tough nut to crack. He is very direct, and he's not a guy who will beat around the bush. I've never gotten into an argument with Jack, because I knew I couldn't win it. Yet he really fights for the underdog, he's willing to help anybody.

It's neat to watch him at the race track when a young racer comes by and asks for advice or help. Jack will drop whatever he's doing, even if he's under pressure himself to make the show, and take whatever time that kid needs.

You'd have to look long and hard to find another Jack Hewitt. He's a special racer, and a special friend.

Randy Steenbergen
Print Communications, Inc.
Indianapolis, Indiana

22

RECENT YEARS

My racing activity has slacked off a little bit in recent years. Through the 1980s and early 1990's, I consistently raced 100-plus features every year. But I've seen my schedule begin to change. The biggest factor is just less variety; I haven't gone to Australia since 1993, and I don't race late models or midgets very often.

Still, I've been very, very fortunate in my career. It's a fact of life that as you get older it becomes more difficult to get quality rides. For example, look at my dad: He never officially retired; he just got to where he couldn't get competitive rides any more.

But I've had several guys in recent years who still believed in me, and I'm proud to say I've won some races for just about all of 'em. Of course, I don't win as often as I used to, and certainly not as often as I'd like. But I can still sneak in and grab one every so often.

After I quit Bob Hampshire at the end of the 1997 season, I wound up driving for Bill Biddle. Bill owns Hannig Construction in Terre Haute, and he's fielded race cars for several years under the banner of BWB Racing.

Brian Hayden was driving one of Bill's cars in 1998, but crashed at Winchester in the USAC opener and was sidelined a couple of weeks. I was without a ride, and Bill called and asked if I'd like to drive his car at a race in Wisconsin.

I finished fourth up there, and Brian wasn't healed as quickly as he had hoped, so I stayed in the car a few weeks. When Brian was able to get back into the car, Bill decided to add a third car to his program. So it was Brian, Derek Davidson, and myself in the BWB cars.

A lot of people might take Bill Biddle the wrong way. He's like a lot of guys with money who come into the sport: He thought winning was about how much money you could spend. He didn't understand that with three cars it's no different than any other business: You've got to have the right people. The mistakes he made early on were just those of a guy who didn't know his way around yet.

Bill and I can sit and talk about a lot of different things and we're just fine. Some people might think he's distant, or cold, but he's not. He's a good guy, and I like him. He's been around the sport long enough now to learn about things that are important, so if he is smart enough not to make the same mistakes twice, he'll do fine. The guy is very successful in the construction business, so he's certainly no dummy.

I think I got along better with Bill than his other drivers. Mostly because he and I are closer in age, I suppose. He might walk up and tell me to do something stupid, like wash my car off, and I'd laugh at him and say, "Kiss my ass! Go tell those kids to do that." He'd look at me and grin and walk away. If it made him mad, he never let on.

But the kids would do that: wash the car, wipe the wheels, whatever. He intimidated them.

One day we're at Salem and Derek Davidson says to me, real quiet, "Did you hear I might be getting fired?"

"No, I haven't heard a thing about it."

A half-hour later the entire team is standing there, and I say, "Hey, Bill, are you firing Derek?" Man, Derek couldn't find a rock to crawl under; based on the look on his face, he was wanting to.

Bill just said, "No, I'm not planning on getting rid of him."

Derek felt better, but I tried to tell him later, "Look, if you're worried about something like that, go to Bill and ask him!"

Bill likes to intimidate everybody; he rules his company with an iron fist, and he's tried to run his racing team the same way. That just doesn't work. I think Bill has a hard time getting close to people because of that. But when you get to know him, he's actually a good guy.

I left Biddle after that 1998 season, and went racing with Dick Newkirk. Dick is a really nice guy, kind of quiet. He had Keith Holsapple and Dallas working on the car, and Keith and I really get along well. I brought a tire deal and a shock deal, which made Dick happy, and also brought Print Express along as a sponsor.

I had a lean year with Dick in 1999. We did have some good runs; we won three non-winged races, including a USAC race at Lawrenceburg. But we also struggled at times.

Probably the one that was hardest came at the 4-Crown in September. After sweeping all four races there a year earlier, we missed the show in the sprint car. Man, that was a bitter pill to swallow. I ran second in the Silver Crown race in the 6R Racing car, which made it a little easier to take. Still...boy, I'd rather forget about that deal.

Really, though, the biggest drawback to Dick's program was that they weren't able to race as much as I'd like. They all had jobs, and it's hard to get away to go racing as often as I needed. I understand that.

But, hey, I still do this to pay the bills. Jody doesn't work outside the home, and we live on my racing earnings. So I had to make a tough decision at the end of 1999, because I had to find a ride that could keep me racing more.

I wound up going back with Bill Biddle, and bringing Keith as my mechanic. I went through the 2000 season in that deal, and in 2001 Johnny Beaber came over as the mechanic.

I forgot to mention I got hurt again in July 1998, just a few weeks after I ran Indy. We were at Indianapolis Raceway Park, and I got tangled up with another car in my heat race, and we hit the wall a ton. A torsion tube or something came back and smashed through my visor, and just tore the hell out of my face, around my eye and eye socket. I'm extremely lucky it didn't take my head off; after a whole bunch of stitches I was as good as new.

The crash was on a Wednesday night, and two nights later we had a Silver Crown race at Terre Haute. I was all stitched up, but I surprised everybody there when I set quick time. I eventually crashed in the feature but didn't have any injuries.

I just remembered a funny story from that week. My eye looked terrible, because I had a ton of stitches, and because of taking my helmet on and off, I couldn't cover them with a bandage. All I could do was keep ointment on 'em and keep 'em clean. I looked like hell, I know.

Two days after Terre Haute I'm running a sprint car at Kokomo, getting ready to climb in for my heat race. A writer comes walking into the trailer-the same guy helping me with this book-and he leans in real close and looks at all those stitches.

"Man, Jack," he said. "How you doin'?"

"I'm fine," I said. "I just try to keep 'em clean and I'll be all right."

"Does it hurt?" he asked.

"Shit, man, I unplugged that wire a long time ago," I bragged.

"Jack," he said, "I hate to tell you this, but that's not the only wire that's been unplugged for some time."

Smart-ass.

Actually, 1998 was a weird year in many respects. Sure, I had two enormous highlights: running Indy and sweeping the 4-Crown. But those two things are so...huge, I almost wish I could have spread 'em out over a few years, to maybe savor and enjoy them more. To have the two biggest things in your career happen within four months of each other, it's kind of difficult to fully appreciate them.

I had some pretty good runs with Biddle. We won a few races, including a USAC feature at Sun Prairie, Wisconsin, in June 2001. Still, I felt like we weren't going in the right direction, and two weeks after the Wisconsin win we split up, and I teamed up with Dennis Kaser.

Dennis has become one of the neatest people I've been with. He and his wife, Chris, are from Lima, and he spent a lot of years helping the Nickles Bros. on their car.

Dennis is definitely a "hands-on" car owner. He's a hard-working guy who is out there sweating like a dog, working on that race car till all hours of the night. I think the world of him, and Chris, too. We call her "Kitten" and both of 'em are just a blast to be around.

The Sun Prairie deal, by the way, was a neat story. USAC had a sprint/midget doubleheader that night, with a $50,000 bonus to any driver who could win both features. The midget feature came first, which Dave Darland won. Then came the sprint car feature, which I won with Darland finishing second. Dave was telling me later, "Man! I should have talked to you before the race, and had you pull over for me so I could win that 50 grand!"

My suspicion is that Dave didn't figure I was a threat to win, so he didn't talk with me before the race. Nobody was worried about us, the old fellow on the front row. I know it would be hard to back off and let somebody pass you, but for $25,000 I would have let him by.

Dave says, "If I'd known you would've let me by, I'd have given you four or five thousand."

"Yeah, I'll bet you would!" I said. "There's only one way to figure that kind of a deal, big boy...HALF! That's what you get when you make a deal like that, HALF! That's the only kind of deal out there."

Actually, I should have got first place money PLUS $25,000. Next time, maybe he'll ask me in advance.

When you bounce around and win less frequently, it's hard to adjust. You never like not winning, or not being competitive. And I know I don't win as much. But there are still times when the track is just right, and I can give 'em as much trouble as I ever did.

You can say what you want, and deny it, but age does catch up with you. Whether it's reflexes or brains or whatever, the kids are usually going to win out. On the tracks today, with the cars like we have today, the bravest guys are usually going to beat the guys with brains. Even on the dry-slick tracks, the kids are learning how to do well on those tracks.

So it's a challenging deal. You're still racing and trying to win, because you're not ready to give up. That means a lot, that you're still out there competing.

Truthfully, I don't have to win to have fun. I learned a long time ago that you lose a lot more than you win. The closest exception is Steve Kinser, and he still loses more than he wins. That's just the reality of sprint car racing; I don't care who you are.

So you have to learn how to be a graceful loser. If you're not a graceful loser, you'll have no fans. Win, lose, or draw, I'm always there for the fans. Then again, maybe you can look at it this way: win, lose, or draw, the fans are there for me. It makes no difference if I win or lose, they still come down after the races and I'll talk with them the same way.

It comes full circle, because when I was winning a lot I gave a lot of attention to the fans. Now they're there for me, to give some of it back. Not money, that's not what I mean. I'm talking about love and attention. They still look at me like I'm somebody special, like it's special when we can hang out together. They're a fan only at that first race; after that they're a friend. When you can still get out and renew your old friendships, that's pretty cool.

One thing I was able to do in the 1990s was run the Little 500 sprint car race a few times. That's a cool deal, with 33 sprint cars on a quarter-mile track for 500 laps. Awesome! That track is so small, so tight. I had seen the race before-Dad was leading there in 1970 when he crashed-and had always thought about running it. I got the chance with Hamp in 1991, when we qualified 11ᵗʰ and finished 24ᵗʰ after breaking a u-joint. We came back in 1996 and finished 24ᵗʰ again, after having suspension trouble.

My best run there was 1997 in Bob Parker's car. I ran sixth, making 487 laps. That deal is two hours of non-stop traffic, and I love driving traffic. So I had a ball.

I've probably had my best runs over the past few years in John Orr's modified. I realize the level of competition isn't quite as strong as in, say, a USAC sprint car race, but it's still a rush to win.

Hey, you never get tired of winning. Never, ever, ever.

I still think of myself as a sprint car driver. Absolutely. Sure, I still run most of the Silver Crown races, but they'll only race 10, 15 times a year, not nearly enough to earn a living. You've also got to race other things to get the laps you need to stay sharp.

The last few years have been an adjustment, and I've tried to be graceful and patient as my career has changed. It's hard, though. I think any man would admit that if you've been on top, it's pretty tough to be anywhere else. And I was fortunate enough to be on top for a long while. For that I'm very grateful.

Talking about Jack...

Jack Hewitt is a helluva guy. He was always my hero, and it was exciting to race with him. We've had some good ones.

He's very generous about offering his help to other racers. When I began running at Eldora, Jack came to me and offered some good advice on how to get around the place. I didn't even have to ask; he came and offered. His advice on how to drive the track, race setups, things like that, were really a help to me.

He's a super-competitive man, and if you cross his path you've got to be careful because if you do him wrong, he's going to come tell you about it. No doubt about it! But if you run him clean, you'll never have a problem, even when you beat him. I'm really proud of the fact that through all our years racing with each other, he and I never once had a problem.

When I was first starting out, Jack was really in his heyday, just an awesome racer. He could do things with the car that most guys just couldn't. You could tell he had it under control (most of the time!) and it wasn't a fluke. If you watched him long enough, you couldn't help but be impressed.

He did cost me a bunch of money at Sun Prairie one night, though. I finished second to him in a sprint car race that would have paid me a $50,000 bonus if I'd won. A lot of people have asked me why I didn't talk with him before the race to make arrangements for him to "help" me get the bonus. The truth is, I didn't have enough time between races to talk to anyone. Plus, Jack is such a racer, he wasn't out there for the money, anyway. I don't think he would have been interested in any deals; he was there to win the race. You know, if I could have gotten close enough, I probably would have given Jack a big ol' slider if that's what it took to win. I wouldn't have hurt him; I'd never do that. But maybe bumped him just enough to win. I would have taken an ass whippin' for 50 grand! But he was just faster than me, and I couldn't catch him.

I've sure got some good memories of racing with Jack. It's been fun, all along the way.

Dave Darland
Walton, Indiana

23

2 MUCH FUN

I've said it a million times: racing is all about the fans. For all these years, the highlight for me has been meeting people and signing autographs back in the pits after the races. Even when you've had a bad night, those people just pick you right up and by the time everybody is gone, you feel really good.

A lot of guys say that, but I mean it from my heart. For a long time I wished I could give more back to the fans, to help them feel closer and more in touch with sprint car racing. But how do you do that? A couple of years ago, I got an idea.

I was over in Indy one afternoon, and I stopped by the PDM Racing garage on the west side. Those guys are a blast; they're goof balls, just totally fun to be around, always clowning around. We're in their shop, and they're telling me they're gonna build a two-seater Indy car. I don't know if they were serious or just joking; this was before anyone had actually built one. They were saying that they were going to have to get Jimmy Kite to drive it, because he's the only one with short enough legs to fit.

After I left the shop I was driving back to Troy, with the radio down and just thinking. I had seen the Richard Petty deal, a ride-along program with a stock car. I thought, "You know what? The neatest race car on the face of the earth has got to be a sprint car. It's just got to be."

Some time earlier, I had urged Larry Moore to build a two-seater late model, and he had C.J. Rayburn build him one. Then Jerry Russell made that two-seater race car that looked like a roadster. In my mind I started thinking about a two-seater sprint car, and how I would build it. I would need to do this, and this, and this, thinking about how I'd lay it out. But I didn't know exactly what I wanted.

I called Johnny Beaber, who has a successful chassis building business up in Gibsonburg, Ohio, and told him what I wanted: I wanted the second seat right behind mine, and we needed to lengthen the car to add that seat back there. By the time he and I sat down, we had a car there, in our minds, and we figured up how much room the extra seat would take. We figured about 20 inches.

I had talked with Johnny on a Thursday night, and told him I'd be up there on Monday. When I got there he kind of had it sketched out on a legal pad. The next morning, we went downstairs and started bending tubing and putting it together. One thing I noticed right away, he had the roll cage real tall, he had based it on the length. I didn't like that; it just didn't look right. So we cut the roll cage down about four inches (it's still higher than a normal car, but you don't really notice it).

We worked maybe 12 hours that Tuesday, and the next several days, too. Beaber knew how to build a sprint car, so that was no problem. By the time I left Friday, we had it pretty much finished. Tony Beaber was a big help, and Johnny's wife, Pam, was right out there with us, getting it all together.

So I was now the proud owner of a two-seater sprint car. I was excited. Absolutely fired up.

I tried to make it as close to a real sprint car as I possibly could. I put in a full 410-inch engine; a 410 is the same engine that makes sprint cars the most bad-ass deal going.

People ask me if it's different to drive, and I tell them it isn't. It's a little longer, yes, but it's not all that different. They ask if it's like a Silver Crown car, but I tell 'em I don't know, because I've never had a 410 in a Silver Crown car. It actually handles better than a Silver Crown car, I think. It's a longer wheelbase, but you don't have that 70-gallon fuel tank sitting behind you. And our motor is a lot farther forward than any pavement Silver Crown car. It's pretty different.

The car works really, really well. I wouldn't be afraid to run it at a Silver Crown race. Just make me a long, skinny tank, and I think I'd outrun 'em. It would be about 10 inches longer than the other Silver Crown cars.

It drives off the corner so hard...if it wasn't so long, I know I could get it to do a wheelie. And the torsion bars I put in there, I use bars that will keep it real loose, because I need to be able to spin it out if I have to. I always want to be able to slide; I don't want it to be hooked up so tight that it might bicycle. So I use, I think it's a 1050 bar in the right front and a 1075 bar in the right rear, which as a setup is just unheard of. I've got an inch on the left front, which really loosens the car up to get into the corner, and I've got a inch-and-a-quarter on the left rear, which loosens it up more.

One of these days, I'd like to set the car up for speed just to see how fast it would go. We took it to Gas City for a test-and-tune day, and I was taking some people for rides in between hot laps. Finally I wanted to go out in the hot-lap session, without a passenger, and I passed several cars. I wanted people to see that it was a real race car, capable of going fast. I got to thinking on the way home, I've got a car that's kind of a play car, and these guys are out there with their serious sprint cars, and we're passing them. I probably made those guys feel bad. I didn't like that. But I did want people to understand that it is a real race car, with just a little longer wheelbase. That's the only difference.

I wanted people to get out of the car knowing it is as realistic as I could possibly make it. Dave Blaney also has a two-seater to give people rides, but his has a grab bar for the passenger. Well, I didn't want mine to be a roller-coaster ride. So I put a steering wheel back there, so the rider can grab that wheel and get the feeling that they're actually driving the car. They aren't, of course; the wheel isn't hooked up to anything. But you'd be surprised how much realism that gives the rider.

The very first rider was Page Jones, at the Chili Bowl in 2000. Page was a great racer who suffered a bad head injury at Eldora in 1994 and has fought back from disability. He still struggles with some things, but he's come a long, long way. He hadn't been in a race car since his accident, and I thought it was only fitting that he was my first rider.

If you look at photos of us during his ride, it's amazing: our arms are in the same position, because he's driving with me. It was instinctive, he was doing what came natural to him. It was so neat.

His dad, Parnelli Jones, was there with us, and when we finished the ride and drove back up to the pits, there was a huge crowd there. Everyone was crying, and Page was so wound up, so cranked up. Randy Steenbergen of Print Express is my sponsor, and back in the rider's compartment Randy put a sticker of a "Panic Button," kind of as a joke. Randy asked Page if he used that button, and it was so funny, Page kind of slurs his words, and he just grinned and said, "I wore it out!"

In my whole racing career, probably the greatest compliment I've ever received came from Parnelli that night. It was neater than any award I've ever received. I told Parnelli, "Parnelli, I'll tell you right now, I wouldn't do anything to hurt Page. I was smart about it, and I didn't do anything that might have hurt him." Parnelli just looked at me and said, "I wouldn't let Page ride with just anybody." Man, you talk about a compliment. I had a big "S" on my chest, it was all swelled up. Here is Parnelli Jones telling me that about his kid. It makes my hair stand up just thinking about it.

When Page got out of the car, he was telling me, real excited, "You drive just like me, the way you set the car with the throttle and stuff." I kind of blew it off, and ignored it. We were back in the pits five minutes later, and Page is pretty sharp, he doesn't forget what he said. "I'm telling you, Jack, you drive just like I do. Identical!" I looked at him and said, "I know, Page...that's why we're both fucking hurt!" And he got to laughing again.

People take the ride, and they go back and tell their friends about it, and you can't believe how it gets people excited. We had an ol' guy take a ride at Gas City one night, he was probably 70 years old. He goes back to the coffee shop every morning, and he drove those people crazy, telling them about his ride. Finally this other guy, his friend, came all the way over to Terre Haute for a ride, saying, "I've got to ride in that car, just to see what he's talking about." It brings more people in.

We took the car to Grandview, Pennsylvania, and we had a huge line of people wanting to ride. This one guy is a writer for the Philadelphia paper, and in the Philadelphia newspaper he wrote a story about his ride that covered one whole page in the sports section. He compared it to riding with the Blue Angels, and just wrote about how awesome it was. Then he wrote a little different article, and got three-quarters of a page in the Reading paper. You can write about racing all day long; and people watch it all day long. But until you get inside and ride...

The neatest thing a guy said to us last year, and I'd seen him around forever, he said, "You know, I've been around racing all my life. I'll never, ever make fun of the guy running last again. Because that's still a pretty hard job."

When you've got people seeing something from the seat of that car, it's very different than from what you watch from the grandstand. Writers tell the story from a fan's perspective, not a racer's. We get out there and act like it's no big deal, like it's easy. But when somebody thinks it looks easy, when they go out there and feel what it's like in the car on the race track, it's an eye-opener.

Even when you're just rolling around, you think you're breaking the track record, but a push truck can drive by you. It's just the way a sprint car feels. Bobby Snead's dad got in Dad's car one time at Winchester, and he was reaching down there pulling up on the gas pedal. "The throttle is stuck," he kept saying. And it was idling, that's all it was doing. A sprint car is going to get your attention, no matter who you are. It's just that neat of a race car.

Even after you take the ride, then you've got to imagine what it's like with 19 other cars out there. That's a different experience! It's like Randy Steenbergen, he ran Legends cars for a little while, but when he took his ride at Terre Haute, I gave him a good ride. He got out and all he is wanting is a beer. But I said, "Okay, Randy, now you've got to drive this thing." And it's the only time I've been in the back seat of it around the track. But by then he was so scared of it, he had seen what it could do, that he probably didn't get past quarter-throttle.

Terre Haute is an ideal place, because it's so wide open, and you really can't get yourself into trouble. Unless your name is Cody Hewitt. I mean, when you're 16 and you're braver than you are smart, that changes things. Yes, it's true: Cody crashed my two-seater at Terre Haute.

It was an open-competition race, a run-what-you-brung deal, in late 2000. We told Cody he could drive it in the race. I'm thinking, "It's a pretty forgiving little race car." The only other cars he had driven were those mini-cup cars, on pavement. So he kept driving the car in the corner straight, saying it was pushing. Well, it wasn't pushing, he just wasn't turning the wheel. He was driving it like he was on pavement. He was going in so hard, there is no way he could turn it that close. So there wasn't any doubt it was a matter of time before he turned it over. It wasn't if; it was when.

I watched him in the heat and it scared me to death. He came in and I told him what he was doing, and he said, "Yeah, I know, I know..." Those are our worst words together: "I know." When I'm trying to tell him something and he's saying, "I know, I know..." I kind of lose control then. But I talked to him, and I think I had him understanding what was going on. But the second I left, all these other people are coming up to him, saying, "Man, you were doing great!" So there went everything I said. Because he wasn't doing great; he was scary, out of control. He was a SCUD missile. But everybody else told him he was great, and he listened to 'em. That was a mistake. They talked him into being something he wasn't.

He went out in the B-main and was trying to make the show, but he had no idea of what he was doing. He just kept going harder and harder until he got the front end into the wall down in turn one, then banged into the wall with the right rear, and got to flipping, end-over-end.

Jody took off running from the stands in turn four, she probably broke the track record getting there. I was racing in the B-main with Cody, so I didn't see the crash. I was running second, but when I saw the red flag I knew who it was. I knew who, but I didn't know where he was. You're supposed to stop where you are, but I kept going until I found him. Then I saw them taking Jody across the track on a four-wheeler.

I use a head-strap that I hook to the roll cage, and he broke the pop rivet that holds it on. But he didn't even have a stiff neck the next day.

Cody's crash cost about $3,000 to repair. We fixed the frame and the rear end, but the crash got the torque tube and driveshaft, front axle, some shocks, wheels...all the bolt-on stuff. We also took the engine to Gaerte Engines for a rebuild, and found out we're not on a rebuild deal with them any more, so it cost us $7,600 to rebuild the engine.

Cody doesn't remember anything. He covered it up good. The only thing I said to him was, "You're not as good as you thought you were, are you?" That's all I said.

I was pretty surprised about the engine rebuild cost. Next time I'll take it to Hamp and have him rebuild it, I know that will be less. And I'm not badmouthing Earl Gaerte and his guys, not in any way. Because the previous year, he rebuilt it twice, even though our deal only called for once. It's not that I'm mad at him or anybody there; it's just that I've got to find a more affordable solution to keeping the engine fresh.

Part of my comfort in letting Cody race the thing was safety equipment. I insist on using the same equipment I've raced with for years, and I've tried to be innovative to help guys like Bill Simpson come up with new stuff to keep us safe. That helmet strap I use, the one that attaches to the roll cage, Simpson makes that part for me, but they don't push it much. They still think it's safer to hook the strap to your body. I think the strap to the cage is going to help you, though. If it's hooked at your body, it's still got to pivot at your neck. With ours, you've have to tear the whole roll cage off for it to come loose. But if you tear the roll cage off, you're probably in trouble anyways.

After I broke my neck in '93, I knew I needed additional support. Simpson started making them for me, and now I see them all over the place.

They make another belt I use, the lower seat belt, and it's called the "Hewitt belt." I had them lengthen the belt eight inches so the buckle didn't dig into you when they tightened it up. Before, you felt like it was tight enough, but it wasn't; it just felt tight because that buckle was digging into you. But they didn't put that belt in the catalog, and I don't understand that. Shirley Kears of Kears Speed Shop told me she sold 100 sets of them last year, but they still don't put it in the catalog. It's crazy.

And the head restraint, it's called the "Jack strap," and it's not in the catalog either. I told 'em, "Listen, I don't care if you use my name, because this is just a way for me to pay you back." I've bought helmets from Simpson since 1978. Sometimes when guys are on a deal with a manufacturer, they forget they're also the test pilot for them. They need to try new things, and tell the manufacturer if it isn't right. But most guys won't do it, because they think they're bad-mouthing the product. It's not about bad-mouthing anything; it's about trying to make it better.

The best year I ever had, the most McCreary Tires I sold for them was the right rear, because they had a great tire. Racers would come down and ask me, and I'd say, "Whatever you do, don't buy their left rear. They are junk (at that time, they were)." So when I told them what right rear to buy, they wouldn't even question it. Because they knew I was being honest about it.

It doesn't bother me if more people build two-seaters. I think I'll still do okay with mine, because half the people want to ride in the a two-seater, period; the other half want to ride with Jack Hewitt. Or Jimmy Sills, or Davey Hamilton. That's the difference. Not everybody has that luxury, that they have a following of fans to support them.

The two-seater is going to be perfect for Jimmy Sills. We told him everything we were doing, we didn't hold anything back. Davey Hamilton called, he built a two-seater supermodified, and we told him exactly what we had done. I think the more people who get in and ride, they'll spread the word about how cool it is.

Part of it, too, is that there isn't a two-seater in the country I wouldn't race, title-for-title. There just isn't. Kenny Schrader built one, and he put a 360-inch engine in his. Mine is a real sprint car, with a 410. I don't know about 'em all, but I think everybody else has detuned the cars a little bit. But I feel like I'm cheating the riders if I do that. I want 'em to have an experience as close to a real sprint car as possible. Maybe the people wouldn't even be able to tell the difference, but if you want a real, honest-to-goodness sprint car ride, that's what you get with me. If they're setting the idle back and detuning the motor, you're not really getting the real ride. When you're out there with me, you're getting probably 95 percent of the ride of a real sprint car. Ninety percent at the very least. And that's why we're always changing tires on the thing, and wing angle, all kinds of things to make it faster.

We did a bunch of laps, maybe 225, at Fremont one day. I'm continuing to change the car, change the setup, getting the car better. If it can still get me excited, I know the person in the back is excited. And the people really like seeing you working on the car, changing tires, jacking the weight bolts, all that, because it's a more realistic situation.

Jody is always in there joking with them, getting them dressed up, fitting them up. Cody is there changing tires, and I drive. I get out with each and every one to take a picture. I don't just sit there while they're buckling in.

Mine isn't a sprint car ride; it's a sprint car *experience*. We get letters, and it's not, "Thank you Jack for giving me the ride of my life." It's more like, "Thank you Jack, Jody, and Cody..." Because they are a big part of it. We've all done everything we could to make it fun for the rider. And it shows, I'm sure. I know others aren't going to go that far; they're not as proud as I am. And if they don't think the same way they're not going to give the same ride.

I don't really fear a crash with 'em. Because I've got 'em strapped in as safe as I possibly can. The biggest fear I have is a heart attack. I worry about that. I can see it happening. We had a guy ride with us East Bay Raceway, and that's the first time I actually got scared afterward, because I thought he was going to have a heart attack. He was white as a ghost. I always ask 'em beforehand, "Do you want a ride, or do you want *A RIDE*?" And he said, "Well, give me *A RIDE*." His buddies were right there watching. He was maybe in his 50s, I think. I gave him the ride, and to me it wasn't all that radical. But man, he looked like he was dying.

I said, "Sir, we're in no hurry here. You take your time, until you calm down, and when you're ready you can get out of the car." He wasn't panting or anything, but he was totally white, and his eyes were wide. We had his arm restraints off him, had his uniform unzipped, trying to make him comfortable. And I told him, "Sir, I promise you this: if you have a heart attack in my race car, I will get you out of the car." And he kind of started looking at me while I was talking to him. Then I said, "I'll tell you one other thing: I will beat on your chest. But how you get air, that's entirely up to you. No way am I giving you mouth-to-mouth." And he got to laughing, and started to feel better.

You know, he came back the next night and bought another ticket. I guess he wanted to beat it, to overcome his fear, and that's how he did it.

We had another guy last year, and after the ride he told Jody, "I just had open-heart surgery six weeks ago." "No kidding!" "Yeah, I was afraid to tell you before, I thought maybe you wouldn't let me ride!" Well, we don't care. We would have let him ride.

We've just had so much fun with all the things that have been said in those situations. I wish we had been writing them down, or recording them. All the things people say when they get out. We've had guys who have both driven and ridden in the Richard Petty Experience, and they've all said there is no comparison. We had another guy in Florida say, "I've skydived, I've bungee-jumped; and that didn't even compare to this." That kind of blew me away, because I didn't think there was anything that would compare to jumping out of an airplane.

We had a promoter who asked us to give a ride to the trophy girl (a few years ago, that request would have had a whole different meaning), and we took her for a ride. She looked younger than she really was. She was complaining that something was cutting into her, that she was uncomfortable. We were sitting in the car waiting for a heat race to finish. I asked her, "How old are you?" She balked for a minute, and she said, "Well...I'm 30." She had told the track she was younger than that. I said, "Well, never mind then. I know you've had sex before that really wasn't all that comfortable when you got started, but the end result was pretty good, wasn't it? That's just what this ride is gonna be." She never said another word.

I'll tell you a secret: The ride is an aphrodisiac, because when you're done with the ride, you're excited. It just gets you going. It can be anybody, a truck driver, a secretary, whatever, and they'll ask you questions. You try to tell them something they can compare it to. Now I've got it figured out. I just tell 'em it compares to sex, and they know exactly what I'm talking about.

I had already taken Page Jones for a ride, and a year later at the Chili Bowl I took Dean Billings out, Dean had been hurt badly in a midget crash at Sun Prairie. That was a tear-jerker, because he liked the ride so much. He had us all crying. Me, Kevin Olson, all his friends, everybody.

Probably the toppers so far have been these two young boys in Oklahoma, both of whom have cerebral palsy. That was an awesome experience, for everyone. One was at the Chili Bowl, the other was at the big race track in Tulsa. The one boy, we had to use duct tape to help him hold his head up a little bit. His step-dad, Terry Henry, raced a 360-inch sprinter with a two-barrel carburetor there. I said to Terry, "Why don't you take a ride in the car to show folks what we'll be doing tomorrow night?" So he did. The track was really dry from top to bottom, just nasty. You know me, I'm up just about brushing the wall, gassin' it up. We came in, and this guy is plumb scared to death. And he had raced for a year or two. His buddies were making fun of him because he was so scared, and he finally said, real soft..."But I run the bottom!"

I don't know if you've been around people with cerebral palsy, but they talk in a way that's really hard to understand. When the boy came in from that ride, he did a TV interview, and you could almost understand him like normal conversation. It was amazing. They need to look at adrenaline, and the affects it has on the body, because it helped that kid.

They were both good boys, just so thankful for the opportunity. The 16-year-old kid who rode at the Chili Bowl, his dad had raced for 20 years. And his dad came up afterward, and he's in tears. "You've made that boy the happiest boy in the world," he said. "You've made his life complete." Me and my mouth, I speak before I have a chance to think. "No I haven't," I said. "Now you've got to take him to a whorehouse." Well, I didn't know if he wanted to hit me or turn and walk away. I probably shouldn't have said that. Oh, well.

When I tallied up how the thing has worked financially, I figured we were doing okay until the motor bill came in. Part of my problem is that I don't know how to charge for sponsorship, because I don't know for sure how many times we'll race during the course of the season. Print Express and Turbines, Inc. have been a huge help, and Tommy Worth sponsored us some in 2001. We haven't tried too hard to find more money, and I've turned down a couple of offers because they were just too low. I'd rather not do it if the money isn't at least close to what it's worth. I'll just make the Print Express name bigger.

I hope I can get a handle on the costs, and keep the thing going. One thing I'm very sure of: I don't want it to be a rich man's ride. Rich people get to do all the stuff. And right now, to do it and do it right, you've got to charge some money. You can't justify going completely in the hole with the car. But before I raise the price to $150 a lap, or $200, or $250, I would quit. Because I'm not going to make it just for rich people. They get enough breaks as it is. If I can't keep it to where a regular race fan can afford it, I wouldn't want to do it. I just wouldn't.

Talking about Jack...

The first thing I can tell you about Jack Hewitt is that he is a racer's racer. You can underline that, double-double. He is respected more by his peers than just about anybody in the entire sport. Jack is a dirt tracker, the kind of guy who thrills the people, and treats the fans fabulous. I love to watch him race, because he's always giving it all he's got. We should all be like him, in a lot of different ways. For sure, Jack is a man's man.

He's never uncomfortable in a crowd. He's unique in that way. People love him, and they love his style of driving. He's very colorful.

Jack has had a scrap or two, but we've all done that. Racers are like brothers: We'll fight among ourselves, but don't let an outsider come in. As a racer you live in a dangerous atmosphere, and when you do that for a period of time, it gives you an extra intensity. And it also helps you learn to appreciate life, to appreciate what you have and what you've done.

Jack is very unique. Nobody is quite like him. Some guys might have part of what he has, but nobody has a package like Jack. He is truly an individual character.

What I like is that everybody loves him. All the racers love him, all his peers love him, and they respect him. He's a good race driver, and he's been a good race driver for many, many years at just about every dirt track in the country. He's a special guy, and you've got to respect all the things he's done, and the blessings he's given to his fans. He's made a lot of people happy.

When my son Page got hurt, Jack was there to do whatever he could to help us. He's that kind of a guy. I'll never forget that. I have the utmost respect for Jack Hewitt.

Parnelli Jones
Torrance, California

24

HALL OF FAME

On Saturday, June 1, 2002, I was inducted into the National Sprint Car Hall of Fame in Knoxville, Iowa.

I say that not to brag; but because I'm so humbled and proud to join so many awesome racers in the Hall of Fame.

When you're going through your career, you don't think about things like that. In the beginning you're so hungry for success, just a little shred of success, that it hurts your gut. Then you have a tiny success, then a little more, and a little more, and you look around and realize you're winning some races. Then you take that for granted, and maybe win more races. Before you know it, you're looking back at your career and wondering where the time went.

That's when you start to appreciate things like the Hall of Fame.

Truthfully, I didn't dare dream it would happen. In 1999 the National Sprint Car Poll voted to select the top 25 sprint car drivers of the 20th century, and I was fortunate to be selected. When I made that list, I began to think maybe I had a shot at the Hall of Fame.

But I didn't dwell on it, because of two reasons: one, I didn't want to get my hopes up in case it didn't happen; and two, I try not to think about things I can't control.

When the Hall of Fame called to mention I was eligible for induction in 2002, I was surprised. I turned 50 on July 8, 2001, and I thought the rules for induction required you to be 50 years old, and be out of racing for at least five years. I was surprised to learn that if you're 50 you're eligible, even if you're still active.

The Hall of Fame had a reception in Indianapolis in December, where they announced the balloting results. I was so excited when they called my name, and I'm glad Jody and Cody were there with me.

I had a bit of a scheduling problem with the induction ceremony, because it was set for Saturday afternoon and we had a Silver Crown race that night at Terre Haute. My buddy Jim Mills of Turbines, Inc. in Terre Haute came to my rescue, and provided an airplane to shuttle me from Terre Haute to Knoxville early in the day, then fly me back when the inductions were over.

When I got up there to accept my induction plaque, I was so excited I didn't really know what to say. That really pisses me off when I do that, because after it's over and I sit down I'll think of all the people I want to thank and things I want to say. I guess I get so excited I just lose track.

This much I remember: I'm standing up there, looking out at the audience. There is Junie Heffner, who gave me my start in this business and has been a lifelong friend. At that same table was Johnny Rutherford, and sitting nearby was Jim McElreath. Tom Bigelow was at another table, along with a bunch of other great racers. I admire them all so much, deep in my heart, that I almost started to cry. The emotion was very strong, because the moment meant so much to me...so many people have inspired me and helped me and motivated me, I absolutely didn't get there all by myself.

Somebody mentioned later that, "It's too bad your dad couldn't have been there with you." Oh, he was there, all right. You couldn't see him, but he was there, with me all the way. Just like always.

I've had a great career. If I checked out to the big house tomorrow, I'd die a happy man. I've got more friends than I can possibly count, a good family, and a ton of great experiences that will never leave me.

When I started, just about everybody I raced against was older than me. Now, nearly all the guys racing are younger. That's a natural deal, but only if you're lucky enough to stick around for a long time. Think about this: When I started I raced with Sheldon Kinser, Larry Rice, Jim Hines, Joe Saldana, Brent Kaeding, and Pancho Carter. Later on, I raced against their sons.

I've seen some great racers on both ends. When I started, there was some great talent out there, and I was in awe of those guys: Pancho,

Gary Bettenhausen, Larry Dickson, Sheldon, Rollie Beale, Sam Sessions, and Rick Ferkel, to name a few. Today, I look around and see some really, really good racers: Tracy Hines, Dave Darland, J.J. Yeley, they could win in any type of car they climbed into. Anything.

When I started, if a guy was talking about "moving up," that meant the Indy 500. Today it's obviously different, because Winston Cup has grabbed the limelight and attracted most of the great young talent.

That's fine for these young guys, but there is a danger in trying to move up too soon. You need several seasons in a sprint car to be fully experienced, I think. Jimmy Kite, for example, moved up too quickly in my opinion. He won a Silver Crown race at Phoenix, and right away he got into an Indy car. Then when his Indy car deal went away, he didn't have the solid short track background to fall back on. That's a tough deal, because you can find yourself on the outside looking in awfully quickly in this business. I think Kasey Kahne might have moved up a little early, because he's struggled a little bit. Both those guys are good little racers, don't get me wrong; I just think they ought to do the short-track deal a little longer to get more education and experience. But sponsors want to invest in kids, that's just a part of today's business reality.

You've got to look at Tony Stewart and figure he got it just about exactly right. He raced on the short tracks for five, maybe six full seasons before he moved to Indy cars. When he stepped up, he was ready. Today, I think you'd be hard pressed to find a better pure race driver in the country than Stewart.

I watched a bunch of guys leave the short tracks and go on to bigger things. Kenny Schrader, Jeff Gordon, Stewart, Ryan Newman, Dave Blaney, and Doug Kalitta all come to mind.

Do I envy them? Do I regret not trying to move up earlier?

Nope.

See, Jeff Gordon can't go to Wal-Mart, and he can't go to Wendy's and get a sandwich, without being mobbed. He's got all the money in the world, and nowhere to hide. I wouldn't trade places with him for anything. I'm not trying to make an example of Jeff; really, I wouldn't trade places with *anybody*. I'm very content with the life I've got.

I raced for the love of the sport. Sometimes the money isn't all that great, but so what?

Truth is, I'll bet some of those guys think about their situation and say, "Man, I envy that Hewitt. I wish I'd stayed back there with him." They might not admit it, but I'd bet they've said it a time or two.

If they're in this deal for money, they're in exactly the right situation. There is big, big money in the big leagues now, and they're raking it in. But if a kid gets into this sport just for money, he's making a big mistake.

You've got to race for the love of the sport. Over the long haul, that's the only way.

I know there are lots of guys out there who are richer than I am. But you'd have a hard time finding anybody happier than me.

I'm pretty satisfied with what I've accomplished in my racing career. I've won plenty of races, and reached most of my goals, so overall I can't bitch.

I never dreamed I'd be able to race so long. Now, don't misunderstand me: I also didn't think I'd quit; I just didn't think I'd have the opportunity to be competitive into my 50s. A couple of years ago I came to the conclusion that at this point every race is a bonus, so you've got to be a little bit happy to just be there.

Sure, I still want to do well at every race. But if I have a bad night, I don't get mad and throw my helmet. I just know that I did the best I could that night, and try to do better tomorrow.

Talking about Jack...

When I first met Jack Hewitt, he was a rough, tough character. A little hotheaded at times, but when you got to know him you found he would bend over backward to help you. I had a wrong first impression of the man, I think. With his long hair and beard, he looked rough and rowdy.

He's turned out to be one heckuva race driver, and a fierce competitor. He would stand on the gas! He also turned out to be a very good friend.

Jack was always a clean racer. He wouldn't give you any room, but he wouldn't drive dirty, either. You could go in the corner with him, and he wouldn't put you in danger. You felt safe racing beside him.

I always liked how he took so much time with people; he's so fan-friendly. A lot of guys today forget that the fans drive this sport, but Jack was all about the fans from the beginning. Whenever I see him, even if he's in a crowd and we're not able to talk, he'll give me a wink and a thumb's up. He's like that; he's really good with people.

I've told many people that if anybody had to beat my USAC sprint car record (52 wins), I'd feel very comfortable with Jack doing it. Records are made to be broken, and of course I'd like to hang on to that one as long as I can, but I really figured Jack would get it. I'd be tickled for him if he did.

Jack is not just my competitor, or my rival. He's my friend. And I'm glad.

Tom Bigelow
Winchester, Indiana

25

THE FUTURE

I know this sounds stupid, but I've gone through my entire life not worrying about tomorrow.

I never worried about money, or getting my next ride, or any of that stuff. I'm just a happy-go-lucky guy spending almost no time worrying. Some might say that's irresponsible, but I guarantee you I'm not in any danger of getting an ulcer.

These days I'm toward the end of my career, and I'm starting to think about what lies beyond the horizon. I'm not sitting around stewing and worrying, but I am wondering what's in store.

This latest crash obviously changed some things. I had hoped to race until I couldn't get good rides, and maybe that's still the way it will be, but my recent injuries will keep me occupied and recovering for a little bit. So at this point I can honestly say I don't know if I'm finished racing, because I don't yet know how much I'll have physically when I'm all healed up.

I plan on racing again. Somewhere, somehow; that's my goal.

Hey, I'm a racer. Racing is just about all I know. So as long as there is a sliver of hope, I'm going to try.

I'm actually pretty fortunate as a race driver, because I reached most of my goals. It's tough when you're a driven person, and you've fallen short of what you wanted to accomplish. That gnaws at you. I got to Indy, I won the 4-Crown, I've won lots of races, so I don't have anything to cry about.

As far as my career, the only thing still hanging out there is Tom Bigelow's USAC sprint car victory record. He has 52 wins, and as of today

I have 46. I've been the first guy to challenge Tom's mark in years, so that tells you it's a tough number to reach. When I started inching closer I began to think a little bit about it, because nobody else has been able to get as close as I have.

But I'm not going to cry or pout if I don't get his record. I'll just figure it wasn't meant to be.

That wasn't why I was still racing, anyway. I wasn't just chasing his record. The only race I was worried about was the one I was in at that moment; I wanted to win that baby. It was always about the here-and-now, not just about some number.

Besides, I'm pretty sure I'm leading him in another category: I've probably kissed more girls than Tom. That counts for something, doesn't it?

My lifestyle has never been extravagant. I don't need new cars or expensive clothes, so I can live on the cheap. Hey, if money gets tight, I'll dig for worms instead of buying fishing lures. That's how I look at it.

Maybe I'll get a job. Of course, I tremble and shake just thinking about that idea. I've spent the better part of 30 years *avoiding* a job, so it isn't easy to think about joining the work force. Besides, maybe it's Jody's turn to get a job. I've paid the bills all these years, now it's her turn. She looks at me kind of funny when I say that.

Every year I was racing, we started the year with zero. We just don't spend a lot of money, and if we had a great year we might buy some things, but we don't go through a lot of money. In the winter we go to the movies, that's our hobby. We might go out to eat a little bit, but it's Wendy's or Kentucky Fried Chicken. We don't go to the expensive places.

It's just not a big deal. You're going to eat tomorrow; you'll find something to eat. And I'm not afraid to ask for something. If I'm hungry and I know you have a spare loaf of bread, I'm not afraid to come to your house and ask you for that spare loaf. By the same token, if I have two loaves, I'm going to ask you if you need one of mine.

I never thought about the day when I couldn't race. Just never thought about it. The time might be getting close, but I'm still not panicked. I'm gonna do something to get by, just like anybody else.

If worse comes to worse, I'd be one of the best Wal-Mart greeters in the world. I know I can say, "Hello, welcome to Wal-Mart!" better than anybody out there. I know I can! And when the older ladies come in and smile at me, the better I'll like it.

Since my recent injuries I've had a couple of job offers, but I've told 'em it's too early to decide what I want to do. Besides, I tell people that the job idea is setting back my recovery, because the longer I'm hurt the longer I can postpone getting a job!

I wouldn't be afraid to stay in racing in some capacity. Maybe I could go to work in Illinois at Red Hill Speedway for Jim Mills, and Earl Baltes has often told me that someday I could work at Eldora.

Would I consider being a racing official? I think I could do that job and be fair. Norm Shields is a really good USAC official, and you see him operate and be fair. Before Norm there was Rollie Beale, who was also a very good official. The problem with their job, though, is that they don't have the final say. I don't know if it's different now that Rollie Helmling has taken over as USAC president, but in the past I've seen instances where Norm has made a call on Saturday night but was overruled back in the office on Monday morning.

I couldn't live with that. I'm either the official in charge or I'm not, pure and simple. Maybe one of the top guys bitched, or was a crybaby, and they bent for him. I think you'd only overrule me one time and I'd quit.

But Norm is one of the fairest guys out there, and when he makes a call it's as fair as it can possibly be. Bill Carey is another USAC official like that. You know that with those guys they're being as honest and fair as they can possibly be. I have a lot of respect for both Norm and Bill.

I've also thought about working for McCreary Tires, now called American Racer. They inquired through Bob Hampshire, right after I got hurt, but I was still in a halo and my vision wasn't where it needed to be, so I said no. But maybe they'll still be interested later on, and we can talk further.

I'm not interested in relocating, so that's probably an obstacle. I love Troy, and I can't imagine living anywhere else.

Would I be interested in doing television work? I don't think I could be politically correct enough to make it work. I say "ain't" too much, and if I saw a guy on the track stick somebody in the fence, I'm going to say so. And if it looks like he did it on purpose, I might call him an asshole. There isn't one network willing to put up with that.

I can't candy coat it. Lots of times you'll hear on the Winston Cup broadcasts, "It's a racing incident." Don't give me that crap! If a guy runs into the side of your race car, say what really happened!

The idea of getting back in the race car has actually helped in my recovery. In my mind, that's a goal, an incentive to heal up as quickly as possible. The day they say, "Look, you'll never race again..." Well, why are you trying to get better at that point? What's the purpose? You've got to have a reason to get better. Just being alive is not enough, at least not for me.

God has a plan for everybody, but we don't always know what it is. It's a mystery, trying to figure out which door you're supposed to go through. I've never been the smartest guy in the world anyway, and I never listened to anybody, and it's not that I won't listen to God...but it's going to have to be a lot more clear before I follow a certain path and know that it's right. I'll do anything. If He said right now, "You stop racing tomorrow," that would make it easier for me, because then I'd know what He wants. But He doesn't work that way. So I've got to figure out where I go from here, and what He expects from me.

I've been awfully lucky to have so many friends and acquaintances. My dad used to tell me that when you quit racing, people forget about you pretty quickly. He's right; but I've made so many friends that have grown beyond the racing part of it, I know I'll continue to have a lot of friends after I quit. They're not going to stop being my friend just because I'm not racing.

I realize this is an old cliché, but I don't have any regrets. Now, there are things I wish I'd learned earlier; for example, I wish I'd gotten involved in Indy car racing much earlier than I did. I don't know that I could have enjoyed it any more than I enjoyed sprint car racing, though.

If they told me today that I could go back and change my career, I would say no. I'll leave it just as it is. I've lived my life, and I've enjoyed what I've been doing.

What will I be like at age 75? The way I look at it, I'll be three-quarters of the way through my life. I figured when I hit 50, I saw the crossed flags for halfway. But I don't want to just be *alive* at 75, or 100; I want to be *living*. There is a big difference between those two things.

If I can still fish, or do the things I enjoy, I'm okay. Plus, they have Viagra today, and by then they'll probably have something even better, so that area is handled. As long as Jody can keep up with me, Viagra and all, 75 will just be a number.

I'm not scared of getting old, not yet. I don't ever want to go into a home, but who can control that? I just want to live my life where I'm happy with it.

Seeing Cody graduate has kind of reminded me of the passing years. Our relationship is changing, and since he's gotten a girlfriend-her name is Ruthann-it's gotten better. As a teenager he knows it all, and we struggle with that. The biggest problem is that he's so much like me. Back then, Don Hewitt couldn't tell me anything, either.

It's a shame I had to learn so many things the hard way, because I was too stubborn to listen. If you can learn 'em the easy way, you'll learn faster.

Cody has talked about wanting to race, but we'll see what happens. Who knows, maybe I'll be like Dad and continue my racing through my son.

My recent crash has probably strengthened my relationship with Jody. I watch her, and think about what she's been willing to do for me, and I'm amazed. I told her after my first big crash in 1993, "You know it's true love when you're so far down somebody has to wipe your butt for you." I've told Jody I don't think I could do that for somebody else. My mom made fun of me when Cody was growing up because I only changed one dirty diaper in my life. Problem was, when Jody got home the diaper was laying out in the yard next to the water hose. I just peeled him out of the diaper and hosed him off. My mom said that was terrible; but I'm just not able to do a dirty diaper, no matter who it is. I'll change a wet diaper, but if it's chunky I'm not the guy to take care of it.

As Jody and I get older, we kind of redefine our relationship, and we get stronger. In '93 I felt like I owed her so much because of all she did for me; this time, I can see that it's just Jody being Jody, helping someone else. That's just her way. She's just the ultimate wife, but what can you say? She still bitches and raises hell with me, and there is always stuff I haven't done around the house, but when it comes down to crunch time she's right there beside me. So you've got to say there is lots of love there.

A couple of months after my recent accident, I was lying in bed one night when I woke Jody up. "God just spoke to me," I told her. "He said I was going to be healed in front of a bunch of people." Later on I interpreted that to mean I was to appear at one of the rallies featuring Benny Hinn, the spiritual healer. To make a long story short that wasn't how it worked out, but it was good because waking her up that night and talking with her about what God wanted has helped our spiritual relationship.

Jody was always a Christian, and when I accepted Jesus that was another bond Jody and I could share. She and I are on the same page. Now, when we walk through the pearly gates of Heaven, we'll be together. That makes a big difference, knowing that.

That's the one positive that came out of my crash at North Vernon. Our faith has been strengthened, together.

The last time I was recovering from a big crash, I went through much of the process without a strong faith in God. I didn't know if there was anything in life that would interest me when my racing career was over, but now I figure maybe I'm supposed to be around just to talk about Jesus, and that's why God is keeping me here, protecting me, keeping me alive.

I'm glad I did this book. It's good to talk about all this stuff. The best part, as far as I'm concerned, is that people can see what kind of a shithead I was in the beginning, and know I'm still kind of a shithead, but at least now I'm on a winning team. If I can go from the bad-as-you-can-be team to the winning team, so can anybody else.

If people can see how I was, and how much happier I am now, they've got to realize there is something to it. If I can find Him, so can they. If these words help one kid out, or one adult, this book is a total success, as far as I'm concerned. I'm glad I spoke up.

I'm happier now than at any period in my life. I'm content with my career, I'm happy with my relationship with Jody, and I'm glad I have so many friends. Yes, God is a big part of being content, but I've also mellowed out (some) and learned to accept that life changes as the years pass.

Wow! Look how many years I did this! Man, it flew past me. But I hope I haven't changed, and I don't believe I have. I'm still just Jack as far as I'm concerned. That's how it's always going to be: just Jack. Period.

EPILOGUE

November 25, 2002
7:30 p.m.
Pleasant Hill, Ohio

I'm sitting here at the Mountaintop, and this is where I'll finish it up.

Not *on* the mountaintop, *at* the Mountaintop. VFW Post 6557, out in the country a few miles west of Troy. It sits up on a big hill overlooking a pretty valley, and everybody calls it the Mountaintop.

My friends are here, sitting at this old bar and telling stories. It's kind of smoky, and there's a lot of laughter and good times. There are beer signs and neon lights and this place is very comfortable.

I very seldom drink alcohol, so I'll sip a Diet Coke while everyone else has a beer. Or two.

There aren't any rich people here. These folks work for a living and they don't wear fancy clothes or drive exotic cars. I've learned to fit in with rich people and famous people; my racing career taught me that. But these are *my* people; I hang around here by choice.

I have known some of the guys in here nearly all my life. They were with me in the early parts of my career and they're still with me. When times were good I shared my success with them, and when times were tough they were right there with me. I don't ever tell 'em this because I'm not that way, but they mean almost everything to me.

I wanted to end this book by sharing a few minutes of a night here with Jody and me at the Mountaintop. It's kind of amazing, really, that my circle of friends has endured so well through all these years. We all still live very close to each other, still do stuff together, and we absolutely have a helluva time giving each other grief.

Sitting here are Bobby Snead, Rick Mohler, Mark Ralidak (Rad), and Dennis Hall (Denny). Bobby was my second car owner, but we were friends both before and after the racing adventure. At one time or another every one of those guys helped me with race cars, or traveled with me. It's been a great friendship for all of us.

We're all sitting at the bar, giving each other hell. When you hang around here, the stories are fast and furious and funny and sometimes pretty off-color. Here, listen in:

Bobby: We used to run Eldora on Sunday afternoon, and Findlay on Sunday night. One day we left Eldora at the same time as Rick Ferkel, and we followed him toward Findlay. He crossed a railroad track, and then the gate came down. We had to wait just a minute for the train to pass, and then we were right back going again. We got to Findlay just a few minutes after Ferkel, and they weren't going to let us run. Said we were too late. We were pissed, and there was a big argument. I look around and Jack has the official by the throat. Remember that?

Jack: I don't remember. (Laughter.)

Rad: He started on the tail of the semi and passed everybody, and won that. Then he started on the tail of the feature and he was running like a wild man. Running off the track, then back on, it was the damnedest thing I've ever seen. He finished fifth.

Bobby: When Jack got started, we had a lot of welding to do, because he hit a lot of shit!

Rad: Remember the snowmobile, when you hit that ditch?

Jack: Oh, man.

Rad: We had these John Deere snowmobiles...

Jack: The snow was real deep, and I didn't realize the ditch was there. I had never been on one before. Well, this snowmobile would haul ass...it just wouldn't turn. It was a real deep ditch, and I almost made it across. Almost. I hit the side and bounced up and wiped out.

Rad: He was trying to jump it.

Jack: No, I wasn't, I just couldn't get 'er turned. Jump it, my ass! It wouldn't turn.

Rad: That was another concussion... (Laughter.)

Jack: No...

Denny: That might be where it started!

Bobby: The first feature we ever won, we got rained out at Eldora so we hauled ass to Chillicothe. The only reason we won was because we got there late, and (Jack) had no time to screw us up.

Jack: Aw, bullshit!

Bobby: We had our Eldora gear in there, and our Eldora setup when we qualified. We had no time to change anything. He qualified seventh or eighth, got the invert, and was on the pole. That's how we won. If we'd got there at four o'clock, ain't no way we would have won, because he would have screwed us up.

Jack: Sometimes we over-engineered ourselves...

Bobby: Yeah, he liked to change things.

Rad: Especially the gear!

Jack: Well, when I start to tell stories on you guys, you're like turtles...everybody just goes back in their shells!

Bobby: Another time, ol' whistle-dick Hewitt is working on the little pond behind his house, and he comes over to the gravel pit and wants to borrow a pump. The only thing I've got is a big four-inch sumbitch that will suck the rocks right up off the bottom of the lake, it's so strong. So I'm telling him, "Anchor this thing down before you fire it up, because when it gets water, it's going to take off." So he gets the pump down on his dam in his back yard, and pulls his van down there to jump-start it. Poor ol' Billy Anderson is sitting in the van with the window down, minding his own business, and numb-nuts Hewitt hadn't paid any attention and had the outlet pipe turned at 90 degrees, pointing right toward the window. The pump takes off and shoots one helluva stream of water right into the passenger compartment of the van, and liked to drowned Billy before Hewitt could get it shut off. They filled the van half-full of water, sand, dirt, gravel; it was a real pretty sight.

Rick: Now, *that* was a wild day.

Jack: Billy took it pretty well, though. He knew he wasn't gonna be for shit anyway, when I was around.

Bobby: We were going to Chillicothe one day, and we're getting close to time to leave. There's this bar that locks down the tool box, and we can't find it. This is a good example of how Jack treats his friends. He grabs a big three-eighths-inch ratchet extension, and I saw him try to put it in the hole in the toolbox. He takes off with it. "Where's he goin'?" we're wondering. "He's gonna grind the lip off that extension, to lock that box." "Aw, he wouldn't do that..." About that time here he comes, with my $30 extension "modified" for something else.

So we get in his van, and take off for Chillicothe. Jack and I are in front with Jody and Cody in the back of the van. Now, he always drove from his house to Troy-about seven miles-and he'd pull over and say, "I'm tired, somebody else needs to drive!" (Laughter, and agreement all around.)

Cody had this little radio-controlled car, and he runs it up by us on the floor. Jack tells him not do run it up there again. He does it again, and Jack tells him again. Jack and I are talking, and here comes the little car. Finally Jack reaches down and grabs the toy and pitches it out the window. So Jody is pissed, Cody is pissed, this sumbitch goes to sleep, and I've got to drive all the way to Chillicothe in total silence! Nobody is saying anything!

Jack: Well, I like it quiet when I sleep! (Laughter.)

Bobby: We got to Chillicothe, it was an All Stars race. Brad Doty was there, in a No. 48, I think. Pretty tough. We're getting ready for the feature, and Jack reaches over and pokes me in the chest a little bit and says, "I'll meet you on the front stretch in 20 minutes." Twenty minutes later, that's where we were, on the front stretch in victory lane.

Jack: What car were we in?

Bobby: The 23 car (Stan Shoff).

Bobby: And then I got home that night, and said to myself, "I ain't ever, ever doin' that again." (Laughter.)

Jack: We had some good racing trips together, though. Late in 1975 we went to Reading, Pennsylvania, for four straight weekends of racing. Lynn Paxton, Smokey Snellbaker, they were all there. We made the feature every trip, and led one of 'em.

Rad: How about some of those girls that used to come around? Oh, that was before you, Jody!

Bobby: All we ever got were seconds...but then, some of 'em weren't too bad. I'll give you "A" for effort.

Jack: I came back from Australia one year, and I called my girlfriend up on the phone...

Bobby: Now that was seconds, don't be lyin...

Jack: No answer! No answer! So I drive over, and there's Bobby's car in the driveway. Man, he shot me in the back so fast! Cowboys don't do that to their friends, they only do it to bad guys.

Bobby: You *were* the bad guy.

Jack: My buddy, Bobby.

Bobby: I was just trying to take care of your interests. Somebody had to!

Denny: You guys didn't talk for how many years after that deal?

Jack: Too many, because we both ended up married.

Bobby: Seriously, though, we always knew Jack would be a race driver. Early on, we were fast everywhere we went. The first break we ever got was when Jack and I went to Shreveport (Louisiana). Ted Johnson's World of Outlaws deal hadn't been done yet, but I think he was one of the promoters. We were there and the four-wheel drive trucks had rutted it up so badly you could hardly race on it. Shithead (Hewitt) is out there, and did pretty good, but he always wanted to get out on the fence. I'm out there, trying to point to the inside rail where everybody else is running.

We had nine barrels of fuel in this old Ford truck, Johnson had given us the fuel because he had no way to transport it, and I think he felt sorry for us. We're sleeping with this fuel, just in love with it. We won the qualifier, and Lanny Edwards came down and said, "You guys want a motel room?" "Hell, yes, we want a motel room! You kiddin' me? You want a barrel of fuel?"

We always passed cars, no matter where we went. He was always up front, before something happened. Somebody stopped in front of him; his steering went out a few times-questionable of course-so we had some bad luck. But it was obvious the guy had talent.

You know, there was a period there, '86, '87, '88, I'd go watch him race and I wanted him to screw up qualifying just so he'd have to start farther back. Because it really wasn't even a show. He had 'em covered. Non-winged, winged, it didn't make any difference.

Jack: I remember one time I was racing somewhere, and Dad was there. Jeff Crawford, he owned the Kozy Kitchen, he was there with us, and he told Dad, "Don, you want to go down and see how he's gettin' into the corner?" "Hell, we know he's gonna go in," Dad says. "Let's see if he comes *out* of the corner!"

Bobby: We went to Selinsgrove (Pennsylvania) one time, it's one of those eight-hour drives that's really ten, and when we got there almost everything was over. Qualifying, heats, done. They put us on the back of the semi, dead last. There was a bunch of goons up in the front, and I'm telling Jack, "Watch yourself." Well, Hewitt tries to smoke the whole damned field coming out of two. One of the goons got sideways and hit him, and when he came walking back from the wreck the only thing I said to him was, "Did you learn anything up there?" Now, it's cold enough that it's trying to snow and this sumbitch was so mad he wouldn't ride in the cab with us going home. He sat in the back. I think that might have been my last race. Cost us $35 to get in, and we raced for three minutes.

Rad: A 20-hour trip for a three-minute crash!

Bobby: We were leaving the parking lot at Eldora, and Jack is already pissed because he missed his first USAC race. That's 1975, maybe. There's a line of traffic where we're merging, and this guy runs right into Jack's door. He was pissed off because Jack wouldn't let him in. He had a brand new Torino. Jack can't open his door, so he's got to go out the passenger door. His girlfriend, Julie, is sitting in the middle, and I'm riding shotgun. I no sooner lifted the door handle, and I'm on the ground, Julie and I all tangled up, and Jack's over there whippin' on this guy.

Jack: We're on the ground, fightin', and this woman is pulling on my hair, "All right, get off him, hippie!" Well, I'm no hippie. But we get up off the ground and get back in our cars. He pulls his car up behind me, and I've got about three feet between us. I'm in an old '66

Nova; I cranked it up to about 5,800 rpm and did a reverse drop. Aw, man, it was beautiful! Took care of that guy!

Bobby: We went to Devil's Bowl for a Saturday-night race, and got rained out. The race was rescheduled for the next Saturday night, so we're staying. Sunday afternoon we're sitting around, you know, "What you wanna do?" "Let's go to a movie across the street." "What's playin'?" "*Car Wash.*" So we see the movie. Next afternoon, I'm sitting out there looking at the race car, drinking beer. Hewitt comes walking up. "Where you goin'?" I ask. "To see a movie." "What's playin'?" "*Car Wash.*" The next afternoon, same deal. "What's playin'?" "*Car Wash.*" Sumbitch did it every day, all week long.

Jack: Hey, Bobby, what about the time you got pulled over for speeding?

Bobby: We were in Texas, and Jack invited this kid to ride with us. I'm running 45 in a 35 zone, and a cop pulls us over from behind a billboard. I'm not sure why he searched us...

Denny: Maybe it was the long hair.

Bobby: That might be it. They're searching us, and they reach in this kid's pocket and pull out a joint. Jack and I look at each other, thinking, "This ought to be good." We're in Texas, and this kid has a joint on him. They took me to jail, because I was driving, and Jack's outside in the lobby mouthing off. They handcuff me to this big black guy, and Jack points to the black guy and says, "If that crazy sumbitch takes off running, don't shoot my buddy!"

So I'm sitting in the cell, locked up, not worrying about a thing. Jack's got my race car, and I knew he wouldn't go racing without me...unless I can't get out.

Denny: How long did they keep you?

Bobby: Just overnight, I think....

Jack: Aw, bullshit! They didn't keep you overnight!

Bobby: Well, when did I get out?

Jack: That afternoon! Don't be starting that overnight bullshit...

Bobby: Maybe I didn't spend the night, but I don't understand how you got me out. I mean, I *know* you didn't have the cash to bail me out...

Jack: I didn't usually have a lot of cash...

Bobby: You got it honest. We went to Australia with Don Hewitt one time, and that was a helluva adventure. We almost missed the plane in Dayton because we were drinking, and when we returned I was taking Don home and he whipped out his wallet and says, "That ain't bad, Bobby! I went halfway around the world, I left with $12, and I have $56 now!"

Rick: Jack says he's the greatest fisherman who ever lived, and he is...when he goes with us.

Jack: We've had some good fishing trips, haven't we? Except for Dennis. Ain't that right, Dennis?

Denny: Yep.

Jack: He came to Canada with us one year, fishing, and his idea of fun was to sit in the motel and drink. Instead of drinking out among that beautiful scenery, he's sitting back at the motel. Travel 1,000 miles to sit in the motel. So we came to an understanding about Canada after that: We wouldn't let him come, and he wouldn't ask. (Laughter.)

Denny: They talked me into fishing, I didn't want to go, so I got out there, and...

Jack: If one of us went we all went!

Denny: Well, bullshit! I was ready to go home. I'm standing on the front of the boat, fishing, and I hear this "click" sound. I look around, and that was Jack turning on the ignition. He hauls ass real quick, I fell backward and broke Bobby's windshield, and felt like an idiot. I didn't even want to go out that night!

Rick: Man, when you heard that "click" sound, hold on. Because we're hauling ass.

Jack: It's kind of amazing, really, that these five guys were together through all that, all those years ago, and here we are.

Rick: At all kinds of places...on the road, and right around here.

Jack: Like at the Kozy...

Rick: You know, it's funny. You could be having a plain, ordinary day, nothing going on. You'd walk into the Kozy, and within five minutes it was, "WOW! I ain't never seen *that* before!"

Jack: Always something new there. Never ordinary.

All: Hell, no!

Rad: Good old days, weren't they?

There is a lot of background noise, as someone across the way is leaving, with lots of big, boisterous goodbyes, and laughter.

The waitress walks over to where we're all sitting.

"Last call," she says. "We're closing in just a few minutes."

So I guess that's it. Time to wrap it up.

It's been fun, doing this book and telling all these stories. I'm sure that as soon as this book is printed, I'll think of some more tales that I'll wish I had remembered.

I guess I'll just save 'em for the next book. Volume 1 is over. It's time to go home.

STATISTICS

JACK HEWITT'S USAC CAREER

Date	Location (-dirt, -paved)	Car	Finish	Entrant
10/5/75	Eldora Speedway, Rossburg, Ohio - d	sprint	DNQ	Bob Snead 90
10/12/75	Winchester Speedway, Winchester, Ind. - p	sprint	DNQ	Doug Trost 30
3/28/76	Eldora Speedway, Rossburg, Ohio - d	sprint	DNQ	Larry Snead 65
4/4/76	Salem Speedway, Salem, Ind. - p	sprint	DNQ	Larry Snead 65
4/11/76	Eldora Speedway, Rossburg, Ohio - d	sprint	DNQ	Larry Snead 65
4/18/76	New Bremen Speedway, New Bremen, Ohio - p	sprint	DNQ	Larry Snead 65
5/1/76	Terre Haute Action Track, Terre Haute, Ind. - d	sprint	DNQ	Larry Snead 65
5/9/76	Dayton Speedway, Dayton, Ohio - p	sprint	DNQ	Larry Snead 65
5/16/76	Indianapolis Raceway Park, Clermont, Ind. - p	sprint	DNQ	Larry Snead 65
5/23/76	Millstream Motor Speedway, Findlay, Ohio - d	sprint	DNQ	Larry Snead 65
6/4/76	Indiana State Fairgrounds, Indianapolis, Ind. - d	sprint	23	Larry Snead 65
6/4/76	Indiana State Fairgrounds, Indianapolis, Ind. - d	sprint	DNS	Larry Snead 65
6/20/76	Eldora Speedway, Rossburg, Ohio - d	sprint	18	Max Britton 27
7/3/76	Millstream Motor Speedway, Findlay, Ohio - d	sprint	14	Max Britton 27
7/10/76	Eldora Speedway, Rossburg, Ohio - d	sprint	DNQ	Max Britton 27
7/11/76	New Bremen Speedway, New Bremen, Ohio - p	sprint	DNQ	Max Britton 27
7/17/76	Toledo Speedway, Toledo, Ohio - p	sprint	DNQ	Max Britton 27
7/25/76	Winchester Speedway, Winchester, Ind. - p	sprint	DNQ	Max Britton 27
7/31/76	Indiana State Fairgrounds, Indianapolis, Ind. - d	sprint	17	Larry Snead 65
7/31/76	Indiana State Fairgrounds, Indianapolis, Ind. - d	sprint	DNS	Larry Snead 65
9/9/78	Indiana State Fairgrounds, Indianapolis, Ind. - d	Silver Cr.	15	POB Sealants 50
6/29/80	Terre Haute Action Track, Terre Haute, Ind. - d	sprint	16	Radar Racing 30
7/25/80	Santa Fe Park Speedway, Hinsdale, Ill. - d	sprint	7	Radar Racing 30
8/19/80	Illinois State Fairgrounds, Springfield, Ill. - d	Silver Cr.	21	Radio Hospital 58
8/24/80	DuQuoin State Fairgrounds, DuQuoin, Ill. - d	Silver Cr.	15	Radio Hospital 58
4/25/81	Eldora Speedway, Rossburg, Ohio - d	sprint	4	Larry Farno 30
4/26/81	Eldora Speedway, Rossburg, Ohio - d	Silver Cr.	2	Coons Construction 58
5/2/81	Indiana State Fairgrounds, Indianapolis, Ind. - d	Silver Cr.	6	Coons Construction 58
5/3/81	Terre Haute Action Track, Terre Haute, Ind. - d	sprint	18	Larry Farno 30
5/22/81	Indiana State Fairgrounds, Indianapolis, Ind. - d	sprint	11	Larry Farno 30
6/5/81	Lakeside Speedway, Kansas City, Kan. - d	sprint	8	Larry Farno 30
6/6/81	Knoxville Raceway, Knoxville, Ia. - d	Silver Cr.	19	Coons Construction 58
7/3/81	Eldora Speedway, Rossburg, Ohio - d	sprint	3	Larry Farno 30
7/5/81	Williams Grove Speedway, Mechanicsburg, Pa. - d	Silver Cr.	3	Coons Construction 58
7/31/81	Santa Fe Park Speedway, Hinsdale, Ill. - d	sprint	9	Larry Farno 30
8/9/81	Terre Haute Action Track, Terre Haute, Ind. - d	sprint	14	Larry Farno 30
8/15/81	Illinois State Fairgrounds, Springfield, Ill. - d	Silver Cr.	4	Coons Construction 58
8/19/81	Whitewater Valley Speedway, Liberty, Ind. - d	sprint	9	Cecilia Smith 14
8/30/81	DuQuoin State Fairgrounds, DuQuoin, Ill. - d	Silver Cr.	4	Coons Construction 58
9/4/81	Whitewater Valley Speedway, Liberty, Ind. - d	sprint	2	Larry Farno 30
9/9/81	Paragon Speedway, Paragon, Ind. - d	sprint	DNQ	Larry Farno 30
9/12/81	Indiana State Fairgrounds, Indianapolis, Ind. - d	Silver Cr.	13	Club 30 26
10/11/81	Eldora Speedway, Rossburg, Ohio - d	sprint	4	Larry Farno 30
10/11/81	Eldora Speedway, Rossburg, Ohio - d	Silver Cr.	4	Coons Construction 58

4/24/82	Eldora Speedway, Rossburg, Ohio - d	sprint	1	Johnny Vance 32
4/25/82	Eldora Speedway, Rossburg, Ohio - d	Silver Cr.	19	Johnny Vance 3
5/2/82	Illinois State Fairgrounds, Springfield, Ill. - d	Silver Cr.	19	Johnny Vance 3
5/5/82	Millstream Motor Speedway, Findlay, Ohio - d	sprint	16	Ray Smith 14
5/8/82	Indiana State Fairgrounds, Indianapolis, Ind. - d	Silver Cr.	4	Johnny Vance 3
5/9/82	Terre Haute Action Track, Terre Haute, Ind. - d	sprint	DNQ	Johnny Vance 32
5/14/82	Paducah Intl. Raceway, Paducah, Ken. - d	sprint	16	Johnny Vance 32
5/15/82	Paragon Speedway, Paragon, Ind. - d	sprint	3	Johnny Vance 32
5/28/82	Indiana State Fairgrounds, Indianapolis, Ind. - d	sprint	14	Johnny Vance 32
6/5/82	Knoxville Raceway, Knoxville, Ia. - d	sprint	4	Johnny Vance 32
6/6/82	I-70 National Speedway, Odessa, Mo. - d	sprint	18	Johnny Vance 32
6/20/82	Terre Haute Action Track, Terre Haute, Ind. - d	sprint	2	King & Powers 51
6/23/82	Mansfield Raceway Park, Mansfield, Ohio - d	sprint	8	Nickles Bros. 31
7/17/82	Eldora Speedway, Rossburg, Ohio - d	sprint	4	Johnny Vance 32
8/8/82	Terre Haute Action Track, Terre Haute, Ind. - d	sprint	3	Blackie Fortune 39a
10/3/82	Eldora Speedway, Rossburg, Ohio - d	sprint	DNQ	Nickles Bros. 31x
3/26/83	Nazareth National Speedway, Nazareth, Pa. - d	Silver Cr.	12	Amerling 34
5/8/83	Terre Haute Action Track, Terre Haute, Ind. - d	sprint	1	King & Powers 51
5/20/83	Santa Fe Park Speedway, Hinsdale, Ill. - d	sprint	8	King & Powers 51
5/21/83	Indiana State Fairgrounds, Indianapolis, Ind. - d	sprint	20	King & Powers 51
5/25/83	Lincoln Park Speedway, Putnamville, Ind. - d	sprint	9	King & Powers 51
6/4/83	Eldora Speedway, Rossburg, Ohio - d	sprint	2	King & Powers 51
6/19/83	Terre Haute Action Track, Terre Haute, Ind. - d	sprint	DNQ	Doug Trost 30
7/1/83	Flemington Fair Speedway, Flemington, N.J. - d	Silver Cr.	3	Amerling 34
7/27/83	Paragon Speedway, Paragon, Ind. - d	sprint	1	King & Powers 51
8/2/83	Eldora Speedway, Rossburg, Ohio - d	sprint	1	King & Powers 51
8/20/83	Illinois State Fairgrounds, Springfield, Ill. - d	Silver Cr.	19	Amerling 34
8/24/83	Lincoln Park Speedway, Putnamville, Ind. - d	sprint	DNQ	King & Powers 51
8/28/83	Terre Haute Action Track, Terre Haute, Ind. - d	sprint	1	King & Powers 51
9/4/83	Tri-State Speedway, Haubstadt, Ind. - d	sprint	8	G & R 37
9/5/83	DuQuoin State Fairgrounds, DuQuoin, Ill. - d	Silver Cr.	19	Amerling 34
9/10/83	Indiana State Fairgrounds, Indianapolis, Ind. - d	Silver Cr.	15	Amerling 34
9/15/83	Paragon Speedway, Paragon, Ind. - d	sprint	8	G & R 37
9/25/83	Eldora Speedway, Rossburg, Ohio - d	sprint	1	G & R 37
9/25/83	Eldora Speedway, Rossburg, Ohio - d	Silver Cr.	3	Amerling 34
4/1/84	Eldora Speedway, Rossburg, Ohio - d	sprint	7	Richard Briscoe 5x
4/28/84	Eldora Speedway, Rossburg, Ohio - d	sprint	3	Richard Briscoe 5x
5/12/84	Indiana State Fairgrounds, Indianapolis, Ind. - d	sprint	13	Richard Briscoe 5x
5/23/84	Lincoln Park Speedway, Putnamville, Ind. - d	sprint	9	Richard Briscoe 5x
5/28/84	Tri-State Speedway, Haubstadt, Ind. - d	sprint	18	Richard Briscoe 5x
7/11/84	Kokomo Speedway, Kokomo, Ind. - d	sprint	1	Richard Briscoe 5x
7/14/84	Eldora Speedway, Rossburg, Ohio - d	sprint	3	Richard Briscoe 5x
7/18/84	Lincoln Park Speedway, Putnamville, Ind. - d	sprint	5	Richard Briscoe 5x
8/16/84	Eldora Speedway, Rossburg, Ohio - d	sprint	1	Richard Briscoe 5x
8/26/84	Terre Haute Action Track, Terre Haute, Ind. - d	sprint	20	Richard Briscoe 5x
9/1/84	Tri-City Speedway, Granite City, Ill. - d	sprint	24	Richard Briscoe 5x
9/2/84	Tri-State Speedway, Haubstadt, Ind. - d	sprint	20	Richard Briscoe 5x
9/3/84	DuQuoin State Fairgrounds, DuQuoin, Ill. - d	Silver Cr.	21	Brake-O 75
9/15/84	Indiana State Fairgrounds, Indianapolis, Ind. - d	Silver Cr.	4	Racing Associates 97
9/16/84	Lawrenceburg Speedway, Lawrenceburg, Ind. - d	sprint	2	Richard Briscoe 5x

2/10/85	Florida State Fairgrounds, Tampa, Fla. - d	Silver Cr.	2	Kenneth Jarrett 10
4/27/85	Eldora Speedway, Rossburg, Ohio - d	sprint	3	Bob Hampshire 63
4/28/85	Eldora Speedway, Rossburg, Ohio - d	sprint	13	Bob Hampshire 63
5/24/85	Indiana State Fairgrounds, Indianapolis, Ind. - d	Silver Cr.	4	Wayne Subaru 98
6/9/85	Terre Haute Action Track, Terre Haute, Ind. - d	sprint	18	G & R 37
6/28/85	Bloomington Speedway, Bloomington, Ind. - d	sprint	3	Bob Hampshire 63
7/11/85	Expo Speedway, Danville, Ill. - d	sprint	2	Bob Hampshire 63
8/4/85	Kokomo Speedway, Kokomo, Ind. - d	sprint	1	Bob Hampshire 63
8/17/85	Illinois State Fairgrounds, Springfield, Ill. - d	Silver Cr.	4	Pro-Am Trailer 79
8/23/85	Bloomington Speedway, Bloomington, Ind. - d	sprint	2	Bob Hampshire 63
8/25/85	Terre Haute Action Track, Terre Haute, Ind. - d	sprint	8	Bob Hampshire 63
9/2/85	DuQuoin State Fairgrounds, DuQuoin, Ill. - d	Silver Cr.	8	Pro-Am Trailer 79
9/7/85	Lincoln Park Speedway, Putnamville, Ind. - d	sprint	DNQ	Bob Hampshire 63
9/14/85	Indiana State Fairgrounds, Indianapolis, Ind. - d	Silver Cr.	17	Pro-Am Trailer 79
4/6/86	Eldora Speedway, Rossburg, Ohio - d	sprint	10	Bob Hampshire 63
4/26/86	Eldora Speedway, Rossburg, Ohio - d	sprint	2	Bob Hampshire 63
5/2/86	Bloomington Speedway, Bloomington, Ind. - d	sprint	1	Bob Hampshire 63
5/17/86	Lincoln Park Speedway, Putnamville, Ind. - d	sprint	8	Bob Hampshire 63
5/23/86	Indiana State Fairgrounds, Indianapolis, Ind. - d	Silver Cr.	1	Bob Hampshire 63
6/8/86	Hagerstown Speedway, Hagerstown, Md. - d	Silver Cr.	1	Bob Hampshire 63
7/13/86	Indianapolis Raceway Park, Clermont, Ind. - p	Silver Cr.	6	Bob Hampshire 63
8/3/86	Terre Haute Action Track, Terre Haute, Ind. - d	sprint	6	Bob Hampshire 63
8/15/86	Springfield Speedway, Springfield, Ill. - d	sprint	5	Bob Hampshire 63
8/16/86	Illinois State Fairgrounds, Springfield, Ill. - d	Silver Cr.	1	J.W. Hunt 63
9/1/86	DuQuoin State Fairgrounds, DuQuoin, Ill. - d	Silver Cr.	1	J.W. Hunt 63
9/13/86	Indiana State Fairgrounds, Indianapolis, Ind. - d	Silver Cr.	1	J.W. Hunt 63
9/28/86	Eldora Speedway, Rossburg, Ohio - d	Silver Cr.	1	J.W. Hunt 63
9/28/86	Eldora Speedway, Rossburg, Ohio - d	sprint	4	Bob Hampshire 63
2/7/87	Florida State Fairgrounds, Tampa, Fla. - d	Silver Cr.	12	Bob Hampshire 63
2/8/87	Florida State Fairgrounds, Tampa, Fla. - d	sprint	2	Bob Hampshire 63
3/28/87	Eldora Speedway, Rossburg, Ohio - d	sprint	3	Bob Hampshire 63
4/25/87	Eldora Speedway, Rossburg, Ohio - d	sprint	15	Bob Hampshire 63
5/22/87	Indiana State Fairgrounds, Indianapolis, Ind. - d	Silver Cr.	2	Bob Hampshire 63
5/23/87	Terre Haute Action Track, Terre Haute, Ind. - d	sprint	4	Bob Hampshire 63
6/13/87	Eldora Speedway, Rossburg, Ohio - d	sprint	16	Bob Hampshire 63
6/18/87	Indianapolis Speedrome, Indianapolis, Ind. - p	midget	13	Tom Piascik 12
6/18/87	Indianapolis Speedrome, Indianapolis, Ind. - p	midget	19	Tom Piascik 12
6/20/87	K-C Raceway, Chillicothe, Ohio - d	sprint	17	Bob Hampshire 63
6/25/87	Indianapolis Speedrome, Indianapolis, Ind. - p	midget	2	Tom Piascik 12
7/2/87	Indianapolis Speedrome, Indianapolis, Ind. - p	midget	4	Tom Piascik 12
7/9/87	Indianapolis Speedrome, Indianapolis, Ind. - p	midget	8	Tom Piascik 12
7/11/87	Indiana State Fairgrounds, Indianapolis, Ind. - d	Silver Cr.	2	Bob Hampshire 63
7/23/87	Indianapolis Speedrome, Indianapolis, Ind. - p	midget	7	Tom Piascik 12
8/12/87	Indianapolis Speedrome, Indianapolis, Ind. - p	midget	19	Tom Piascik 12
8/21/87	Springfield Speedway, Springfield, Ill. - d	sprint	17	Bob Hampshire 63
8/22/87	Illinois State Fairgrounds, Springfield, Ill. - d	Silver Cr.	1	Bob Hampshire 63
9/7/87	DuQuoin State Fairgrounds, DuQuoin, Ill. - d	Silver Cr.	1	Bob Hampshire 63
9/12/87	Indiana State Fairgrounds, Indianapolis, Ind. - d	Silver Cr.	3	Bob Hampshire 63
9/27/87	Eldora Speedway, Rossburg, Ohio - d	sprint	2	Bob Hampshire 63
9/27/87	Eldora Speedway, Rossburg, Ohio - d	Silver Cr.	4	Bob Hampshire 63

9/27/87	Eldora Speedway, Rossburg, Ohio - d	Late Mod.	10	Bob Hampshire 63
11/1/87	Phoenix Intl. Raceway, Phoenix, Ariz. - p	Silver Cr.	15	Bob Hampshire 63
1/23/88	Hoosier Dome, Indianapolis, Ind. - p	midget	16	Tom Piascik 2j
2/7/88	Florida State Fairgrounds, Tampa, Fla. - d	Silver Cr.	4	Bob Hampshire 63
3/27/88	Eldora Speedway, Rossburg, Ohio - d	sprint	2	Bob Hampshire 63
4/23/88	Eldora Speedway, Rossburg, Ohio - d	sprint	1	Bob Hampshire 63
5/7/88	Paragon Speedway, Paragon, Ind. - d	sprint	6	Bob Hampshire 63
5/14/88	Eldora Speedway, Rossburg, Ohio - d	sprint	1	Bob Hampshire 63
5/27/88	Indiana State Fairgrounds, Indianapolis, Ind. - d	Silver Cr.	4	Bob Hampshire 63
6/4/88	Lawrenceburg Speedway, Lawrenceburg, Ind. - d	sprint	1	Bob Hampshire 63
6/18/88	Eldora Speedway, Rossburg, Ohio - d	sprint	1	Bob Hampshire 63
6/26/88	State Fair Park Speedway, Milwaukee, Wisc. - p	Silver Cr.	4	Bob Hampshire 63
7/9/88	Indianapolis Raceway Park, Clermont, Ind. - p	Silver Cr.	9	Bob Hampshire 63
7/16/88	Eldora Speedway, Rossburg, Ohio - d	sprint	20	Bob Hampshire 63
7/17/88	Millstream Motor Speedway, Findlay, Ohio - d	sprint	7	Bob Hampshire 63
8/7/88	Tri-State Speedway, Haubstadt, Ind. - d	sprint	DNS	McBride & Shoff 23s
8/18/88	Indianapolis Raceway Park, Clermont, Ind. - p	sprint	6	McBride & Shoff 23s
8/20/88	Illinois State Fairgrounds, Springfield, Ill. - d	Silver Cr.	14	Bob Hampshire 63
9/5/88	DuQuoin State Fairgrounds, DuQuoin, Ill. - d	Silver Cr.	28	Bob Hampshire 63
9/10/88	Indiana State Fairgrounds, Indianapolis, Ind. - d	Silver Cr.	1	Bob Hampshire 63
9/18/88	Salem Speedway, Salem, Ind. - p	Silver Cr.	3	Bob Hampshire 63
9/25/88	Eldora Speedway, Rossburg, Ohio - d	Silver Cr.	1	Bob Hampshire 63
9/25/88	Eldora Speedway, Rossburg, Ohio - d	Late Mod.	5	J.W. Hunt 63
9/25/88	Eldora Speedway, Rossburg, Ohio - d	sprint	10	McBride & Shoff 23s
10/8/88	Lawrenceburg Speedway, Lawrenceburg, Ind. - d	midget	23	Brey Racing 21
5/26/89	Indiana State Fairgrounds, Indianapolis, Ind. - d	Silver Cr.	5	Bob Hampshire 63
6/4/89	CalExpo State Fairgrounds, Sacramento, Calif. - d	Silver Cr.	19	Bob Hampshire 63
6/16/89	Attica Raceway Park, Attica, Ohio - d	sprint	7	Stan Shoff 23s
6/25/89	Kokomo Speedway, Kokomo, Ind. - d	sprint	1	Stan Shoff 23s
6/29/89	Indianapolis Raceway Park, Clermont, Ind. - p	sprint	17	Stan Shoff 23s
7/13/89	Indianapolis Raceway Park, Clermont, Ind. - p	sprint	4	Stan Shoff 23s
8/10/89	Indianapolis Raceway Park, Clermont, Ind. - p	sprint	14	Stoops Racing 1
8/19/89	Illinois State Fairgrounds, Springfield, Ill. - d	Silver Cr.	8	Bob Hampshire 63
8/24/89	Indianapolis Raceway Park, Clermont, Ind. - p	sprint	11	Jack Nowling 66x
8/27/89	Indiana State Fairgrounds, Indianapolis, Ind. - d	Silver Cr.	1	Bob Hampshire 63
9/2/89	Tri-City Speedway, Granite City, Ill. - d	sprint	2	Chuck Merrill 5m
9/4/89	DuQuoin State Fairgrounds, DuQuoin, Ill. - d	Silver Cr.	21	Bob Hampshire 63
9/24/89	Eldora Speedway, Rossburg, Ohio - d	Silver Cr.	1	Bob Hampshire 63
9/24/89	Eldora Speedway, Rossburg, Ohio - d	Late Mod.	3	J.W. Hunt 21
9/24/89	Eldora Speedway, Rossburg, Ohio - d	sprint	17	Bob Hampshire 3
4/7/90	Eldora Speedway, Rossburg, Ohio - d	sprint	1	Don Murphy 23
5/28/90	Indiana State Fairgrounds, Indianapolis, Ind. - d	Silver Cr.	1	Bob Hampshire 63
6/24/90	Kokomo Speedway, Kokomo, Ind. - d	sprint	19	Nickles Bros. 31
6/30/90	Indianapolis Raceway Park, Clermont, Ind. - p	Silver Cr.	7	Bob Hampshire 63
7/8/90	Terre Haute Action Track, Terre Haute, Ind. - d	sprint	1	Don Murphy 23
7/14/90	Richmond Raceway, Richmond, Ken. - d	sprint	1	Don Murphy 23
7/15/90	Comtrax Motor Speedway, Glasgow, Ken. - d	sprint	1	Don Murphy 23
8/3/90	Attica Raceway Park, Attica, Ohio - d	sprint	9	Don Murphy 23
8/11/90	Indiana State Fairgrounds, Indianapolis, Ind. - d	Silver Cr.	23	Bob Hampshire 63

8/18/90	Illinois State Fairgrounds, Springfield, Ill. - d	Silver Cr.	21	Bob Hampshire 63
8/19/90	Springfield Speedway, Springfield, Ill. - d	midget	4	6R Racing 5R
8/24/90	I-96 Speedway, Lake Odessa, Mich. - d	sprint	1	Bob Hampshire 63
8/29/90	Wilmot Speedway, Wilmot, Wisc. - d	sprint	1	Bob Hampshire 63
9/1/90	Tri-City Speedway, Granite City, Ill. - d	midget	8	6R Racing 5R
9/3/90	DuQuoin State Fairgrounds, DuQuoin, Ill. - d	Silver Cr.	20	Bob Hampshire 63
9/12/90	Tri-City Speedway, Granite City, Ill. - d	sprint	1	Bob Hampshire 63
9/15/90	Terre Haute Action Track, Terre Haute, Ind. - d	midget	DNS	6R Racing 5R
9/30/90	Eldora Speedway, Rossburg, Ohio - d	sprint	1	Bob Hampshire 63
9/30/90	Eldora Speedway, Rossburg, Ohio - d	Silver Cr.	2	Bob Hampshire 63
9/30/90	Eldora Speedway, Rossburg, Ohio - d	Late Mod.	16	J.W. Hunt 21x
9/30/90	Eldora Speedway, Rossburg, Ohio - d	midget	21	6R Racing 5R
11/4/90	Winchester Speedway, Winchester, Ind. - p	sprint	DNQ	Bob Hampshire 63
11/22/90	Ascot Park, Gardena, Calif. - d	midget	5	Wilke Racing 11w
4/7/91	Winchester Speedway, Winchester, Ind. - p	sprint	5	Bob Hampshire 63
4/7/91	Winchester Speedway, Winchester, Ind. - p	midget	8	6R Racing 5R
4/27/91	Tri-City Speedway, Granite City, Ill. - d	sprint	3	Bob Hampshire 63
5/26/91	Tri-City Speedway, Granite City, Ill. - d	sprint	20	Bob Hampshire 63
6/1/91	I-96 Speedway, Lake Odessa, Mich. - d	midget	1	6R Racing 63
6/1/91	I-96 Speedway, Lake Odessa, Mich. - d	sprint	4	Bob Hampshire 63
6/23/91	Kokomo Speedway, Kokomo, Ind. - d	sprint	5	Bob Hampshire 63
7/7/91	Terre Haute Action Track, Terre Haute, Ind. - d	sprint	1	Bob Hampshire 63
8/7/91	Kokomo Speedway, Kokomo, Ind. - d	midget	1	6R Racing 63
8/10/91	Indiana State Fairgrounds, Indianapolis, Ind. - d	Silver Cr.	27	M & L Plumbing 4
8/17/91	Springfield Speedway, Springfield, Ill. - d	midget	24	6R Racing 63
8/17/91	Illinois State Fairgrounds, Springfield, Ill. - d	Silver Cr.	36	Clare Pattee 37
8/24/91	K-C Raceway, Chillicothe, Ohio - d	sprint	19	Don Murphy 23
8/25/91	Kokomo Speedway, Kokomo, Ind. - d	sprint	2	Don Murphy 23
8/31/91	Tri-City Speedway, Granite City, Ill. - d	sprint	1	Don Murphy 23
8/31/91	Tri-City Speedway, Granite City, Ill. - d	midget	1	6R Racing 63
9/22/91	Eldora Speedway, Rossburg, Ohio - d	sprint	1	Don Murphy 23
9/22/91	Eldora Speedway, Rossburg, Ohio - d	Silver Cr.	1	Bob Hampshire 63
9/22/91	Eldora Speedway, Rossburg, Ohio - d	Late Mod.	2	Kistler 21K
9/22/91	Eldora Speedway, Rossburg, Ohio - d	midget	10	6R Racing 63
11/3/91	Winchester Speedway, Winchester, Ind. - p	midget	DNS	6R Racing 63
2/2/92	Phoenix Intl. Raceway, Phoenix, Ariz. - p	Silver Cr.	16	Don Murphy 21
3/28/92	Eldora Speedway, Rossburg, Ohio - d	sprint	3	Robert Milleville 21
5/22/92	Indiana State Fairgrounds, Indianapolis, Ind. - d	Silver Cr.	3	Don Murphy 21
6/27/92	Indianapolis Raceway Park, Clermont, Ind. - p	Silver Cr.	20	Don Murphy 21
7/12/92	Terre Haute Action Track, Terre Haute, Ind. - d	sprint	5	Robert Milleville 21
8/22/92	Illinois State Fairgrounds, Springfield, Ill. - d	Silver Cr.	5	Don Murphy 21
8/29/92	K-C Raceway, Chillicothe, Ohio - d	sprint	1	Robert Milleville 21
9/5/92	Portsmouth Raceway Park, Portsmouth, Ohio - d	midget	16	Dan Drinan 33az
9/7/92	DuQuoin State Fairgrounds, DuQuoin, Ill. - d	Silver Cr.	26	Don Murphy 21
9/12/92	Indiana State Fairgrounds, Indianapolis, Ind. - d	Silver Cr.	4	Don Murphy 21
9/13/92	Terre Haute Action Track, Terre Haute, Ind. - d	midget	27	6R Racing 21
10/4/92	Eldora Speedway, Rossburg, Ohio - d	sprint	6	Robert Milleville 21
10/4/92	Eldora Speedway, Rossburg, Ohio - d	midget	6	6R Racing 21
10/4/92	Eldora Speedway, Rossburg, Ohio - d	Late Mod.	18	Kistler 21
10/4/92	Eldora Speedway, Rossburg, Ohio - d	Silver Cr.	24	Don Murphy 21

2/28/93	Phoenix Intl. Raceway, Phoenix, Ariz. - p	Silver Cr.	29	Leonard Faas 27
3/27/93	Eldora Speedway, Rossburg, Ohio - d	sprint	2	Bob Hampshire 63
5/2/93	Terre Haute Action Track, Terre Haute, Ind. - d	sprint	2	6R Racing 26R
5/28/93	Indiana State Fairgrounds, Indianapolis, Ind. - d	Silver Cr.	20	6R Racing 26
6/27/93	Kokomo Speedway, Kokomo, Ind. - d	sprint	6	6R Racing 26R
7/10/93	Lawrenceburg Speedway, Lawrenceburg, Ind. - d	sprint	1	6R Racing 26R
7/11/93	Terre Haute Action Track, Terre Haute, Ind. - d	sprint	20	6R Racing 26R
7/31/93	State Fair Park Speedway, Milwaukee, Wisc. - p	Silver Cr.	3	Leonard Faas 27
8/11/93	Eldora Speedway, Rossburg, Ohio - d	sprint	1	6R Racing 26R
8/21/93	Illinois State Fairgrounds, Springfield, Ill. - d	Silver Cr.	1	6R Racing 26
8/28/93	K-C Raceway, Chillicothe, Ohio - d	sprint	1	6R Racing 26R
9/5/93	State Fair Speedway, Sedalia, Mo. - d	sprint	1	6R Racing 26R
9/6/93	DuQuoin State Fairgrounds, DuQuoin, Ill. - d	Silver Cr.	1	6R Racing 26
9/26/93	Eldora Speedway, Rossburg, Ohio - d	Late Mod.	DNS	Kistler 21
10/3/93	Eldora Speedway, Rossburg, Ohio - d	midget	1	Streicher 8s
10/3/93	Eldora Speedway, Rossburg, Ohio - d	sprint	21	6R Racing 26R
4/2/94	Eldora Speedway, Rossburg, Ohio - d	sprint	DNQ	Bob Hampshire 63
5/1/94	Terre Haute Action Track, Terre Haute, Ind. - d	sprint	9	Bob Hampshire 63
5/27/94	Indiana State Fairgrounds, Indianapolis, Ind. - d	Silver Cr.	29	6R Racing 63
6/18/94	Lawrenceburg Speedway, Lawrenceburg, Ind. - d	sprint	14	Bob Hampshire 63
6/23/94	Indianapolis Raceway Park, Clermont, Ind. - p	sprint	10	Bob Parker 22
6/25/94	Eldora Speedway, Rossburg, Ohio - d	sprint	10	Bob Hampshire 63
7/17/94	Terre Haute Action Track, Terre Haute, Ind. - d	sprint	18	Jack Hewitt 11
7/30/94	I-96 Speedway, Lake Odessa, Mich. - d	sprint	1	Bob Hampshire 63
8/4/94	Indianapolis Raceway Park, Clermont, Ind. - p	Silver Cr.	16	6R Racing 63
8/10/94	Eldora Speedway, Rossburg, Ohio - d (disq. for contaminated fuel)	sprint	Disq.	Bob Hampshire 63
8/20/94	Illinois State Fairgrounds, Springfield, Ill. - d	Silver Cr.	2	6R Racing 63
8/27/94	K-C Raceway, Chillicothe, Ohio - d	sprint	20	Bob Hampshire 63
9/3/94	Indiana State Fairgrounds, Indianapolis, Ind. - d	Silver Cr.	5	6R Racing 63
9/10/94	DuQuoin State Fairgrounds, DuQuoin, Ill. - d	Silver Cr.	26	6R Racing 63
9/25/94	Eldora Speedway, Rossburg, Ohio - d	Silver Cr.	1	6R Racing 63
9/25/94	Eldora Speedway, Rossburg, Ohio - d	midget	20	Don Murphy 21m
9/25/94	Eldora Speedway, Rossburg, Ohio - d	sprint	DNQ	Bob Hampshire 63
10/1/94	Portsmouth Raceway Park, Portsmouth, Ohio - d	sprint	5	Bob Hampshire 63
10/8/94	CalExpo State Fairgrounds, Sacramento, Calif. - d	Silver Cr.	6	6R Racing 63
10/15/94	Mesa Marin Raceway, Bakersfield, Calif. - p	Silver Cr.	9	6R Racing 63
1/28/95	RCA Dome, Indianapolis, Ind. - p	midget	23	Don Murphy 21
2/5/95	Phoenix Intl. Raceway, Phoenix, Ariz. - p	Silver Cr.	8	6R Racing 63
2/5/95	Phoenix Intl. Raceway, Phoenix, Ariz. - p	midget	20	Don Murphy 121
4/1/95	Eldora Speedway, Rossburg, Ohio - d	sprint	7	Bob Hampshire 63
4/2/95	Winchester Speedway, Winchester, Ind. - p	sprint	18	Jack Steck 2x
4/30/95	Terre Haute Action Track, Terre Haute, Ind. - d	sprint	1	Bob Hampshire 63
5/13/95	Indianapolis Raceway Park, Clermont, Ind. - p	sprint	11	Bob Hampshire 63
5/26/95	Indiana State Fairgrounds, Indianapolis, Ind. - d	Silver Cr.	17	6R Racing 63
6/10/95	Indianapolis Raceway Park, Clermont, Ind. - p	sprint	18	Bob Hampshire 63
6/17/95	Richmond Intl. Raceway, Richmond, Va. - p	Silver Cr.	1	6R Racing 63
7/1/95	Lawrenceburg Speedway, Lawrenceburg, Ind. - d	sprint	1	Bob Hampshire 63
7/5/95	Evans' Kokomo Speedway, Kokomo, Ind. - d	sprint	5	Bob Hampshire 63
7/7/95	Terre Haute Action Track, Terre Haute, Ind. - d	Silver Cr.	2	6R Racing 63

7/8/95	Paragon Speedway, Paragon, Ind. - d	sprint	1	Bob Hampshire 63
7/16/95	Terre Haute Action Track, Terre Haute, Ind. - d	sprint	1	Bob Hampshire 63
7/21/95	Indianapolis Raceway Park, Clermont, Ind. - p	sprint	8	Bob Hampshire 63
7/28/95	Santa Fe Park Speedway, Hinsdale, Ill. - d	sprint	4	Bob Hampshire 63
7/29/95	I-96 Speedway, Lake Odessa, Mich. - d	sprint	1	Bob Hampshire 63
7/30/95	Wilmot Speedway, Wilmot, Wisc. - d	sprint	1	Bob Hampshire 63
8/2/95	Indianapolis Raceway Park, Indianapolis, Ind. - p	Silver Cr.	16	6R Racing 63
8/9/95	Eldora Speedway, Rossburg, Ohio - d	sprint	2	Bob Hampshire 63
8/10/95	Winchester Speedway, Winchester, Ind. - p	sprint	9	Bob Hampshire 63
8/19/95	Springfield Speedway, Springfield, Ill. - d	midget	17	Don Murphy 121
8/19/95	Illinois State Fairgrounds, Springfield, Ill. - d	Silver Cr.	27	6R Racing 63
8/20/95	Salem Speedway, Salem, Ind. - p	sprint	5	Bob Hampshire 63
8/23/95	Kokomo Speedway, Kokomo, Ind. - d	midget	18	Don Murphy 121
8/26/95	Portsmouth Raceway Park, Portsmouth, Ohio - d	sprint	2	Bob Hampshire 63
8/31/95	Louisville Motor Speedway, Louisville, Ken. - p	sprint	16	Bob Hampshire 63
9/2/95	Indiana State Fairgrounds, Indianapolis, Ind. - d	Silver Cr.	3	6R Racing 63
9/3/95	Tri-City Speedway, Granite City, Ill. - d	sprint	2	Bob Hampshire 63
9/4/95	DuQuoin State Fairgrounds, DuQuoin, Ill. - d	Silver Cr.	4	6R Racing 63
9/10/95	Terre Haute Action Track, Terre Haute, Ind. - d	midget	8	Don Murphy 121
9/23/95	Eldora Speedway, Rossburg, Ohio - d	Silver Cr.	1	6R Racing 63
9/23/95	Eldora Speedway, Rossburg, Ohio - d	sprint	5	Bob Hampshire 63
9/23/95	Eldora Speedway, Rossburg, Ohio - d	midget	DNQ	Don Murphy 121
10/7/95	CalExpo State Fairgrounds, Sacramento, Calif. - d	Silver Cr.	20	6R Racing 63
10/22/95	Winchester Speedway, Winchester, Ind. - p	sprint	DNQ	Bob Hampshire 63
1/20/96	RCA Dome, Indianapolis, Ind. - p	midget	12	Steele 80
2/4/96	Phoenix Intl. Raceway, Phoenix, Ariz. - p	Silver Cr.	9	6R Motorsports 63
5/11/96	Indianapolis Raceway Park, Clermont, Ind. - p	midget	22	Don Murphy 121
5/12/96	Terre Haute Action Track, Terre Haute, Ind. - d	sprint	20	Bob Hampshire 63
5/18/96	Indianapolis Raceway Park, Clermont, Ind. - p	Silver Cr.	11	6R Motorsports 63
5/25/96	Indiana State Fairgrounds, Indianapolis, Ind. - d	Silver Cr.	12	6R Motorsports 63
6/1/96	I-96 Speedway, Lake Odessa, Mich. - d	sprint	9	Bob Hampshire 63
6/15/96	Richmond Intl. Raceway, Richmond, Va. - p	Silver Cr.	3	6R Motorsports 63
6/15/96	Richmond Intl. Raceway, Richmond, Va. - p	midget	10	Don Murphy 121
6/30/96	Evans' Kokomo Speedway, Kokomo, Ind. - d	sprint	12	Bob Hampshire 63
7/5/96	Terre Haute Action Track, Terre Haute, Ind. - d	Silver Cr.	18	6R Motorsports 63
7/6/96	Paragon Speedway, Paragon, Ind. - d	sprint	17	Bob Hampshire 63
7/12/96	Terre Haute Action Track, Terre Haute, Ind. - d	sprint	DNQ	Bob Hampshire 63
7/17/96	Indianapolis Raceway Park, Clermont, Ind. - p	midget	16	Don Murphy 121
7/26/96	Bloomington Speedway, Bloomington, Ind. - d	sprint	6	Bob Hampshire 63
7/27/96	Paragon Speedway, Paragon, Ind. - d	sprint	7	Bob Hampshire 63
7/28/96	Evans' Kokomo Speedway, Kokomo, Ind. - d	sprint	15	Bob Hampshire 63
7/31/96	Indianapolis Raceway Park, Indianapolis, Ind. - p	Silver Cr.	7	6R Motorsports 63
8/1/96	Belleville High Banks, Belleville, Kan. - d	midget	DNQ	Don Murphy 121
8/7/96	Eldora Speedway, Rossburg, Ohio - d	sprint	18	Bob Hampshire 63
8/10/96	Red Hill Raceway, Sumner, Ill. - d	sprint	2	Bob Hampshire 63
8/16/96	Macon Speedway, Macon, Ill. - d	midget	DNQ	Don Murphy 121
8/21/96	Hales Corners Speedway, Hales Corners, Wisc. - d	sprint	DNQ	Bob Hampshire 63
8/31/96	Lawrenceburg Speedway, Lawrenceburg, Ind. - d	sprint	5	Bob Hampshire 63
9/2/96	DuQuoin State Fairgrounds, DuQuoin, Ill. - d	Silver Cr.	23	6R Motorsports 63
9/4/96	Terre Haute Action Track, Terre Haute, Ind. - d	midget	DNQ	Don Murphy 121
9/28/96	Eldora Speedway, Rossburg, Ohio - d	Silver Cr.	1	6R Motorsports 63

9/28/96	Eldora Speedway, Rossburg, Ohio - d	sprint	2	Bob Hampshire 63
9/28/96	Eldora Speedway, Rossburg, Ohio - d	midget	12	Don Murphy 121
10/5/96	Terre Haute Action Track, Terre Haute, Ind. - d	sprint	1	Bob Hampshire 63
10/5/96	Terre Haute Action Track, Terre Haute, Ind. - d	Silver Cr.*	1	6R Racing 63
10/5/96	Terre Haute Action Track, Terre Haute, Ind. - d	midget	20	Don Murphy 121
10/12/96	CalExpo State Fairgrounds, Sacramento, Calif. - d	Silver Cr.	20	6R Motorsports 63
10/20/96	Del Mar Fairgrounds, Del Mar, Calif. - d	Silver Cr.	16	6R Motorsports 63
1/31/97	Phoenix Intl. Raceway, Phoenix, Ariz. - p	midget	DNQ	Don Murphy 121
2/2/97	Phoenix Intl. Raceway, Phoenix, Ariz. - p	Silver Cr.	16	6R Motorsports 63
3/29/97	Eldora Speedway, Rossburg, Ohio - d	sprint	7	Bob Hampshire 63
5/4/97	Winchester Speedway, Winchester, Ind. - p	sprint	13	Bob Parker 63p
5/8/97	16th Street Speedway, Indianapolis, Ind. - d	midget	8	Don Murphy 121
5/15/97	16th Street Speedway, Indianapolis, Ind. - d	midget	4	Don Murphy 121
5/17/97	Indianapolis Raceway Park, Clermont, Ind. - p	Silver Cr.	3	6R Motorsports 63
5/22/97	16th Street Speedway, Indianapolis, Ind. - d	midget	11	Don Murphy 121
5/23/97	Indiana State Fairgrounds, Indianapolis, Ind. - d	Silver Cr.	25	6R Motorsports 63
6/8/97	Pikes Peak Intl. Raceway, Fountain, Colo. - p	Silver Cr.	16	6R Motorsports 63
6/15/97	Kokomo Speedway, Kokomo, Ind. - d	sprint	3	Bob Hampshire 63
6/20/97	Attica Raceway Park, Attica, Ohio - d	sprint	15	Bob Hampshire 63
6/22/97	Eldora Speedway, Rossburg, Ohio - d	sprint	3	Bob Hampshire 63
6/27/97	Terre Haute Action Track, Terre Haute, Ind. - d	sprint	2	Bob Hampshire 63
6/28/97	16th Street Speedway, Indianapolis, Ind. - d	midget	8	Don Murphy 121
7/4/97	Terre Haute Action Track, Terre Haute, Ind. - d	Silver Cr.	17	6R Motorsports 63
7/5/97	Paragon Speedway, Paragon, Ind. - d	sprint	21	Bob Hampshire 63
7/9/97	Madison Intl. Raceway, Oregon, Wisc. - p	sprint	9	Bob Parker 23x
7/12/97	Winchester Speedway, Winchester, Ind. - p	sprint	18	Bob Parker 23x
7/19/97	Lawrenceburg Speedway, Lawrenceburg, Ind. - d	sprint	20	Bob Hampshire 63
7/23/97	Terre Haute Action Track, Terre Haute, Ind. - d	sprint	21	Bob Hampshire 63
7/24/97	Twin Cities Raceway Park, Vernon, Ind. - d	sprint	DNQ	Bob Hampshire 63
7/25/97	Bloomington Speedway, Bloomington, Ind. - d	sprint	DNQ	Bob Hampshire 63
7/27/97	Lincoln Park Speedway, Putnamville, Ind. - d	sprint	1	Bob Hampshire 63
7/30/97	Indianapolis Raceway Park, Clermont, Ind. - p	Silver Cr.	20	6R Motorsports 63
7/31/97	Belleville High Banks, Belleville, Kan. - d	midget	DNQ	Don Murphy 121
8/1/97	Belleville High Banks, Belleville, Kan. - d	midget	19	Don Murphy 121
8/6/97	Eldora Speedway, Rossburg, Ohio - d	sprint	3	Bob Hampshire 63
8/15/97	Illinois State Fairgrounds, Springfield, Ill. - d	Silver Cr.	6	6R Motorsports 63
8/23/97	Lincoln Park Speedway, Putnamville, Ind. - d	sprint	18	Bob Hampshire 63
8/30/97	Lawrenceburg Speedway, Lawrenceburg, Ind. - d	sprint	12	Bob Hampshire 63
9/1/97	DuQuoin State Fairgrounds, DuQuoin, Ill. - d	Silver Cr.	8	6R Motorsports 63
9/3/97	Terre Haute Action Track, Terre Haute, Ind. - d	midget	DNQ	Don Murphy 121
9/14/97	Gateway Intl. Raceway, Madison, Ill. - p	Silver Cr.	22	6R Motorsports 63
9/20/97	Eldora Speedway, Rossburg, Ohio - d	sprint	1	Bob Hampshire 63
9/20/97	Eldora Speedway, Rossburg, Ohio - d	midget	4	Don Murphy 121
9/20/97	Eldora Speedway, Rossburg, Ohio - p	Silver Cr.	24	6R Motorsports 63
10/3/97	Terre Haute Action Track, Terre Haute, Ind. - d	sprint	1	Bob Hampshire 63
10/4/97	Terre Haute Action Track, Terre Haute, Ind. - d	midget	1	Don Murphy 121
10/11/97	CalExpo State Fairgrounds, Sacramento, Calif. - d	Silver Cr.	22	6R Motorsports 63
10/18/97	Las Vegas Motor Speedway, Las Vegas, Nev. - d	Silver Cr.	24	6R Motorsports 63
1/17/98	Walt Disney World Speedway, Orlando, Fla. - p	Silver Cr.	4	Bob Hampshire 63
2/1/98	Phoenix Intl. Raceway, Phoenix, Ariz. - p	Silver Cr.	3	Bob Hampshire 63

4/11/98	Beaver Dam Raceway, Beaver Dam, Wisc. - d	sprint	4	BWB Racing 26
4/19/98	Phoenix Intl. Raceway, Phoenix, Ariz. - p	sprint	12	BWB Racing 26
5/2/98	Eldora Speedway, Rossburg, Ohio - d	sprint	7	BWB Racing 26
5/16/98	Indianapolis Raceway Park, Clermont, Ind. - p	Silver Cr.	DNQ	Bob Hampshire 63
5/21/98	16th Street Speedway, Indianapolis, Ind. - d	midget	19	J S Distributing 26
5/22/98	Indiana State Fairgrounds, Indianapolis, Ind. - d	Silver Cr.	18	Bob Parker 23
5/29/98	Terre Haute Action Track, Terre Haute, Ind. - d	sprint	15	BWB Racing 26
5/30/98	Lawrenceburg Speedway, Lawrenceburg, Ind. - d	sprint	13	BWB Racing 26
6/7/98	Memphis Motorsports Park, Memphis, Tenn. - p	Silver Cr.	15	Bob Hampshire 63
6/19/98	Attica Raceway Park, Attica, Ohio - d	sprint	17	BWB Racing 26
6/20/98	Eldora Speedway, Rossburg, Ohio - d	sprint	4	BWB Racing 26
7/1/98	Indianapolis Raceway Park, Clermont, Ind. - p	sprint	DNQ	BWB Racing 62
7/3/98	Terre Haute Action Track, Terre Haute, Ind. - d	Silver Cr.	18	Bob Parker 23
7/12/98	Pikes Peak Intl. Raceway, Fountain, Colo. - p	Silver Cr.	27	Bob Parker 23
7/18/98	Lawrenceburg Speedway, Lawrenceburg, Ind. - d	sprint	6	BWB Racing 16
7/19/98	Kokomo Speedway, Kokomo, Ind. - d	sprint	DNQ	BWB Racing 16
7/23/98	Twin Cities Raceway Park, Vernon, Ind. - d	sprint	DNQ	BWB Racing 16
7/24/98	Bloomington Speedway, Bloomington, Ind. - d	sprint	DNQ	BWB Racing 16
7/25/98	Paragon Speedway, Paragon, Ind. - d	sprint	21	BWB Racing 16
7/26/98	Lincoln Park Speedway, Putnamville, Ind. - d	sprint	DNQ	BWB Racing 16
7/29/98	Indianapolis Raceway Park, Clermont, Ind. - p	Silver Cr.	8	Bob Parker 23
8/9/98	Kokomo Speedway, Kokomo, Ind. - d	sprint	DNQ	BWB Racing 16
8/14/98	Terre Haute Action Track, Terre Haute, Ind. - d	sprint	8	BWB Racing 16
8/15/98	Lincoln Park Speedway, Putnamville, Ind. - d	sprint	18	BWB Racing 16
8/22/98	Illinois State Fairgrounds, Springfield, Ill. - d	Silver Cr.	3	Bob Parker 23
8/23/98	Salem Speedway, Salem, Ind. - p	sprint	15	BWB Racing 16
8/29/98	Lawrenceburg Speedway, Lawrenceburg, Ind. - d	sprint	17	BWB Racing 16
9/7/98	DuQuoin State Fairgrounds, DuQuoin, Ill. - d	Silver Cr.	15	Bob Parker 23
9/26/98	Eldora Speedway, Rossburg, Ohio - d	sprint	1	BWB Racing 16
9/26/98	Eldora Speedway, Rossburg, Ohio - d	Silver Cr.	1	Bob Parker 23
9/26/98	Eldora Speedway, Rossburg, Ohio - d	midget	1	Bob Parker 37
10/3/98	Red Hill Raceway, Sumner, Ill. - d	sprint	9	BWB Racing 16
10/10/98	CalExpo State Fairgrounds, Sacramento, Calif. - d	Silver Cr.	6	Bob Parker 23
10/17/98	Gateway Intl. Raceway, Madison, Ill. - p	Silver Cr.	24	Bob Parker 23
10/25/98	Winchester Speedway, Winchester, Ind. - p	sprint	19	BWB Racing 26
1/24/99	Walt Disney World Speedway, Orlando, Fla. - p	Silver Cr.	25	Dewit Motorsports 23
1/30/99	RCA Dome, Indianapolis, Ind. - p	midget	15	Bob Parker 24
2/7/99	Phoenix Intl. Raceway, Phoenix, Ariz. - p	Silver Cr.	14	Dewit Motorsports 23
2/7/99	Phoenix Intl. Raceway, Phoenix, Ariz. - p	midget	DNQ	Bob Parker 24
3/27/99	Eldora Speedway, Rossburg, Ohio - d	sprint	3	Richard Newkirk 17
4/30/99	Attica Raceway Park, Attica, Ohio - d	sprint	19	Richard Newkirk 17
5/1/99	Eldora Speedway, Rossburg, Ohio - d	sprint	21	Richard Newkirk 17
5/8/99	Terre Haute Action Track, Terre Haute, Ind. - d	sprint	21	Richard Newkirk 17
5/22/99	Indianapolis Raceway Park, Clermont, Ind. - p	Silver Cr.	12	Dewit Motorsports 23
5/27/99	16th Street Speedway, Indianapolis, Ind. - d	midget	DNQ	Bob Parker 23
5/28/99	Indiana State Fairgrounds, Indianapolis, Ind. - d	Silver Cr.	19	Dewit Motorsports 23
5/30/99	Eldora Speedway, Rossburg, Ohio - d	sprint	9	Tim Clark 11
6/5/99	Lawrenceburg Speedway, Lawrenceburg, Ind. - d	sprint	7	Richard Newkirk 17
6/17/99	Terre Haute Action Track, Terre Haute, Ind. - d	sprint	7	Richard Newkirk 17
6/19/99	Terre Haute Action Track, Terre Haute, Ind. - d	sprint	5	Richard Newkirk 17
6/27/99	Pikes Peak Intl. Raceway, Fountain, Colo. - p	Silver Cr.	3	Dewit Motorsports 23

Date	Track	Type	Pos	Team
7/17/99	Nazareth Speedway, Nazareth, Pa. - p	Silver Cr.	13	Dewit Motorsports 23
7/21/99	Terre Haute Action Track, Terre Haute, Ind. - d	sprint	2	Richard Newkirk 17
7/22/99	Lawrenceburg Speedway, Lawrenceburg, Ind. - d	sprint	1	Richard Newkirk 17
7/23/99	Bloomington Speedway, Bloomington, Ind. - d	sprint	20	Richard Newkirk 17
7/24/99	Lincoln Park Speedway, Putnamville, Ind. - d	sprint	DNQ	Richard Newkirk 17
7/25/99	Evans' Kokomo Speedway, Kokomo, Ind. - d	sprint	15	Richard Newkirk 17
7/28/99	Eldora Speedway, Rossburg, Ohio - d	sprint	2	Richard Newkirk 17
7/30/99	Gateway Intl. Raceway, Madison, Ill. - p	Silver Cr.	3	Dewit Motorsports 23
8/4/99	Indianapolis Raceway Park, Clermont, Ind. - p	Silver Cr.	6	Dewit Motorsports 23
8/8/99	Kokomo Speedway, Kokomo, Ind. - d	sprint	21	Richard Newkirk 17
8/21/99	Illinois State Fairgrounds, Springfield, Ill. - d	Silver Cr.	5	Dewit Motorsports 23
8/27/99	Bloomington Speedway, Bloomington, Ind. - d	sprint	15	Richard Newkirk 17
8/28/99	Lawrenceburg Speedway, Lawrenceburg, Ind. - d	sprint	9	Richard Newkirk 17
9/1/99	Terre Haute Action Track, Terre Haute, Ind. - d	midget	33	Bob Parker 23
9/6/99	DuQuoin State Fairgrounds, DuQuoin, Ill. - d	Silver Cr.	14	Dewit Motorsports 23
9/17/99	Terre Haute Action Track, Terre Haute, Ind. - d	Silver Cr.	1	Dewit Motorsports 23
9/25/99	Eldora Speedway, Rossburg, Ohio - d	Silver Cr.	2	Dewit Motorsports 23
9/25/99	Eldora Speedway, Rossburg, Ohio - d	midget	8	Bob Parker 23
9/25/99	Eldora Speedway, Rossburg, Ohio - d	sprint	DNQ	Richard Newkirk 17
10/9/99	CalExpo State Fairgrounds, Sacramento, Calif. - d	Silver Cr.	13	Dewit Motorsports 23
10/16/99	Irwindale Speedway, Irwindale, Cal. - p	Silver Cr.	8	Dewit Motorsports 23
10/31/99	Memphis Motorsports Park, Memphis, Tenn. - p	Silver Cr.	15	Dewit Motorsports 23
1/29/00	Walt Disney World Speedway, Orlando, Fla. - p	Silver Cr.	20	Dewit Motorsports 23
2/6/00	Phoenix Intl. Raceway, Phoenix, Ariz. - p	Silver Cr.	23	Dewit Motorsports 23
3/11/00	RCA Dome, Indianapolis, Ind. - p	midget	DNQ	Bob Parker 23
4/1/00	Eldora Speedway, Rossburg, Ohio - d	sprint	19	BWB Racing 16
4/2/00	Anderson Speedway, Anderson, Ind. - p	sprint	5	BWB Racing 16
4/8/00	Nazareth Speedway, Nazareth, Pa. - p	Silver Cr.	20	Dewit Motorsports 23
4/29/00	Eldora Speedway, Rossburg, Ohio - d	sprint	7	BWB Racing 16
4/30/00	Winchester Speedway, Winchester, Ind. - p	sprint	19	BWB Racing 16
5/6/00	Tri-City Speedway, Granite City, Ill. - d	sprint	2	BWB Racing 16
5/7/00	Gateway Intl. Raceway, Madison, Ill. - p	Silver Cr.	6	Dewit Motorsports 23
5/12/00	Hawkeye Downs Speedway, Cedar Rapids, Ia. - p	sprint	DNQ	BWB Racing 16
5/20/00	Indianapolis Raceway Park, Clermont, Ind. - p	Silver Cr.	10	Dewit Motorsports 23
5/24/00	Anderson Speedway, Anderson, Ind. - p	sprint	19	BWB Racing 16
5/28/00	Eldora Speedway, Rossburg, Ohio - d	sprint	DNQ	BWB Racing 16
6/3/00	Knoxville Raceway, Knoxville, Ia. - d	Silver Cr.	5	Dewit Motorsports 23
6/10/00	Indianapolis Raceway Park, Clermont, Ind. - p	sprint	8	BWB Racing 16
6/15/00	Terre Haute Action Track, Terre Haute, Ind. - d	sprint	10	BWB Racing 16
6/18/00	Terre Haute Action Track, Terre Haute, Ind. - d	sprint	DNQ	BWB Racing 16
7/7/00	Toledo Raceway, Toledo, Ohio - p	sprint	21	BWB Racing 16
7/15/00	Indianapolis Raceway Park, Clermont, Ind. - p	sprint	21	BWB Racing 16
7/20/00	Twin Cities Raceway Park, Vernon, Ind. - d	sprint	21	BWB Racing 16
7/21/00	Bloomington Speedway, Bloomington, Ind. - d	sprint	13	BWB Racing 16
7/22/00	Lawrenceburg Speedway, Lawrenceburg, Ind. - d	sprint	19	BWB Racing 16
7/23/00	Kokomo Speedway, Kokomo, Ind. - d	sprint	21	BWB Racing 16
7/28/00	Terre Haute Action Track, Terre Haute, Ind. - d	sprint	8	BWB Racing 16
7/29/00	Lincoln Park Speedway, Putnamville, Ind. - d	sprint	DNQ	BWB Racing 16
7/30/00	Tri-State Speedway, Haubstadt, Ind. - d	sprint	DNQ	BWB Racing 16
8/6/00	Indianapolis Raceway Park, Clermont, Ind. - p	Silver Cr.	20	Dewit Motorsports 23
8/11/00	Hartford Speedway Park, Hartford, Mich. - d	sprint	8	BWB Racing 16

8/19/00	Illinois State Fairgrounds, Springfield, Ill. - d	Silver Cr.	1	Dewit Motorsports 23
8/25/00	Attica Raceway Park, Attica, Ohio - d	sprint	23	BWB Racing 16
8/26/00	Lawrenceburg Speedway, Lawrenceburg, Ind. - d	sprint	6	BWB Racing 16
9/4/00	DuQuoin State Fairgrounds, DuQuoin, Ill. - d	Silver Cr.	13	Dewit Motorsports 23
9/22/00	Indiana State Fairgrounds, Indianapolis, Ind. - d	Silver Cr.	2	Dewit Motorsports 23
9/30/00	Eldora Speedway, Rossburg, Ohio - d	Silver Cr.	6	Dewit Motorsports 23
9/30/00	Eldora Speedway, Rossburg, Ohio - d	sprint	22	BWB Racing 16
10/29/00	Memphis Motorsports Park, Memphis, Tenn. - p	Silver Cr.	11	Dewit Motorsports 23
3/10/01	RCA Dome, Indianapolis, Ind. - p	midget	20	Beaber 66
3/18/01	Phoenix Intl. Raceway, Phoenix, Ariz. - p	Silver Cr.	DNQ	Bob Parker 23
4/21/01	Twin Cities Raceway Park, Vernon, Ind. - d	sprint	DNQ	BWB Racing 16
4/27/01	Attica Raceway Park, Attica, Ohio - d	sprint	20	BWB Racing 16
4/28/01	Eldora Speedway, Rossburg, Ohio - d	sprint	9	BWB Racing 16
5/13/01	Tri-State Speedway, Haubstadt, Ind. - d	sprint	DNQ	BWB Racing 16
5/19/01	Terre Haute Action Track, Terre Haute, Ind. - d	sprint	DNQ	BWB Racing 16
6/2/01	Knoxville Raceway, Knoxville, Ia. - d	Silver Cr.	11	Bob Parker 23
6/10/01	Angell Park Speedway, Sun Prairie, Wisc. - d	sprint	1	BWB Racing 16
6/22/01	Eldora Speedway, Rossburg, Ohio - d	sprint	4	BWB Racing 16
6/23/01	Eldora Speedway, Rossburg, Ohio - d	sprint	14	BWB Racing 16
7/21/01	Lincoln Park Speedway, Putnamville, Ind. - d	sprint	31	Dennis Kaser 31
7/22/01	Tri-State Speedway, Haubstadt, Ind. - d	sprint	18	Dennis Kaser 31
7/24/01	Twin Cities Raceway Park, Vernon, Ind. - d	sprint	1	Dennis Kaser 31
7/26/01	Lawrenceburg Speedway, Lawrenceburg, Ind. - d	sprint	DNQ	Dennis Kaser 31
7/27/01	Bloomington Speedway, Bloomington, Ind. - d	sprint	DNQ	Dennis Kaser 31
7/29/01	Kokomo Speedway, Kokomo, Ind. - d	sprint	16	Dennis Kaser 31
8/18/01	Illinois State Fairgrounds, Springfield, Ill. - d	Silver Cr.	12	Bob Parker 23
8/31/01	Route 66 Raceway, Joliet, Ill. - d	sprint	7	Dennis Kaser 31
9/2/01	DuQuoin State Fairgrounds, DuQuoin, Ill. - d	Silver Cr.	23	Bob Parker 23
9/22/01	Eldora Speedway, Rossburg, Ohio - d	sprint	24	Dennis Kaser 31
9/22/01	Eldora Speedway, Rossburg, Ohio - d	Silver Cr.	DNS	Bob Parker 23
9/28/01	Indiana State Fairgrounds, Indianapolis, Ind. - d	Silver Cr.	23	Bob Parker 23
10/20/01	Terre Haute Action Track, Terre Haute, Ind. - d	sprint	12	Dennis Kaser 31
10/20/01	Terre Haute Action Track, Terre Haute, Ind. - d	sprint	13	Dennis Kaser 31
3/17/02	Phoenix Intl. Raceway, Phoenix, Ariz. - p	Silver Cr.	DNQ	Team 6-R 21
4/21/02	Nazareth Speedway, Nazareth, Pa. - p	Silver Cr.		Team 6-R 21
5/11/02	Terre Haute Action Track, Terre Haute, Ind. - d	sprint	19	Dennis Kaser 31
5/24/02	Indiana State Fairgrounds, Indianapolis, Ind. - d	Silver Cr.	DNQ	Team 6-R 21
5/26/02	Eldora Speedway, Rossburg, Ohio - d	sprint	11	Dennis Kaser 31
6/1/02	Terre Haute Action Track, Terre Haute, Ind. - d	Silver Cr.	22	Team 6-R 21
6/16/02	Pikes Peak Intl. Raceway, Fountain, Colo. - p	Silver Cr.	DNQ	Team 6-R 21
6/19/02	Attica Raceway Park, Attica, Ohio - d	sprint	13	Dennis Kaser 31
6/20/02	Fremont Speedway, Fremont, Ohio - d	sprint	16	Dennis Kaser 31
6/21/02	Limaland Motorsports Park, Lima, Ohio - d	sprint	20	Dennis Kaser 31
6/22/02	Eldora Speedway, Rossburg, Ohio - d	sprint	20	Dennis Kaser 31
7/7/02	Angell Park Speedway, Sun Prairie, Wisc. - d	sprint	19	Dennis Kaser 31
7/19/02	Gas City I-69 Speedway, Gas City, Ind. - d	sprint	DNQ	Dennis Kaser 31
7/20/02	Lincoln Park Speedway, Putnamville, Ind. - d	sprint	DNQ	Dennis Kaser 31
7/22/02	Twin Cities Raceway Park, North Vernon, Ind. - d	sprint	DNQ	Dennis Kaser 31

USAC TRADITIONAL RACE VICTORIES

4-Crown Nationals
Eldora Speedway, Rossburg, Ohio
midget: 1987, '93, '98
sprint car: 1983, '90, '91, '97, '98
Silver Crown: 1986, '88, '89, '91, '94, '95, '98

Don Branson/Jud Larson sprint car race
Eldora Speedway
1982, '90

Tony Hulman Classic
Terre Haute Action Track, Terre Haute, Ind.
1983, '95

Hoosier Hundred
Indiana State Fairgrounds, Indianapolis
1986, '88, '89

Hulman Hundred
Indiana State Fairgrounds, Indianapolis
1986, '90

Tony Bettenhausen 100
Illinois State Fairgrounds, Springfield, Ill.
1986, '87, '93, '00

Ted Horn 100
DuQuoin State Fairgrounds, DuQuoin, Ill.
1986, '87, '93

ALL STARS CIRCUIT OF CHAMPIONS
SPRINT CAR VICTORIES

Date	Track
6/21/80	Fremont Speedway, Fremont, Ohio
7/3/80	Fremont Speedway, Fremont, Ohio
7/11/81	Fremont Speedway, Fremont, Ohio
9/11/81	Lincoln Park Speedway, Putnamville, Ind.
8/28/82	Mansfield Raceway Park, Mansfield, Ohio
6/26/83	Millstream Motor Speedway, Findlay, Ohio
6/8/84	Avilla Motor Speedway, Avilla, Ind.
7/8/84	West Virginia Motor Speedway, Pennsboro, W.Va.
7/12/84	Springfield Speedway, Springfield, Ill.
8/5/84	Tri-State Speedway, Haubstadt, Ind.
9/30/84	Avilla Motor Speedway, Avilla, Ind.
6/1/85	Eldora Speedway, Rossburg, Ohio
6/8/85	Fremont Speedway, Fremont, Ohio
6/9/85	Kokomo Speedway, Kokomo, Ind.
6/30/85	Millstream Motor Speedway, Findlay, Ohio
7/2/85	K-C Raceway, Chillicothe, Ohio
7/4/85	Sharon Speedway, Sharon, Ohio
7/21/85	Millstream Motor Speedway, Findlay, Ohio
8/2/85	Vermillion County Speedway, Danville, Ill.
9/14/85	Lawrenceburg Speedway, Lawrenceburg, Ind.
9/22/85	West Virginia Motor Speedway, Pennsboro, W.Va.
9/28/85	Buckeye Speedway, Orrville, Ohio
11/2/85	Dixie Speedway, Woodstock, Ga.
5/10/86	Fremont Speedway, Fremont, Ohio
5/11/86	Sharon Speedway, Sharon, Ohio
5/18/86	Wilmot Speedway, Wilmot, Wisc.
6/1/86	Kokomo Speedway, Kokomo, Ind.
6/14/86	Fremont Speedway, Fremont, Ohio
6/15/86	Millstream Motor Speedway, Findlay, Ohio
7/20/86	Millstream Motor Speedway, Findlay, Ohio
8/2/86	Fremont Speedway, Fremont, Ohio
8/23/86	Tri-City Speedway, Granite City, Ill.

Date	Track
5/16/87	Fremont Speedway, Fremont, Ohio
7/31/87	Vermillion County Speedway, Danville, Ill.
6/17/88	Midstate Raceway, Mt. Olive, Ill.
6/19/88	Whitewater Valley Speedway, Liberty, Ind.
7/29/88	Vermillion County Speedway, Danville, Ill.
8/6/88	Fremont Speedway, Fremont, Ohio
8/7/88	Millstream Motor Speedway, Findlay, Ohio
11/28/88	Dixie Speedway, Woodstock, Ga.
5/19/89	Columbus Motor Speeway, Columbus, Ohio
6/2/89	I-96 Speedway, Lake Odessa, Mich.
6/7/89	Vermillion County Speedway, Danville, Ill.
6/17/89	Fremont Speedway, Fremont, Ohio
6/28/89	Pennsylvania Motor Speedway, Pittsburgh, Pa.
7/5/89	Millstream Motor Speedway, Findlay, Ohio
7/12/89	Vermillion County Speedway, Danville, Ill.
8/25/89	Shady Bowl Speedway, DeGraff, Ohio
9/30/89	K-C Raceway, Chillicothe, Ohio
10/14/89	Eldora Speedway, Rossburg, Ohio
5/26/90	Florence Speedway, Florence, Ky.
7/13/90	I-96 Speedway, Lake Odessa, Mich.
8/5/90	Millstream Motor Speedway, Findlay, Ohio
10/12/90	Bloomington Speedway, Bloomington, Ind.
2/2/91	Jax Raceway, Jacksonville, Fla.
8/18/91	Kokomo Speedway, Kokomo, Ind.

Total All Stars wins: 56

PROMINENT WINS AND CHAMPIONSHIPS

1985 Ohio Speedweek champion
1985 All Stars sprint car champion
1986 USAC Silver Crown champion
1986 Eldora Enterprises champion
1987 USAC Silver Crown champion
1987 Eldora Enterprises champion
1989 Devil's Bowl Winternationals, Mesquite, Texas
1989 Cheater's Day classic, Sioux Empire Fairgrounds, Sioux Falls, S.D.
1990 Marlboro Grand National 100 for stock cars, Liverpool, New South
    Wales, Australia
1990 Brad Doty sprint car classic, Attica, Ohio
1991 Belleville Midget Nationals champion
1991 Jayhawk Nationals, Topeka, Kansas
1991 Grand Annual Sprintcar Classic, Warrnambool, Victoria, Australia

Sanctioned career wins:

USAC Silver Crown:	23 (1st all time)
USAC sprint cars:	46 (2nd all time)
All Stars sprint cars:	56 (3rd all time)
World of Outlaws sprint cars:	3
CRA sprint cars:	5
USAC national midget:	7
Total USAC career feature wins:	76 (7th all time)

OUTSTANDING AWARDS

USAC James McElreath Memorial "Driver of the Year" award for
    outstanding attitude, conduct, and sportsmanship, 1983
USAC Jimmy Caruthers Memorial Award, 1995
Anthony "Tony" Foyt Tenacity Award, 1996
Outstanding Contribution to the Sport Award (National Sprint Car Poll),
    1998
Hoosier Auto Racing Fans (HARF) Hall of Fame, 1998
Voted 19th in the Greatest Sprint Car Drivers of the Century balloting by
    the National Sprint Car Poll, 1999
Inducted into the National Sprint Car Hall of Fame, 2001

THE 25 GREATEST SPRINT CAR DRIVERS OF THE 20TH CENTURY

SELECTED BY THE NATIONAL SPRINT CAR POLL

Gary Bettenhausen
Tom Bigelow
Don Branson
Pancho Carter
Emory Collins
Larry Dickson
Rick Ferkel
A.J. Foyt
Bobby Grim
Jack Hewitt
Tommy Hinnershitz
Ted Horn
Jim Hurtubise
Parnelli Jones
Steve Kinser
Jud Larson
Frank Lockhart
Rex Mays
Jan Opperman
Troy Ruttman
Gus Schrader
Sammy Swindell
Kenny Weld
Tony Willman
Doug Wolfgang

INDEX

Y

Z

Dave Argabright is a writer living in Fishers, Indiana. He has covered auto racing since 1981 for publications including *NATIONAL SPEED SPORT NEWS, Sprint Car and Midget Magazine, Speedvision.com, OPEN WHEEL Magazine, Car and Driver, and AMI Auto World.* His background in broadcasting includes work as a pit reporter for TNN, covering the World of Outlaws.

His professional honors include the "Outstanding Contribution to the Sport" award from the National Sprint Car Poll, the "Frank Blunk Award for Journalism" from the Eastern Motorsports Press Assn., the "Dymag Award of Journalism Excellence," the "Gene Powlen Fan Appreciation Award," and the Hoosier Auto Racing Fans "Media Member of the Year" awards. He is a five-time recipient of the "Media Member of the Year" award from the National Sprint Car Poll.

OTHER BOOKS BY DAVE ARGABRIGHT...

AMERICAN SCENE
A COLLECTION

A collection of nearly 100 columns and feature stories from 1988 to 1997, from auto racing's well-known storyteller. The stories you have loved for years, in a book to be enjoyed forever.

Hardbound, 356 pages

Foreword by Chris Economaki

A portion of the proceeds of *American Scene* are donated to the National Sprint Car Hall of Fame and Museum, and the National Midget Auto Racing Hall of Fame.
ISBN: 1-891390-11-2

STILL WIDE OPEN
By Brad Doty
with Dave Argabright

An amazing, exciting, emotional autobiography, telling the story of one of sprint car racing's most popular stars. Brad Doty soared to the pinnacle of sprint car stardom, only to be cut down in a devastating 1988 crash. A spinal injury stole his ability to walk, but as this heartfelt and critically-acclaimed volume attests, couldn't diminish his will to live.

Forewords by Ron Shuman, Bruce Ellis, Steve Kinser, Paul Wilson, Ed Haudenschild, and Laurie Doty.

Hardbound, 282 pages, with 50 photographs
ISBN: 0-9719639-0-8

Book reorder information:

Books by Dave Argabright
P.O. Box 84
Fishers, IN 46038
(317) 598-9773 (voice)
(317) 598-1269 (fax)
orders@daveargabright.com

www.daveargabright.com

ISBN: 0-9719639-1-6

"The sky was blue,
The track was fast.
I started first,
And finished last.
Send me another $100 to get
home on."

- Don Hewitt